ROY -

I AM SO THANKFUL TO KNOW MY BROTHER SHARES MY LOVE FOR JESUS. THIS IS ONE OF MY FAVORITES TO READ - HOPE YOU ENJOY IT AS MUCH AS I DID

TOZER

ON THE SON OF GOD

TOZER

ON THE SON OF GOD

A 365-DAY DEVOTIONAL

Moody Publishers

CHICAGO

All Scripture quotations in the body text are taken from the King James Version.

Interior Design: Brandi Davis
Cover design and illustration: Faceout Studio, Tim Green

Library of Congress Cataloging-in-Publication Data

Names: Tozer, A. W. (Aiden Wilson), 1897-1963, author.
Title: Tozer on the Son of God : a 365-day devotional / A. W. Tozer.
Description: Chicago : Moody Publishers, 2020. | Includes index. | Summary: "Spend a year encountering the Son of God alongside A. W. Tozer. In this 365-day devotional, you can intentionally pursue Christ daily. Encounter the character of Christ, His work on the cross, and His limitless love for you. With each page, may your heart be filled and your worship increased"-- Provided by publisher.
Identifiers: LCCN 2020020569 (print) | LCCN 2020020570 (ebook) | ISBN 9780802419705 (paperback) | ISBN 9780802498663 (ebook)
Subjects: LCSH: Jesus Christ--Person and offices--Prayers and devotions. | Devotional calendars.
Classification: LCC BT203 .T696 2020 (print) | LCC BT203 (ebook) | DDC 232--dc23
LC record available at https://lccn.loc.gov/2020020569
LC ebook record available at https://lccn.loc.gov/2020020570

Originally delivered by fleets of horse-drawn wagons, the affordable paperbacks from D. L. Moody's publishing house resourced the church and served everyday people. Now, after more than 125 years of publishing and ministry, Moody Publishers' mission remains the same—even if our delivery systems have changed a bit. For more information on other books (and resources) created from a biblical perspective, go to www.moodypublishers.com or write to:

Moody Publishers
820 N. LaSalle Boulevard
Chicago, IL 60610

1 3 5 7 9 10 8 6 4 2

Printed in the United States of America

Preface

Aiden Wilson Tozer was born April 21, 1897, on a small farm among the spiny ridges of Western Pennsylvania. Within a few short years, Tozer, as he preferred to be called, would earn the reputation and title "twentieth-century prophet."

When he was fifteen years old, Tozer's family moved to Akron, Ohio. One afternoon as he walked home from his job at Goodyear, he overheard a street preacher say, "If you don't know how to be saved . . . just call on God." When he got home, he climbed the narrow stairway to the attic where, heeding the preacher's advice, Tozer was launched into a lifelong pursuit of God.

In 1919, without formal education, he was called to pastor a small storefront church in Nutter Fort, West Virginia. That humble beginning thrust him and his wife, Ada, into a forty-four-year ministry with The Christian and Missionary Alliance.

Thirty-one of those years were spent at Chicago's Southside Alliance Church. The congregation, captivated by Tozer's preaching, grew from eighty to 800.

His humor, written and spoken, has been compared to that of Will Rogers—honest and homespun. Congregations could one moment be swept by gales of laughter and the next sit in a holy hush.

But Tozer's forte was his prayer life which often found him walking the aisles of a sanctuary or lying face down on the floor. Tozer biographer James L. Snyder notes that "his preaching as well as his writings were but extensions of his prayer life." An earlier biographer and confidante, David J. Fant, wrote, "He spent more time on his knees than at his desk."

Tozer's final years of pastoral ministry were at Avenue Road Church in Toronto, Canada. On May 12, 1963, his pursuit of God was realized when he died of a heart attack at age 66. In a small cemetery in Akron, Ohio, his tombstone bears this simple epitaph: "A Man of God."

As Tozer once affirmed, "Because Jesus Christ is the eternal Son, because He is of the eternal generation and equal with the Father as pertaining to His substance, His eternity, His love, His power, His grace, His goodness, and all of the attributes of deity, He is the channel through which God dispenses all His blessing."

Our prayer for these pages is that they and He will make a difference in your life.

Please note:
Each excerpt is followed by a code and number representing the name of the book and the page from which the quote was taken. A list of the reference codes is provided in the back of the book.

JANUARY

JANUARY 1

Faith in Which Jesus?

You are righteous, LORD, and your laws are right. The statutes you have laid down are righteous; they are fully trustworthy.

—PSALM 119:137–138

To manipulate the Scriptures so as to make them excuse us, compliment us and console us is to do despite to the written Word and to reject the Living Word. To believe savingly in Jesus Christ is to believe all He has said about Himself and all that the prophets and apostles have said about Him. Let us beware that the Jesus we "accept" is not one we have created out of the dust of our imagination and formed after our own likeness.

True faith commits us to obedience. "We have received grace and apostleship," says Paul, "for obedience to the faith among all nations, for his name" (Rom. 1:5). That dreamy, sentimental faith which ignores the judgments of God against us and listens to the affirmations of the soul is as deadly as cyanide.

That faith which passively accepts all the pleasant texts of the Scriptures while it overlooks or rejects the stern warnings and commandments of those same Scriptures is not the faith of which Christ and His apostles spoke. OGM062

Loving and gracious Savior, I repent of the ways in which I have believed the truth about You selectively. Grant that I would believe everything the Scriptures reveal about You so that I would know You fully and honor You with my whole life. Amen.

JANUARY 2

True Christian Equals Practicing Christian

For we know that if the earthly tent we live in is destroyed, we have a building from God, an eternal house in heaven, not built by human hands.

—2 CORINTHIANS 5:1

The supreme purpose of the Christian religion is to make men like God in order that they may act like God. In Christ the verbs *to be* and *to do* follow each other in that order.

True religion leads to moral action. The only true Christian is the practicing Christian.

Such a one is in very reality an incarnation of Christ as Christ is the incarnation of God; not in the same degree and fullness of perfection, for there is nothing in the moral universe equal to that awful mystery of godliness which joined God and man in eternal union in the person of the Man Christ Jesus; but as the fullness of the Godhead was and is in Christ, so Christ is in the nature of the one who believes in Him in the manner prescribed in the Scriptures. OGM063

Lord Jesus, You are the way to true life. Grant by Your Spirit that I would practice what You have taught in the Scriptures. Amen.

JANUARY 3

Fruit, Not Trees

Make a tree good and its fruit will be good, or make a tree bad and its fruit will be bad, for a tree is recognized by its fruit.
—MATTHEW 12:33

Rightly understood, faith is not a substitute for moral conduct but a means toward it. The tree does not serve in lieu of fruit but as an agent by which fruit is secured. Fruit, not trees, is the end God has in mind in yonder orchard; so Christlike conduct is the end of Christian faith.

To oppose faith to works is to make the fruit the enemy to the tree; yet that is exactly what we have managed to do. And the consequences have been disastrous.

A miscalculation in laying the foundation of a building will throw the whole superstructure out of plumb, and the error that gave us faith as a substitute for action instead of faith in action has raised up in our day unsymmetrical and ugly temples of which we may well be ashamed and for which we shall surely give a strict account in the day when Christ judges the secrets of our hearts. OGM065

Lord Jesus, You know all my thoughts, intentions, and ambitions. Empower me this day to put my faith into action, that I may bear much fruit and You may be glorified. Amen.

JANUARY 4

Word Made Flesh—Happily

The Word became flesh and made his dwelling among us. We have seen his glory, the glory of the one and only Son, who came from the Father, full of grace and truth.

—JOHN 1:14

Redemption is not a heavy work for God. God didn't find Himself in a fix and have to rush off somewhere and try to get "foreign policy" straightened out with the archangels. God did what He did joyfully. He made the heaven and the earth joyfully. That's why the flowers look up and smile, and the birds sing and the sun shines, and the sky is blue and rivers trickle down to the sea. God made the creation and He loved what He did!

He took pleasure in Himself, in His own perfection and in the perfection of His work. And when it comes to redemption, I repeat that this was not a heavy task laid upon God by moral necessity. God wanted to do this. There was no moral necessity upon God to redeem mankind. He didn't have to send His Son Jesus Christ to die for mankind. He sent Him, but at the same time Jesus did it voluntarily. If God was willing, it was the happy willingness of God.

Thank You, Father, that because Jesus became human, I can fellowship with You once again. Amen.

JANUARY 5

God—Acting Like God

The one and only Son, who is himself God and is in closest relationship with the Father, has made him known.

—JOHN 1:18

When Jesus walked and taught in Galilee 2,000 years ago, many asked, "Who is that Man?"

The Bible's answer is clear: That Man walking in Galilee was God, acting like God! It was God, limited deliberately, having crossed the wide, mysterious gulf between God and not God, between God and creature. No man had seen God at any time.

In John 1:18, the English translators have said, "The only begotten Son . . . hath declared him." Other versions skirt around it, doing everything to try to say what the Holy Spirit said, but when we have used up our words and synonyms, we still have not said all that God revealed when He said, "Nobody has ever looked at God, but when Jesus Christ came He showed us what God is like" (paraphrase of John 1:18).

He has revealed Him—He has shown us what God is like!

He has declared Him! He has set Him forth! He has revealed Him!

He is in the Father's bosom. It is stated in present, perpetual tense, the language of continuation. Therefore, when Jesus hung on the cross, He did not leave the bosom of the Father! MWT247

Lord Jesus, that You are the Son of God is the bedrock of our faith. Thank You for revealing what God is like during Your brief sojourn on earth. Amen.

JANUARY 6

Christ Unchanging

He made himself nothing by taking the very nature of a servant, being made in human likeness.
—PHILIPPIANS 2:7

Because change is everywhere around us at all times on this earth and among human beings, it is difficult for us to grasp the eternal and unchanging nature and person of Jesus Christ.

Nothing about our Lord Jesus Christ has changed down to this very hour. His love has not changed. His compassionate understanding of us has not changed. His interest in us and His purposes for us have not changed.

He is Jesus Christ, our Lord. He is the very same Jesus. Even though He has been raised from the dead and seated at the right hand of the Majesty in the heavens, and made Head over all things to the Church, His love for us remains unchanged.

It is hard for us to accept the majestic simplicity of this constant, wonder-working Jesus. We are used to getting things changed so that they are always bigger and better!

He is Jesus, easier to approach than the humblest friend you ever had! He is the sun that shines upon us, He is the star of our night. He is the giver of our life and the rock of our hope. He is our safety and our future. He is our righteousness, our sanctification, our inheritance.

You will find that He is all of this in that instant that you move your heart towards Him in faith! This is the journey to Jesus that must be made in the depths of the heart and being. This is a journey where feet do not count! EWT208

Lord Christ, how amazing that You do not change! I trust in Your unfailing love and compassion this day. Amen.

JANUARY 7

God and the Individual

Blessed is the one whose sin the Lord will never count against them.
—ROMANS 4:8

When the eternal Son of God became the Son of Man and walked on this earth, He always called individuals to His side. Jesus did not come into the world to deal with statistics!

He deals with individuals and that is why the Christian message is and always has been: "God loves the world! He loves the masses and throngs only because they are made up of individuals. He loves every individual person in the world!"

In the great humanistic tide of our day, the individual is no longer the concern. We are pressed to think of the human race in a lump. We are schooled to think of the human race in terms of statistics. In many nations, the state is made to be everything and the individual means nothing at all.

Into the very face and strength of this kind of humanism comes the Christian evangel, the good news of salvation, wondrously alight with the assurance for all who will listen:

"You are an individual and you matter to God! His concern is not for genes and species but for the individuals He has created!" MWT 359

Father God, Your Word says that You knew each one of us before we were born (see Jer. 1:5), You personally knit us together in our mother's womb (see Ps. 139:13), and You planned each day of our life (see Ps. 139:16). I praise You, Lord! My only response to this can be to live every day for Your glory. Amen.

JANUARY 8

We Must Have Kindness

The Son is the radiance of God's glory and the exact representation of his being, sustaining all things by his powerful word. After he had provided purification for sins, he sat down at the right hand of the Majesty in heaven.

—HEBREWS 1:3

Jesus is God. And Jesus is the kindest man ever to live on this earth. His kindness is something we must have. It must be a reflection, a lingering flavor, like an old vase that once held beautiful flowers. Though the vase is broken, the scent of the roses hangs round the vase. So mankind, fallen like a broken vase, dashed to the pavement and splintered into a million pieces, yet has something we call kindness.

God is not revolted by our wretchedness. He has no despite of anything that He has made, nor does He disdain the service in the simplest office that to our body belongeth. The Lord will be your Nurse, your Caretaker, your Helper, and He's not revolted by anything about you. He wills that you joy along with Him. The everlasting marvel and the high, overpassing love of God, the irresistable love of God, out of His goodness sees us perfect even though we are not perfect. And He wants us to be glad in Him. AOG052-053

Lord, You know the secrets of my heart, yet You love me unconditionally, even when I am unkind. I confess my sins to You, Lord. Forgive me when I fall and make me more like You. Amen.

JANUARY 9

Infinite Mercy

But because of his great love for us, God, who is rich in mercy, made us alive with Christ even when we were dead in transgressions—it is by grace you have been saved.
—EPHESIANS 2:4-5

When Jesus died on the cross the mercy of God did not become any greater. It could not become any greater, for it was already infinite. We get the odd notion that God is showing mercy because Jesus died. No—Jesus died because God is showing mercy. It was the mercy of God that gave us Calvary, not Calvary that gave us mercy. If God had not been merciful, there would have been no incarnation, no babe in the manger, no man on a cross, and no open tomb.

The intercession of Christ at the right hand of God does not increase the mercy of God toward His people. If God were not already merciful, there would be no intercession of Christ at the right hand of God. And if God is merciful at all, then He is infinitely merciful. It is impossible for the mediatorship of Jesus at the right hand of the Father to make the mercy of God any more than it is now. AOG082-083

Lord, show me what it means to be merciful and how to extend to others the mercy You have shown me. Amen.

JANUARY 10

All the Grace You Need

Let us then approach God's throne of grace with confidence, so that we may receive mercy and find grace to help us in our time of need.
—HEBREWS 4:16

Jesus was saying to us, "You went away in Adam, but you're coming back in Christ. And when you come back you'll find the Father hasn't changed. He's the same Father that He was when you all went out, every man to his own way. But when you come back in Jesus Christ you'll find Him exactly the same as you left Him—unchanged." And the Father ran and threw His arms around him and welcomed him and put a robe and a ring on him and said, "This my son was dead, and is alive again" (Luke 15:24). This is the grace of God. Isn't it worth believing in, preaching, teaching, singing about while the world stands?

If you're out of the grace of God, do you know where the grace is? Turn your eyes upon Jesus, and there's the grace of God flowing free for you—all the grace you need. If you set your teeth against Him, the grace of God might as well not exist for you. And Christ might as well not have died. But if you yield to Him and come home, then all the overwhelming, incomprehensible plentitude of goodness and kindness in the great illimitable reaches of God's nature are on your side. Even justice is on the side of the returning sinner: "He is faithful and just to forgive us our sins" (1 John 1:9). All the infinite attributes of God rejoice together when a man believes in the grace of God and returns home. AOG115

Lord, I confess that I am a sinner—but one who has been saved by Your grace. I look to You, Jesus, for everything I need. Amen.

JANUARY 11

So Man Can Come Home

God is light; in him there is no darkness at all.
—1 JOHN 1:5

I'd rather go to hell than go to a heaven presided over by a god who would compromise with sin, and I believe every true man and woman would feel the same. We want God to be the holy God that He is. God can never compromise; it doesn't work that way. . . .

God never compromises and comes halfway down. God stays the God that He is. This is the God we adore—our faithful, unchangeable Friend whose love is as great as His power and knows neither limit nor end. We don't want God to compromise. We don't want God to wink at our iniquity. We want God to do something about it.

What did He do about it? He came down and became flesh and became both God and man, sin excepted, in order that by His death He might remove everything out of the way so that man could come back. He couldn't come back if Christ had not come and died. But now because He came and died, He removed every moral obstacle out of the way so man can come home. AOG131-132

Holy Father, I praise You that You do not change or compromise, and that You have revealed Yourself fully in Your blessed Son, Jesus Christ. Thank You that He has made a way back to You. Amen.

JANUARY 12

Be Like Christ

Follow God's example, therefore, as dearly loved children and walk in the way of love, just as Christ loved us and gave himself up for us as a fragrant offering and sacrifice to God.

—EPHESIANS 5:1–2

This desire, this yearning to be near to God is, in fact, a yearning to be like Him. It's the yearning of the ransomed heart to be like God so there can be perfect communion, so the heart and God can come together in a fellowship that is divine.

There is a similarity which makes it compatible and proper for God to commune with His children—even the poorest and weakest of His children. But there are also dissimilarities, such that there isn't the degree of fellowship that there ought to be. There isn't that perfection of the sense of God's presence that we want and yearn and pray for and sing about.

How are we going to know what God is like so that we may know whether we're like God? The answer is: God is like Christ, for Christ is God manifest to mankind. By looking at our Lord Jesus we will know what God is like and will know what we have to be like to experience the unbroken and continuous presence of God. AOG145-146

Jesus, my Lord, You are the express image of the Father! May I become more like and bring glory to the Father this day. Amen.

JANUARY 13

The Holiness of Christ

But just as he who called you is holy, so be holy in all you do; for it is written: "Be holy, because I am holy."

—1 PETER 1:15–16

Our God is holy and our Lord is holy, and we call the Spirit the Holy Spirit. Now think how stained and how spotted and how carnal the average Christian is. We allow stains—months go by without repentance. Years go by without asking for cleansing or taking it. Then we sing, "Draw me nearer, nearer, nearer, blessed Lord." Or we pray, "Come, Lord, come to this meeting." Well, the Lord is there.

What we're praying is, "Oh Lord, show Thyself," but the Lord cannot; a holy God cannot show Himself in full communion to an unholy Christian. You ask, "Is it possible to be a Christian and be unholy?" It's possible to be a carnal Christian. You can have the seed of God in you, be regenerated and justified and still be unholy in some of your inner feelings and desires and willingness. AOG146-147

Lord, I pray that each member of the church will so earnestly seek holiness that many unsaved people in the world will be pointed to Jesus Christ. Amen.

JANUARY 14

Confusing Truths with "Truth"

By wisdom the LORD laid the earth's foundations, by understanding he set the heavens in place.

PROVERBS 3:19

The celebrated prayer of the great German astronomer, Kepler, has been a benediction to many: "O God, I thank Thee that Thou has permitted me to think Thy thoughts after Thee!"

This prayer is theologically sound because it acknowledges the priority of God in the universe. Whatever new thing anyone discovers is already old, for it is but the present expression of a previous thought of God. The idea of the thing precedes the thing itself; and when things raise thoughts in the thinker's mind, these are the ancient thoughts of God, however imperfectly understood.

Should an atheist, for instance, state that two times two equals four, he would be stating a truth and thinking God's thoughts after Him, even though he might deny that God exists.

In their search for facts, men have confused truths with truth. The words of Christ, "Ye shall know the truth and the truth shall make you free," have been wrenched from their context and used to stir people to the expectation of being made "free" by knowledge. Certainly, this is not what Christ had in mind when He uttered the words.

It is the Son who is the Truth that makes men free. Not facts, not scientific knowledge, but eternal Truth delivers men, and that eternal Truth became flesh to dwell among us! EWT058

Son of God, I acknowledge that You are the Truth! May I testify faithfully to who You are before others. Amen.

JANUARY 15

God Is Sovereign

We are in him who is true by being in his Son Jesus Christ.
1 JOHN 5:20

Oh, how I wish that I could adequately set forth the glory of the One who is worthy to be the object of our worship!

I do believe that if our new converts—the babes in Christ—could be made to see His thousand attributes and even partially comprehend His being, they would become faint with a yearning desire to worship and honor and acknowledge Him, now and forever!

I know that many discouraged Christians do not truly believe in God's sovereignty. In that case, we are not filling our role as the humble and trusting followers of God and His Christ.

And yet, that is why Christ came into our world. The old theologians called it "theanthropism"—the union of the divine and human natures in Christ. This is a great mystery, and I stand in awe before it!

The theanthropy is the mystery of God and man united in one Person—not two persons but two natures. So, the nature of God and the nature of man are united in this One who is our Lord Jesus Christ! MWT162

Lord Jesus, You are the only hope for this world. You provided the perfect plan for our redemption. Though Your supernatural being may be beyond our human comprehension, Your grace and mercy and love are worthy of all our praise. Amen.

JANUARY 16

The Kindness and Forgiveness of Christ

But when the kindness and love of God our Savior appeared, he saved us, not because of righteous things we had done, but because of his mercy. He saved us through the washing of rebirth and renewal by the Holy Spirit, whom he poured out on us generously through Jesus Christ our Savior.

—TITUS 3:4–6

Another quality of Christ is kindness. Think how utterly kind our Lord Jesus is. The love of God is kinder than the measure of man's mind. Think of the kindness of Jesus in contrast to the harshness, the severity, the sharpness, the bitterness, the acidity in so many people's lives. How can a kind Savior feel perfectly at home with a harsh Christian?

Then there is forgiveness. He is a forgiving Lord and He forgave them while they beat Him. He forgave them while they put Him on the cross. But how hard and vengeful so many of the Lord's children are! Can you remember bad things that happened to you twenty years ago? You can't get over it; you say you've forgiven it, but you haven't. You're vengeful; He is forgiving. And He proved He was forgiving by dying in blood. You prove that you're vengeful and hard by many proofs and demonstrations. AOG149-150

Lord Jesus, You are holy and righteous, yet You are also kind. You are gentle and love the lowly. Thank You for showing me Your kindness and may I extend it to others this day. Amen.

JANUARY 17

Faith and Experience

Taste and see that the LORD is good.
—PSALM 34:8

I insist that the effective preaching of Jesus Christ, rightly understood, will produce Christian experience in Christian believers. Moreover, if preaching does not produce spiritual experience and maturing in the believer, that preaching is not being faithful to the Christ revealed in the Scriptures.

Let me say it again another way: The Christ of the Bible is not rightly known until there is an experience of Him within the believer, for our Savior and Lord offers Himself to human experience.

When Jesus says, "Come unto me, all ye that labour and are heavy laden" (Matt. 11:28), it is an invitation to a spiritual experience. He is saying, "Will you consent to come? Have you added determination to your consent? Then come; come now!"

Yes, our Lord gives Himself to us in experience. David says in Psalm 34: "O taste and see that the LORD is good." I think David said exactly what he meant.

Surely the Holy Spirit was saying through David: "You have taste buds in your soul for tasting, for experiencing spiritual things. Taste and experience that God is good!" MWT147

Lord, the great need of people within and outside our churches today is to experience the "real thing"—God in all His power and majesty and personal involvement in our lives. Help me to inspire others to "taste" You, Lord. Amen.

JANUARY 18

The Incarnation

Today in the town of David a Savior has been born to you; he is the Messiah, the Lord. This will be a sign to you: You will find a baby wrapped in cloths and lying in a manger.

—LUKE 2:11–12

"Let the beauty of the LORD our God be upon us" (Ps. 90:17). Was there ever anything more beautiful than the story of Jesus' birth? Was there ever anything more beautiful than the picture of Jesus walking up and down among men in tenderness of humility, healing the sick and raising the dead, forgiving sinners and restoring poor fallen people back to society again? Is there anything more wonderful than His going out to the cross to die for those who were crucifying Him?

Was there anything lovelier than to be the Creator of His own mother, to have made the very body that gave Him protection and bore Him at last into the world? Was anything more awful and awesome and mysterious than that God-Man walking about among men, saying, "I beheld Satan as lightning fall from heaven" (Luke 10:18) and "Before Abraham was, I am" (John 8:58)? He was "the only begotten Son, which is in the bosom of the Father" (John 1:18). AOG189-190

Lord God, thank You for willingly coming to earth and becoming so vulnerable. You are a selfless, loving God. I stand in awe of You, O Lord. Amen.

JANUARY 19

A Great Moral Blunder

By the name of Jesus Christ of Nazareth, whom you crucified. . . . Jesus is "the stone you builders rejected."
—ACTS 4:10–11

Of all the people on the earth, the nation of Israel surely was the best prepared to receive the Christ of God. The children of Abraham, they were called to be a chosen people in an everlasting covenant with God, the Father.

Yet they failed to recognize Jesus as Messiah and Lord. There is no doubt that theirs was the greatest moral blunder in the history of mankind. He came to His own people, and they rejected Him!

Jesus taught frankly that He was asking His followers to throw themselves out on the resources of God. For the multitude, He was asking too much. He had come from God but they received Him not!

It seems to be a comfort to some Christians to sit back and blame and belabor the Jews, refusing to acknowledge that they have information and benefits and spiritual light that the Jews never had.

It is surely wrong for us to try to comfort our own carnal hearts by any emphasis that Israel rejected Him. If we do that, we only rebuild the sepulchres of our fathers as Jesus said! MWT169

Lord, would I have mocked You? Denied You? Ignored who You really were? I know only that I wholeheartedly worship You today as the King of kings and Lord of lords! Amen.

JANUARY 20

Humanity and Deity

But when the set time had fully come, God sent his Son, born of a woman, born under the law, to redeem those under the law, that we might receive adoption to sonship.
—GALATIANS 4:4–5

Christ the eternal Son is timeless. When you think about Jesus, you have to think twice. You have to think of His humanity and His deity. He said a lot of things that made it sound as if He wasn't God. He said other things that made it sound as if He wasn't human. He said, for instance, "Before Abraham was, I am" (John 8:58). That made it sound as if He antedated creation. Then He said, "I can of mine own self do nothing: as I hear, I judge" (5:30), and that made it sound as if He wasn't divine. He said, "my Father is greater than I" (14:28), and that made it sound as if He wasn't God. And He said, "I and my Father are one" (10:30), and that made it sound as if He wasn't human.

But the fact is, He is both. . . . He could talk like God and then He could talk like man. So we've always got to think about the Son of Man, Jesus Christ the Lord, in two ways. AOGII65-66

Christ, while I do not understand the mystery of the Incarnation, I believe that You are fully human and fully divine. May those who do not know You come to a saving knowledge of You, Son of God and Son of Man. Amen.

JANUARY 21

Before the Foundation of the World

"I am the Alpha and the Omega," says the Lord God, "who is, and who was, and who is to come, the Almighty."
—REVELATION 1:8

How could He be slain from the foundation of the world [Rev. 13:8]? When God laid the heaven and the earth and caused the grass to be upon the hills and the trees to be upon the mountains, when God made the birds to fly in the air and the fish to swim in the sea, God had already in His heart lived Calvary and the resurrection and the glory and the crown. So He was slain before the foundation of the world. . . .

God never panics, because God never looks at clocks or watches. "The fulness of time" was the time when God had ordered it; when that time came, Mary gave birth to her Boy and He was born and lived and died, "the just for the unjust, that he might bring us to God" (1 Peter 3:18). So the eternal Son has lived through all time. He who was born in Bethlehem's manger did not take His origin in the womb of the virgin. The human Baby did, but the eternal Son did not. AOGII076-077

Oh, the mystery of God's sovereign plan! I praise You, Lord, for Your infinite wisdom and for ordaining a plan of redemption long before the world was made. Amen.

JANUARY 22

The Timeless One

Father, glorify me in your presence with the glory I had with you before the world began.

—JOHN 17:5

My poor, helpless, dependent self finds a home in God. God is our home! I look forward not so much to heaven as my home but as God is my home, in His heaven and the eternity of God. We poor victims of the passing moment, we have found the Timeless One. When I preach, I notice some people looking at their wristwatch. We're victims of time—counting our pulse beating, tearing off from the calendar the page that tells us that one more month has gone by.

But there is One who contains time in His bosom: the Timeless One, who stepped out of eternity into time, in the womb of the virgin Mary, who died and rose and lives at the right hand of God for us. He invites us into His bosom where time is no more. And instead of getting old, we stay young in Jesus Christ. Do you know that song, "Now rest, my long-divided heart; Fixed on this blissful center, rest!" What did he mean? "If a house be divided against itself, that house cannot stand" (Mark 3:25), said our Lord. There is confusion, revolution and tumult until we find rest in Christ. What is that blissful center? It is none other than the Son of God made flesh, crucified and risen. And He invites us to rest in His bosom. There is a real sense in which nobody knows rest of mind or heart until they find it in Jesus Christ our Lord. AOGII109

Lord Jesus, every day there is indeed some new glimpse of Your glory. Today may I live with a holy anticipation so that I may discover more of who You are! Amen.

JANUARY 23

Life in Christ

The thief comes only to steal and kill and destroy; I have come that they may have life, and have it to the full.
—JOHN 10:10

God offers life, but not an improved old life. The life He offers is life out of death. It stands always on the far side of the cross. Whoever would possess it must pass under the rod. He must repudiate himself and concur in God's just sentence against him.

What does this mean to the individual, the condemned man who would find life in Christ Jesus? How can this theology be translated into life? Simply, he must repent and believe. He must forsake his sins and then go on to forsake himself. Let him cover nothing, defend nothing, excuse nothing. Let him not seek to make terms with God, but let him bow his head before the stroke of God's stern displeasure and acknowledge himself worthy to die.

Having done this, let him gaze with simple trust upon the risen Savior, and from Him will come life and rebirth and cleansing and power. The cross that ended the earthly life of Jesus now puts an end to the sinner; and the power that raised Christ from the dead now raises him to a new life along with Christ. OCN004

Father, I praise You for giving me new life in Your Son! May I walk in abundance of life today. Amen.

The Lord of All Beauty

They will see the glory of the Lord, the splendor of our God.
—ISAIAH. 35:2

Think with me about beauty—and about this matchless One who is the Lord of all beauty, our Savior!

God has surely deposited something within our human beings that is capable of understanding and appreciating beauty—the love of harmonious forms, appreciation of colors, and beautiful sounds.

Brother, these are only the external counterparts of a deeper and more enduring beauty—that which we call moral beauty. It has been the uniqueness and the perfection of Christ's moral beauty that has charmed even those who claimed to be His enemies throughout the centuries of history.

We do not have any record of Hitler saying anything against the moral perfection of Jesus. One of the great philosophers, Nietzsche, objected to Paul's theology of justification by faith, but he was strangely moved within himself by the perfection of moral beauty found in the life and character of Jesus, the Christ.

We should thank God for the promise of heaven being the place of supreme beauty—and the One who is all-beautiful is there! MWT401

Thank You, Lord, for Your beauty that is reflected in the lives of Your servants who have left the comfort of their own home and culture to serve You in distant lands. "How beautiful on the mountains are the feet of him that bringeth good tidings" (Isa. 52:7). Amen.

JANUARY 25

Heavenly Wisdom

For the Lord gives wisdom; from his mouth comes knowledge and understanding.
—PROVERBS 2:6

The writer of the Proverbs in the Old Testament taught that true spiritual knowledge is the result of a visitation of heavenly wisdom. It is a kind of baptism of the Spirit of Truth that comes to God-fearing men and women. This wisdom is always associated with righteousness and humility; it is never found apart from godliness and true holiness of life.

We need to learn and declare again the ministry of wisdom from above. It is apparent that we cannot know God by the logic of reason. Through reason we can only know about God. The deeper mysteries of God remain hidden to us until we have received illumination from above. We were created with a capacity to know spiritual things—that potential died when Adam and Eve sinned. Thus, "dead in sin" is a description of that part of our being in which we should be able to know God in conscious awareness.

Christ's atoning death enabled our Lord and Savior to take God the Father with one hand and man with the other and introduce us. Jesus enables us to find God very quickly! MWT290

Thank You, Father, that You provided a way—the only way—to bring sinful people back into a right relationship with You. That one way is through faith in Jesus Christ. Thank You, Lord, that You did not leave us lost and hopeless. Amen.

JANUARY 26

No Compromise of Deity

Who, being in very nature God, did not consider equality with God something to be used to his own advantage; rather, he made himself nothing by taking the very nature of a servant, being made in human likeness.

—PHILIPPIANS 2:6–7

We can surely know this, at least: that the Incarnation required no compromise of deity. Let us always remember that when God became incarnate, there was no compromise on God's part. . . .

But the holy God who is God, and all else not God, our Father who art in heaven, could never compromise Himself. The Incarnation, the Word made flesh, was accomplished without any compromise of the holy Deity.

The living God did not degrade Himself by this condescension. He did not in any sense make Himself to be less than God.

He remained ever God and everything else remained not God. The gulf still existed even after Jesus Christ had become man and had dwelt among us. Instead of God degrading Himself when He became man, by the act of Incarnation He elevated mankind to Himself. . . .

Thus, we do not degrade God but we elevate man—and that is the wonder of redemption! CES010-011

Lord, You are so powerful that You could humble Yourself, yet remain the majestic God. Thank You, Father, that because Jesus came down to me, I can be raised up to be with You. Amen.

JANUARY 27

The Eternal Verity

Jesus Christ the same yesterday and today and forever.
—HEBREWS 13:8

There is a great deal of discussion now taking place about the lack of spiritual power in our Christian churches. What about the New Testament patterns?

Brethren, the apostolic method was to provide a foundation of good, sound biblical reasons for following the Savior, for our willingness to let the Spirit of God display the great Christian virtues in our lives.

That is why we come in faith and rejoicing to the eternal verity of Hebrews 13:8: "Jesus Christ the same yesterday, and to day, and for ever!" This proclamation gives significance to every other section of teaching and exhortation in the letter to the Hebrews. In this verse is truth that is morally and spiritually dynamic if we will exercise the faith and the will to demonstrate it in our needy world.

I think this fact, this truth that Jesus Christ wants to be known in His church as the ever-living, never-changing Lord of all, could bring back again the power and testimony of the early church! MWT081

Lord, I pray for my pastor and my church, that they will comprehend anew the truth that You are ever-living and never-changing. Amen.

JANUARY 28

Lord and Savior

The Son is the image of the invisible God, the firstborn over all creation. For in him all things were created: things in heaven and on earth, visible and invisible, whether thrones or powers or rulers or authorities; all things have been created through him and for him.

—COLOSSIANS 1:15–16

It is the truth that God has never done anything apart from Jesus Christ. The stars in their courses, the frogs that croak beside the lake, the angels in heaven above, and men on earth below all came out of the channel we call the eternal Word. While we are busy presenting Jesus as Lord and Savior, it is true that we have all received out of His fullness.

Now, some time ago I wrote in an editorial concerning Jesus Christ that there can be no Savior-hood without Lordship. This was not original with me because I believe that the Bible plainly teaches that Jesus Christ is both Lord and Savior; that He is Lord before He is Savior; and that if He is not Lord, He is not Savior.

I repeat: when we present this Word, this eternal Word who was made flesh to dwell among us, as Lord and Savior, we present Him also in His other offices—Creator, Sustainer, and Benefactor. CES020-021

Wonderful Jesus, forgive me for the ways in which I have looked to You as Savior and not as Lord. I submit myself to You today and give You full reign of my life. Amen.

JANUARY 29

Man With God

Who then is the one who condemns? No one. Christ Jesus who died—more than that, who was raised to life—is at the right hand of God and is also interceding for us.

—ROMANS 8:34

Even among those who acknowledge the deity of Christ there is often a failure to recognize His manhood. We are quick to assert that when He walked the earth He was God with men, but we overlook a truth equally as important, that where He sits now on His mediatorial throne He is Man with God.

The teaching of the New Testament is that now, at this very moment, there is a Man in heaven appearing in the presence of God for us. He is as certainly a man as was Adam or Moses or Paul. He is a man glorified, but His glorification did not dehumanize Him. Today He is a real man, of the race of mankind, bearing our lineaments and dimensions, a visible and audible man whom any other man would recognize instantly as one of us.

But more than this, He is heir of all things, Lord of all worlds, Head of the church and the Firstborn of the new creation. He is the way to God, the life of the believer, the hope of Israel, and the high priest of every true worshiper. He holds the keys of death and hell and stands as advocate and surety for everyone who believes on Him in truth. WOS172-173

Father, not only do I have the assurance of my salvation, but I also know that You intercede for me as a man who has experienced life on this earth. Thank You for being both God with men and man with God. Amen.

JANUARY 30

Christ Receives Sinners

God exalted him to his own right hand as Prince and Savior that he might bring . . . repentance and forgive . . . sins.
—ACTS 5:31

What a gracious thing for us that Jesus Christ never thinks about what we have been. He always thinks about what we are going to be!

The Savior who is our Lord cares absolutely nothing about your moral case history. He forgives it and starts from there as though you had been born one minute before.

The woman of Samaria met our Lord at the well and we ask, "Why was Jesus willing to reveal so much more about Himself in this setting than He did in other encounters during His ministry?"

You and I would never have chosen this woman with such a shadow lying across her life, but Jesus is the Christ of God, and He could sense the potential within her innermost being. He gave her the secret of His Messiahship and the secret of the nature of God. Her frankness and her humility appealed to the Savior as they talked of man's need and the true worship of God by the Spirit of God.

In Jesus' day, His critics said in scorn: "This man receives sinners!" They were right—and He lived and died and rose again to prove it. The blessed part is this: He is still receiving sinners! MWT199

Lord, I have many family, friends, and coworkers who need You as their Savior. Will You receive them into Your family today? Amen.

JANUARY 31

Asking In His Name

You may ask me for anything in my name, and I will do it.
—JOHN 14:14

Asking in Jesus' name simply means asking according to His will. This is where the promises come in: you must know the promises to know what is His will. Memorize the Word of God; let it become a part of your being so that you can fully count upon the merit of Jesus.

The merit of Jesus is enough! We will enter paradise because Jesus went out from paradise on our behalf. We will live because Jesus died. We will be with God because Jesus was rejected from the presence of God in the terror of the crucifixion.

Our faith rests upon the character of God and the merit of His Son, Jesus. We do not have anything we can bring—only our poor, miserable souls. The bad person who thinks he or she is good is shut out of God's kingdom forever. But the person who knows he or she is the chief of sinners and totally unworthy, who comes in humility depending upon the merit of Jesus, enters in. FBR049-050

Lord Christ, I look to You for all I need, placing my faith in what You have done for me. Give me all I need this day to accomplish Your will. Amen.

FEBRUARY

FEBRUARY 1

Spirit Anointed

How God anointed Jesus of Nazareth with the Holy Spirit and power, and how he went around doing good and healing all who were under the power of the devil, because God was with him.

—ACTS 10:38

Our Lord Jesus, while He was on earth, did not accomplish His powerful deeds in the strength of His deity. I believe He did them in the strength and authority of His Spirit-anointed humanity.

My reasoning is this: If Jesus had come to earth and performed His ministry in the power of His deity, what He did would have been accepted as a matter of course. Cannot God do anything He wants to do? No one would have questioned His works as the works of deity. But Jesus veiled His deity and ministered as a man. It is noteworthy, however, that He did not begin His ministry—His deeds of authority and power—until He had been anointed with the Holy Spirit.

I know there are erudite scholars and theological experts who will dispute my conclusion. Nevertheless, I hold it true. Jesus Christ, in the power and authority of His Spirit-anointed humanity, stilled the waves, quieted the winds, healed the sick, gave sight to the blind, exercised complete authority over demons, and raised the dead. He did all the miraculous things He was moved to do among men not as God, which would not have been miraculous at all, but as a Spirit-anointed man. Remarkable! JMI060-061

Jesus, You are the perfect human and the image of what I want to be. Fill me with Your Spirit, that I may ever walk in Your steps to the glory of God the Father. Amen.

FEBRUARY 2

Christ Does Not Change

Jesus came to them and said, "All authority in heaven and on earth has been given to me."
—MATTHEW 28:18

You will have to prove it to me if you are among those who claim that Jesus Christ refuses to do for you something that He has done for any other of His disciples!

I address this to all of those who insist that the gifts of the Spirit ended when the last apostle died. They have never furnished chapter and verse for their position.

When some men beat the cover off their Bible to demonstrate how they stand for the Word of God, they should be reminded that they are only standing by their own interpretation!

I find nothing in the Bible that says the Lord has changed. He has the same love, the same grace, the same mercy, the same power, the same desires for the blessings of His children.

Why can we not claim all that God has promised for His redeemed people? What a sad condition for Christians who are in the Church of the mighty Redeemer and Deliverer, who is eternally the Victor, the Rock of Ages. Let us never forget that Jesus Christ is the same yesterday, today, and forever! (see Heb. 13:8). MWT246

Almighty God, I thank You and praise You that You are the same yesterday, today, and forever. This means that You are exactly the same God who personally led the children of Israel in the desert wilderness. Thank You, Lord, for Your patience and guidance in my life today. Amen.

FEBRUARY 3

Total Commitment

When the young man heard this, he went away sad, because he had great wealth.

—MATTHEW 19:22

When the rich young ruler learned the cost of discipleship, he went away sorrowing. He could not give up the sunny side of the brae. But thanks be to God, there are some in every age who refuse to go back! The Acts of the Apostles is the story of men and women who turned their faces into the stiff wind of persecution and loss and followed the Lamb whithersoever He went. They knew that the world hated Christ without a cause and hated them for His sake, but for the glory that was set before them they continued steadfastly on the way.

What is it that Christ has to offer us that is sound, genuine, and desirable?

He offers forgiveness of sins, inward cleansing, peace with God, eternal life, the gift of the Holy Spirit, victory over temptation, resurrection from the dead, a glorified body, immortality, and a dwelling place in the house of the Lord forever! These are a few of the benefits that come to us as a result of faith in Christ and total committal to Him.

To accept the call of Christ changes the returning sinner indeed, but it does not change the world. The wind still blows toward hell and the man who is walking in the opposite direction will have the wind in his face. We had better take this into account: If the unsearchable riches of Christ are not worth suffering for, we should know it now and cease to play at religion! EWT284

Lord Christ, thank You for what You offer me, for it is infinitely greater than what the world offers. May I never turn away from You in unbelief or ingratitude. Amen.

FEBRUARY 4

In the Beginning

In the beginning was the Word . . . and the Word was God.
—JOHN 1:1

John, in his Gospel, provides a beautiful portrait of the eternal Christ, starting with those stark, incredible words: "In the beginning!" My brethren, that is where we start with the understanding and the revelation of Christianity!

Many others have made a variety of claims, but only our Christ is the Christ of God. Certainly it was not Buddha and not Mohammed; not Joseph Smith, not Mrs. Eddy, and not Father Divine! All of these and countless others like them had beginnings—but they all had their endings too.

What an incredible difference! Our Christian life commences with the eternal Son of God. This is our Lord Jesus Christ: the Word who was with the Father in the beginning, the Word who was God, and the Word who is God! This is the only one who can assure us: "No man cometh unto the Father, but by me" (John 14:6). MWT010

Loving Heavenly Father, help me to see this day just how awesome Your Son, Jesus Christ, truly is. Amen.

FEBRUARY 5

A Pain Felt in Heaven

When he had received the drink, Jesus said, "It is finished." With that, he bowed his head and gave up his spirit.
—JOHN 19:30

The Father in heaven so loved the world that He gave His only begotten Son. It was the love of the Father that sent the Son into our world to die for mankind. The Father and Son and Spirit were in perfect agreement that the eternal Son should die for the sins of the world. We are not wrong to believe—and proclaim—that while Mary's Son, Jesus, died alone, terribly alone, on that cross, the loving heart of God the Father was as deeply pained with suffering as was the heart of the holy, dying Son.

We must ask our Lord to help us comprehend what it meant to the Trinity for the Son to die alone on the cross. When the holy Father had to turn His back on the dying Son by the necessity of divine justice, I believe the pain for the Father was as great as the suffering of the Savior as He bore our sins in His body. When the soldier drove that Roman spear into the side of Jesus, I believe it was felt in heaven.

JMI112-113

Christ, the price You paid for my sins is far greater than I could imagine. I thank You and the Father and the Holy Spirit for the sacrifice You made. Amen.

FEBRUARY 6

The Cross Did Not Change God

I the Lord do not change.
—MALACHI 3:6

The work of Christ on the cross did not influence God to love us, did not increase that love by one degree, did not open any fount of grace or mercy in His heart. He had loved us from old eternity and needed nothing to stimulate that love. The cross is not responsible for God's love; rather, it was His love that conceived the cross as the one method by which we could be saved.

God felt no different toward us after Christ had died for us, for in the mind of God Christ had already died before the foundation of the world. God never saw us except through atonement. The human race could not have existed one day in its fallen state had not Christ spread His mantle of atonement over it. And this He did in eternal purpose long ages before they led Him out to die on the hill above Jerusalem. All God's dealings with man have been conditioned upon the cross. . . .

The Scriptures never represent the persons of the Trinity as opposed to or in disagreement with each other. The Holy Three have ever been and will forever be one in essence, in love, in purpose.

We have been redeemed not by one person of the Trinity putting Himself against another, but by the three persons working in the ancient and glorious harmony of the Godhead. TET023-024

Father, thank You for loving me with an everlasting love. I pray that I would always see Your unchanging love and extend it to those around me. Amen.

FEBRUARY 7

The Christ Question

"What shall I do, then, with Jesus who is called the Messiah?" Pilate asked.

—MATTHEW 27:22

"Where is Jesus now?" asks the world, and the Christian answers, "At the right hand of God." He died but He is not dead. He rose again as He said He would. . . . Better than all, His Spirit now reveals to the Christian heart not a dead Christ but a living one. This we are sent to declare with all the bold dogmatism of those who know, who have been there and experienced it beyond the possibility of a doubt.

The gospel is the official proclamation that Christ died for us and is risen again, with the added announcement that everyone who will believe, and as a result of that belief will cast in his lot with Christ in full and final committal, shall be saved eternally.

He . . . will not be popular and . . . he will be called to stand where Jesus stood before the world: to be admired by many, loved by a few, and rejected at last by the majority of men. He must be willing to pay this price, or let him go his way; Christ has nothing more to say to him now. GTM038

Father, I pray You would help me to reach out and speak the truth about Christ to those who do not know Him. May their hearts be good soil to receive His Word and accept Him as Savior. Amen.

FEBRUARY 8

The Word Made Flesh

And a voice from heaven said, "This is my Son, whom I love; with him I am well pleased."
MATTHEW 3:17

I have given much thought and contemplation to the sweetest and tenderest of all of the mysteries in God's revelation to man—the Incarnation! Jesus, the Christ, is the Eternal One, for in the fullness of time He humbles Himself. John's description is plain: The Word was made flesh and dwelt among us.

I confess that I would have liked to have seen the baby Jesus. But the glorified Jesus yonder at the right hand of the Majesty on high was the baby Jesus once cradled in the manger straw. Taking a body of humiliation, He was still the Creator who made the wood of that manger, made the straw, and was Creator of all the beasts that were there.

In truth, He made the little town of Bethlehem and all that it was. He also made the star that lingered over the scene that night. He had come into His own world, His Father's world. Everything we touch and handle belongs to Him. So we have come to love Him and adore Him and honor Him! MWT394

Lord, You became so vulnerable for us by becoming a helpless baby. Thank You for Your intentional humility. Even in Your birth You showed us how to sacrifice what is rightly ours for the benefit of others. Help me to apply this lesson in my own life so that I will become more like You. Amen.

FEBRUARY 9

Christ's Eternal Glory

We have seen his glory, the glory of the one and only Son, who came from the Father.

—JOHN 1:14

The Apostle John speaks for all when he writes of the eternal Son and reminds us that "we beheld his glory." John was speaking of much more than the glory of Christ's wondrous works. Every part of nature had to yield to Him and His authority. Everything our Lord did was meaningful in the display of His eternal glory.

But we may be sure that John had a much greater glory in mind than the gracious and wonderful acts of healing and help.

It was the very person and character of Jesus that was glorious. It was not only what He did—but what He was. What He was in His person primary!

Brethren, there can be no argument about Jesus Christ's glory—it lay in the fact that He was perfect love in a loveless world; that He was perfect purity in an impure world; and that He was perfect meekness in a harsh and quarrelsome world. Patience in suffering, unquenchable life, and God's grace and truth were in the eternal Word, as well.

This is the divine and eternal glory that earth's most famous and capable personalities can never attain! MWT263

Lord, we get so bogged down with our life's responsibilities that we often miss out on the kind of revelation that John had of Jesus Christ's glory. I want to slow down, Lord, to experience more of Your eternal glory. Amen.

FEBRUARY 10

Our Hope

He was taken up before their very eyes, and a cloud hid him from their sight.
—ACTS 1:9

The glory of the Christian faith is that the Christ who died for our sins rose again for our justification. We should joyfully remember His birth and gratefully muse on His dying, but the crown of all our hopes is with Him at the Father's right hand.

Paul gloried in the cross and refused to preach anything except Christ and Him crucified, but to him the cross stood for the whole redemptive work of Christ. In his epistles Paul writes of the incarnation and the crucifixion, yet he stops not at the manger or the cross but constantly sweeps our thoughts on to the resurrection and upward to the ascension and the throne.

"All power is given unto me in heaven and in earth" (Matt. 28:18), said our risen Lord before He went up on high, and the first Christians believed Him and went forth to share His triumph. "With great power gave the apostles witness of the resurrection of the Lord Jesus: and great grace was upon them all" (Acts 4:33).

Should the church shift her emphasis from the weakness of the manger and the death of the cross to the life and power of the enthroned Christ, perhaps she might recapture her lost glory. It is worth a try. WOS118-119

Lord, thank You for raising me up with You. Keep my eyes fixed on You, the resurrected and ascended One, Who reigns in power over all things. Amen.

FEBRUARY 11

The Only Means of Grace

We have seen his glory, the glory of the one and only Son, who came from the Father, full of grace and truth.
—JOHN 1:14

Here are two important truths. (And I want you to take it and the next time you hear a professor or a preacher say otherwise, go to him and remind him of this.) The first truth is that no one ever was saved, no one is now saved, and no one ever will be saved except by grace. Before Moses nobody was ever saved except by grace. During Moses' time nobody was ever saved except by grace. After Moses and before the cross and after the cross and since the cross and during all that dispensation, during any dispensation, anywhere, any time since Abel offered his first lamb before God on the smoking altar—nobody was ever saved in any other way than by grace.

The second truth is that grace always comes by Jesus Christ. The law was given by Moses, but grace came by Jesus Christ. This does not mean that before Jesus was born of Mary there was no grace. God dealt in grace with mankind, looking forward to the Incarnation and death of Jesus before Christ came. Now, since He's come and gone to the Father's right hand, God looks back upon the cross as we look back upon the cross. Everybody from Abel on was saved by looking forward to the cross. Grace came by Jesus Christ. And everybody that's been saved since the cross is saved by looking back at the cross. AOG100-101

Father, may I experience more of Your grace in Christ, the One who freely gave His life for me. Amen.

FEBRUARY 12

Selfish Personal Interest

This is especially true of those who follow the corrupt desire of the flesh and despise authority.
—2 PETER 2:10

Throughout history, the philosophers have pretty well agreed on the conclusion that selfish personal interest is the motive behind all human conduct.

The philosopher Epictetus illustrated his understanding with the fact that two dogs may romp on the lawn with every appearance of friendship until someone tosses a piece of raw meat between them. Instantly, their play turns into savage fight as each struggles to get the meat for himself. Let us not condemn the old thinker for comparing the conduct of men to animals. The Bible frequently does and, humbling as it may be to us, we humans often look bad by comparison.

If we would be wise in the wisdom of God, we must face up to the truth that men and women are not basically good: They are basically evil, and the essence of sin lies in their selfishness! Putting our own interests before the glory of God is sin in its Godward aspects, and the putting of our own interests before those of our fellow man is sin as it relates to society. By the cross, Jesus Christ demonstrated pure, selfless love in its fullest perfection. When He died, He set a crown of beauty upon a God-centered and an others-centered life! MWT220

Lord Jesus, I pray that in every situation today I will put the interests of others before my own, just as You have done. Amen.

FEBRUARY 12

Our Judge

The Father judges no one, but has entrusted all judgment to the Son.

—JOHN 5:22

What is your concept of Jesus Christ, my brother? . . .The Christ we must deal with has eyes as a flame of fire, and His feet are like burnished brass, and out of His mouth comes a sharp, two-edged sword.

He will be the Judge of mankind. And, thank God, you can leave your loved ones who have died in His hands, knowing that He Himself suffered, knowing that He knows all, that no mistakes can be made, that there can be no miscarriage of justice, because He knows all that can be known!

This is one of the neglected Bible doctrines of our day—that Jesus Christ is the judge of mankind. The Father judges no man. When the Lord, the Son of Man, shall come in the clouds of glory, then shall be gathered unto Him the nations, and He shall separate them. God has given Him judgment, authority, to judge mankind, so that He is both the Judge and Saviour of men.

That makes me both love Him and fear Him! I love Him because He is my Saviour and I fear Him because He is my Judge. TS083-084

Christ, You are the just and merciful Judge. Help me to trust that You will right all wrongs in the world, and help me to live my life in a manner that is pleasing to You. Amen.

FEBRUARY 14

Just As He Went

These have come so that the proven genuineness of your faith—of greater worth than gold, which perishes even though refined by fire—may result in praise, glory and honor when Jesus Christ is revealed.

—1 PETER 1:7

Our Lord Jesus Christ has not yet appeared the second time, for if He had, it would have been consistent with the meaning of the word as it was commonly used in the New Testament. He would have to appear as He appeared in the temple, as He appeared by the Jordan or on the Mount of Transfiguration. It would have to be as He once appeared to His disciples after the resurrection—in visible, human manifestation, having dimension so He could be identified by the human eye and ear and touch.

If the word *appearing* is going to mean what it universally means, the appearing of Jesus Christ has to be very much the same as His appearing on the earth the first time, nearly 2,000 years ago.

When He came the first time, He walked among men. He took babies in His arms. He healed the sick and the afflicted and the lame. He blessed people, ate with them, and walked among them, and the Scriptures tell us that when He appears again He will appear in the same manner. He will be a man again, though a glorified man! He will be a man who can be identified, the same Jesus as He went away. . . .

We may, therefore, expect Jesus Christ again to appear on earth to living persons as He first appeared. TSII151-152

Lord, give me the grace to prepare for Your return and the ability to rejoice in my trials as I wait for that glorious day. Amen.

FEBRUARY 15

Decision! Decision!

As God's co-workers we urge you not to receive God's grace in vain.

—2 CORINTHIANS 6:1

I believe there must be great throngs of men and women who keep on assuring themselves that they will "make it" into the kingdom of God by a kind of heavenly osmosis! They have a fond hope that there is a kind of unconscious "leaking through" of their personalities into the walls of the kingdom.

That is a vain hope. No one ever comes to God by an automatic or unconscious process; it does not happen that way at all!

The individual man or woman must make the choice—and on that point we must be dogmatic. We have the Book, the Word of God. We know that God has revealed Himself through the giving of Jesus Christ, the eternal Son. We know that the saving message is the gospel—the good news of our Lord Jesus Christ.

There is no way that God can come to us and forgive us and restore us to the position of son or daughter until we consciously let Him! This is an authentic experience of the grace and mercy of God—we have made our decision! MWT297

Lord, I pray that pastors in our churches will make it clear from their pulpits that in order to be saved, people must acknowledge their sin before God and receive Jesus Christ as their Savior and Lord of their new life. Amen.

FEBRUARY 16

Forever Incarnated

Therefore the Lord himself will give you a sign: The virgin will conceive and give birth to a son, and will call him Immanuel.
—ISAIAH 7:14

Then, too, there is another thing that we can know for sure about the acts of God—and that is that God can never back out of His bargain. This union of man with God is effected unto perpetuity!

In the sense which we have been considering, God can never cease to be man, for the second Person of the Trinity can never un-incarnate Himself, or de-incarnate Himself. The Incarnation remains forever a fact, for "And the Word was made flesh, and dwelt among us" (John 1:14). . . .

They called His name Immanuel, which means God with us. In that first coming of Jesus the Christ, God again came to dwell with men in person. . . .

He appeared to dwell *with* men. He appeared to be united *to* men. He came to ultimately dwell *in* men forever. So, it is with men, and to men, and in men that He came to dwell. CES011, 013

Father, I am amazed at the incarnation of Your Son! How marvelous are Your deeds. May I ever be grateful for what You have done in Christ. Amen.

FEBRUARY 17

Everything By Grace

Out of his fullness we have all received grace in place of grace already given.

—JOHN 1:16

Let us remember this: everything God does is by grace, for no man, no creature, no being deserves anything. Salvation is by grace, the Creation is by grace—all that God does is by grace and every human being has received of His fullness.

This boundless grace must operate wherever that which is not God appeals to that which is God; wherever the voice of the creature crosses the vast gulf to the ears of the Creator. . . .

All that you have is out of His grace. Jesus Christ, the eternal Word, who became flesh and dwelt among us, is the open channel through which God moves to provide all the benefits He gives to saints and sinners.

And what about the years, the rest of your existence?

You cannot believe that you have earned it.

You cannot believe that it has something to do with whether you are good or bad.

Confess that it is out of His grace, for the entire universe is the beneficiary of God's grace and goodness. CES018-019

Precious Lord, I praise You today for the grace You have given me. You act so kindly toward me, and I am ever in awe of who You are. May I honor You this day. Amen.

FEBRUARY 18

Praise the Redeemer

Then I heard every creature in heaven and on earth and under the earth and on the sea, and all that is in them, saying: "To him who sits on the throne and to the Lamb be praise and honor and glory and power, for ever and ever!"
—REVELATION 5:13

In the fifth chapter of Revelation, John bears record of the whole universe joining to give praise to the Lamb that was slain. Under the earth and on the earth and above the earth, John heard creatures praising Jesus Christ, all joining in a great chorus and saying with a loud voice, "Worthy is the Lamb that was slain to receive power, and riches, and wisdom, and strength, and honour, and glory, and blessing" (5:12). . . .

Yes, surely the entire universe is a beneficiary of God's rich grace in Jesus Christ.

When we faithfully witness and present Christ to men and women in our day as Lord and Savior, we should remember that they are already receiving benefits of grace, and we are only presenting Jesus Christ to them in a new office—that of Redeemer.

When we say to an unbelieving man, *Believe on the Lord Jesus Christ,* we are actually saying to him: "Believe on the One who sustains you and upholds you and Who has given you life. Believe on the One who pities you and spares you and keeps you. Believe on the One out of whom you came!" CES019-020

Lord Jesus, I praise You for You are the one who created me, sustains me, has redeemed me, and guards me. Increase my faith in You. Amen.

FEBRUARY 19

Look First to Christ

Built on the foundation of the apostles and prophets, with Christ Jesus himself as the chief cornerstone . . . In him you too are being built together to become a dwelling in which God lives by his Spirit.

EPHESIANS 2:20, 22

The first look of the Church is toward Christ, who is her Head, her Lord, and her All!

After that she must be self-regarding and world-regarding, with a proper balance between the two.

By self-regarding I do not mean self-centered. I mean that the church must examine herself constantly to see if she be in the faith; she must engage in severe self-criticism with a cheerful readiness to make amends; she must live in a state of perpetual penitence, seeking God with her whole heart; she must constantly check her life and conduct against the Holy Scriptures and bring her life into line with the will of God.

By world-regarding I mean that the church must know why she is here on earth; that she must acknowledge her indebtedness to all mankind (Rom. 1:14, 15); that she must take seriously the words of her Lord, "Go ye into all the world, and preach the gospel to every creature" (Mark 16:15) and "Ye shall be witnesses unto me both in Jerusalem, and in all Judaea, and in Samaria, and unto the uttermost part of the earth" (Acts 1:8). EWT366

Holy Spirit, enable the church to look to Christ first and foremost, that we may rely on Him in all things and spread the gospel effectively throughout the world. Amen.

FEBRUARY 20

Law and Truth

For the law was given through Moses; grace and truth came through Jesus Christ.

—JOHN 1:17

The only contrast here is between all that Moses could do and all that Jesus Christ can do. The Law was given by Moses—that was all that Moses could do. Moses was not the channel through which God dispensed His grace.

God chose His only begotten Son as the channel for His grace and truth, for John witnesses that grace and truth came by Jesus Christ.

All that Moses could do was to command righteousness.

In contrast, only Jesus Christ produces righteousness.

All that Moses could do was to forbid us to sin.

In contrast, Jesus Christ came to save us from sin.

Moses could not save but Jesus Christ is both Lord and Savior.

Grace came through Jesus Christ before Mary wept in the manger stall in Bethlehem.

It was the grace of God in Christ that saved the human race from extinction when our first parents sinned in the garden. CES022-023

Father, may I experience more of Your grace and truth in Jesus Christ, the one who freely gave His life for me. Amen.

FEBRUARY 21

The Incarnated Christ

In the beginning was the Word, and the Word was with God, and the Word was God.

—JOHN 1:1

It was the very person and character of Jesus that was glorious. It was not only what He did—but what He was. What He did was secondary. What He was in His person was primary.

Brethren, there can be no argument about Jesus Christ's glory—His glory lay in the fact that He was perfect love in a loveless world; that He was perfect purity in an impure world; that He was perfect meekness in a harsh and quarrelsome world.

There is no end to His glory. He was perfect humility in a world where every man was seeking his own benefit. He was boundless and fathomless mercy in a hard and cruel world. He was completely selfless goodness in a world full of selfishness.

John says, "And we beheld his glory" (John 1:14). He included the deathless devotion of Jesus; the patient suffering and the unquenchable life and the grace and truth which were in the eternal Word. CES025-026

Lord Jesus, what You have done is glorious, and who You are is glorious. I praise You today for all You are and all You have done. Amen.

Believe and Accept

The Word became flesh and made his dwelling among us.
We have seen his glory, the glory of the one and only Son,
who came from the Father, full of grace and truth.
—JOHN 1:14

The Scriptures say that "no man hath seen God at any time, the only begotten Son, which is in the bosom of the Father, he hath declared him" (John 1:18).

The eternal Son came to tell us what the silence never told us.

He came to tell us what not even Moses could tell us.

He came to tell us and to show us that God loves us and that He constantly cares for us.

He came to tell us that God has a gracious plan and that He is carrying out that plan.

Before it is all finished and consummated, there will be a multitude that no man can number, redeemed, out of every tongue and tribe and nation.

That is what He has told us about the Father God. He has set Him forth. He has revealed Him—His being, His love, His mercy, His grace, His redemptive intention, His saving intention.

He has declared it all. He has given us grace upon grace. Now we have only to turn and believe and accept and take and follow. All is ours if we will receive because *the Word was made flesh, and dwelt among us!* CES028-029

Lord Jesus, You are the supreme one! You have done what no one else could ever do. I bow down before You today in humble gratitude. Amen.

FEBRUARY 23

The Brightness

No one has ever seen God, but the one and only Son, who is himself God and is in closest relationship with the Father, has made him known.

—JOHN 1:18

The glory of Jesus Christ shines like the brightness of the sun—for what He was has astonished the world. What He did was wonderful; what He said and taught was amazing; but what He was, the eternal Word made flesh, was the crown upon all that He did and all that He said.

The Bible teaches so clearly and so consistently what John proclaims in the first chapter of his gospel: "And of his fulness have all we received, and grace for grace" (John 1:16).

Out of His fullness we have received. There is no way that it can mean that any of us have received all of His fullness. It means that Jesus Christ, the eternal Son, is the only medium through which God dispenses His benefits to His creation.

Because Jesus Christ is the eternal Son, because He is of the eternal generation and equal with the Father as pertaining to His substance, His eternity, His love, His power, His grace, His goodness, and all of the attributes of deity, He is the channel through which God dispenses all His blessing. CES027

Father, thank You for the fullness that You have given me in Your Son, Jesus. I am complete in Him. Amen.

FEBRUARY 24

Live For Christ? Then Die With Him First

Now if we died with Christ, we believe that we will also live with him.

—ROMANS 6:8

The victorious Christian has known two lives. The first was his life in Adam which was motivated by the carnal mind and can never please God in any way. It can never be converted; it can only die (Rom. 8:5–8).

The second life of the Christian is his new life in Christ (Rom. 6:1–14). To live a Christian life with the life of Adam is wholly impossible. Yet multitudes take for granted that it can be done and go on year after year in defeat. Worst of all, they accept this half-dead condition as normal!

Another aspect of this attitude is the effort of many to do spiritual work without spiritual power. David Brainerd once compared a man without the power of the Spirit of God trying to do spiritual work to a workman without fingers attempting to do manual labor. The figure is striking but it does not overstate the facts.

The Holy Spirit is not a luxury meant to make deluxe Christians, as an illuminated frontispiece and a leather binding makes a deluxe book. The Spirit is an imperative necessity. Only the Eternal Spirit can do eternal deeds! EWT059

Jesus my Lord, give me power by Your Spirit to live the crucified life, that I may experience Your resurrection power. Amen.

FEBRUARY 25

Individuals Matter

For God so loved the world that he gave his one and only Son, that whoever believes in him shall not perish but have eternal life.

—JOHN 3:16

When the eternal Son of God became the Son of Man and walked on the earth, He always called individuals to His side.

He did not preach to the multitudes as though they were a faceless crowd. He preached to them as individuals and with a knowledge of the burdens and the needs of each one.

The individuals mattered to Him. He was emotionally concerned with the individual beings.

The woman whose accusers said she was taken in the act of adultery was lying in the dust ready to be stoned to death, but the Son of Man raised her gently to her feet. He assured her of God's forgiveness for the individual as He told her to go and sin no more. . . .

He deals with individuals and that is why the Christian message is and always has been: God loves the world. CES082

Loving Lord, thank You for caring about individuals. May I be filled with Your love today and point others to You. Amen.

FEBRUARY 26

God Has Not Abandoned Man

He appeared in the flesh, was vindicated by the Spirit, was seen by angels, was preached among the nations, was believed on in the world, was taken up in glory.

1 TIMOTHY 3:16

Man who was made in the image of God has not been forsaken—God promised a plan to restore that which had been made in His image.

Only that creature whom He called "man" did God make in His own image and likeness. So, when man failed and sinned and fell, God said, "I will go down now."

God came down to visit us in the form of a man, for in Christ Jesus we have the incarnation, "God manifest in the flesh." God Himself came down to this earthly island of man's grief and assumed our loss and took upon Himself our demerits, and in so doing, redeemed us back unto Himself. Jesus Christ, the King of glory, the everlasting Son of the Father, in His victory over sin and death opened the kingdom of heaven to all believers!

Beyond His death and resurrection and ascension, the present work of Jesus Christ is twofold. It is to be an advocate above—a risen Saviour with high priestly office at the throne of God; and the ministry of preparing a place for His people in the house of His Father and our Father, as well.

That is what the Bible teaches. That is what the Christian church believes. It is the essence of the doctrines of the Christian church relating to atonement and salvation! EWT111

Father, thank You for not abandoning me and for sending Your Son to become human, so that You might restore me to fellowship with You. Amen.

FEBRUARY 27

He Came to People

For God did not send his Son into the world to condemn the world, but to save the world through him.
—JOHN 3:17

Now, when the Word says that God sent His Son into the world, it is not talking to us merely about the world as geography. It does not just indicate to us that God sent His Son into the Near East, that He sent Him to Bethlehem in Palestine.

He came to Bethlehem, certainly. He did come to that little land that lies between the seas. But this message does not have any geographical or astronomical meaning. It has nothing to do with kilometers and distances and continents and mountains and towns. . . .

What it really means is that God sent His Son into the human race. He came to people. This is something we must never forget—Jesus Christ came to seek and to save people. Not just certain favored people. Not just certain kinds of people. Not just people in general.

We humans do have a tendency to use generic terms and general terms and pretty soon we become just scientific in our outlook. Let us cast that outlook aside and confess that God loved each of us in a special kind of way so that His Son came into and unto and upon the people of the world—and He even became one of those people! CES101-102

Lord Jesus, I praise You for coming to this world to save people, people like me, a sinner. May I become more amazed at what You have done and tell others of Your goodness. Amen.

FEBRUARY 28

Christ, the Blessed One

Take my yoke upon you, and learn from me . . . For my yoke is easy, and my burden is light.

—MATTHEW 11:29–30

I feel great sorrow for those who read the Sermon on the Mount and then conclude that Jesus was providing a word picture of men and women comprising the human race. In this world, we find nothing approaching the virtues of which Jesus spoke in the Beatitudes.

Instead of poverty of spirit, we find the rankest kind of pride. Instead of mourners, we find pleasure seekers.

Instead of meekness, we find only arrogance, and instead of hunger after righteousness, we hear men saying, "I am rich, and increased with goods, and have need of nothing" (Rev. 3:17).

Instead of mercy, we find cruelty. Instead of purity of heart, we encounter corrupt imaginings. Instead of peacemakers, we find men quarrelsome and resentful, fighting back with every weapon at their command.

Jesus said He came to release us from our sad heritage of sin. Blessed is the sinner who finds that Christ's words are the Truth itself, that He is the Blessed One who came from above to confer blessedness upon mankind! MWT248

Thank You, Father, for Your open-armed invitation for Your children to cast all of their worldly cares upon You. Lord, teach me how to trust You more deeply. Amen.

FEBRUARY 29

Bearing Witness

He must become greater; I must become less.
—JOHN 3:30

How do you suppose the Christian church, as we know it today, would be inclined to deal with John the Baptist if he came into our scene?

Our generation would probably decide that such a man ought to be downright proud of the fact that God had sent him. We would urge him to write books and make a documentary film and the seminary leaders would line up to schedule him as guest lecturer.

But in that distant generation of mankind to whom the eternal Son of God presented Himself as suffering Savior and living Lord, John the Baptist gladly stepped down—allowing Jesus the Christ to displace him completely.

This was his example: instead of insisting on recognition as a man sent from God, he pointed to Jesus as the true Light and said in genuine humility, "I am not worthy to unloose his shoe's latchet" (see John 1:27).

That was John, and when his ministry was over, Jesus came. It was then that John said to all who would listen, "Behold the Lamb of God" (1:29). He directed all the eyes away from himself to Jesus. And then? John the Baptist just faded out of the picture. CES109-110

Lord, You alone deserve all honor and praise! May I decrease and You increase, that others would see You in me today. Amen.

MARCH

MARCH 1

"Unfair! Unfair!"

He was oppressed, and afflicted, yet he did not open his mouth. . . . nor was any deceit in his mouth.
—ISAIAH 53:7, 9

Christians who understand the true meaning of Christ's cross will never whine about being treated unfairly. Whether or not they are given fair treatment will never enter their heads. They know they have been called to follow Christ, and certainly the Savior did not receive anything approaching fair treatment from mankind.

In language the word unfair seems altogether innocent, but it indicates an inner attitude that has no place among Christians.

The man who cries "Unfair!" is not a victorious man. He is inwardly defeated and in self-defense appeals to the referee to note that he has been fouled. This gives him an alibi when they carry him out on a stretcher and saves his face while his bruises heal.

It is a certainty that Christians will suffer wrongs; but if they take them in good spirit and without complaint, they have conquered their enemy. They remember that Jesus was reviled—but any thought of His shouting for fair play simply cannot be entertained by the reverent heart! MWT231

Lord, remind me to think of Your example whenever I am tempted to complain that "life is unfair." You suffered the greatest injustice of all; yet You remained silent. Amen.

MARCH 2

The Sacrifice

He came to Jesus at night and said, "Rabbi, we know that you are a teacher who has come from God. For no one could perform the signs you are doing if God were not with him."

—JOHN 3:2

Nicodemus came to Jesus by night, evidently feeling his way. He surely knew something about what it would cost him to show any serious interest in the person or the ministry of this Jesus of Nazareth.

He knew that the disciples of Jesus had abandoned all, left all behind. Their faith in His cause did not come without costing each of them something.

In our day, there is a tendency for enthusiastic Christian promoters to teach that the essence of faith is this: "Come to Jesus—it will cost you nothing! The price has all been paid—it will cost you nothing!"

Brethren, that is a dangerous half-truth. There is always a price connected with salvation and with discipleship. . . . God's grace is free, no doubt about that. No one in the wide world can make any human payment towards the plea of salvation or the forgiveness of sins. CES128-129

Lord, I know that following You is costly. May I count the cost each day and follow You without reservation. Amen.

The Compassion of Christ

Be merciful to those who doubt . . . to others show mercy, mixed with fear.
—JUDE 22, 23

The word "compassion" is a vital New Testament word. Do you realize that compassion is an emotional identification, and that Jesus Christ had that in full perfection? The man who has this wound of compassion is a man who suffers along with other people. Jesus Christ our Lord can never suffer to save us any more. This He did, once and for all, when He gave Himself without spot through the Holy Ghost to the Father on Calvary's cross.

He cannot suffer to save us but He still must suffer to win us. He does not call His people to redemptive suffering for that is impossible; it could not be. Redemption is a finished work!

But He does call His people to feel along with Him and to feel along with those that rejoice and those that suffer. He calls His people to be to Him the kind of an earthly body in which He can weep again and suffer again and love again. For our Lord has two bodies!

One is the body He took to the tree on Calvary; that was the body in which He suffered to redeem us. But He has a body on earth now, composed of those who have been baptized into it by the Holy Ghost at conversion. Paul said he was glad that he could suffer for the Colossians and fill up the measure of the afflictions of Christ in his body for the church's sake.

It is in that body now, on earth, that Christ would suffer to win men! EWT398

Lord Christ, thank You for the compassion You have shown me, which was expressed most fully in the cross. Grant that I would become more compassionate and thus more like You. Amen.

MARCH 4

Jesus Is Enough

Philip found Nathanael and told him, "We have found the one Moses wrote about in the Law, and about whom the prophets also wrote—Jesus of Nazareth, the son of Joseph." "Nazareth! Can anything good come from there?" Nathanael asked.

—JOHN 1:45-46

Nathanael came to Jesus and he was an interesting case. The Bible record does not tell us too much about him—but I think it could well be said that he was a fellow full of prejudice like any other man on the street.

When Philip told him that the disciples had found the Messiah of whom the Old Testament had spoken, Nathanael gave his cynical reply: "Can there any good thing come out of Nazareth?" (John 1:46).

You see, Nathanael was a plain and simple man living from day to day, but he lived under the shadow of his humanness and he just could not get the sun to come out.

But when he came to Jesus and found that Jesus already knew him better than he knew himself, he was suddenly in the radiant sunlight and he confessed to Jesus, "Rabbi, thou art the Son of God; thou art the King of Israel" (1:49).

Truly, the way of man is not in himself, and that is what the Holy Ghost has said. Only Jesus Christ, the eternal Son, is enough. CES141

Lord Christ, You are enough! You know me fully, more than anyone else ever could, and You know all my needs. I look to You for everything I need. Amen.

MARCH 5

Matter of Life and Death

Just as Moses lifted up the snake in the wilderness, so the Son of Man must be lifted up, that everyone who believes may have eternal life in him.

—JOHN 3:14–15

Some things in our human lives are so basically unimportant that we never miss them if we do not have them. Some other things, even some that we just take for granted, are so important that if we do not grasp them and hold them and secure them for all eternity, we will suffer irreparable loss and anguish.

When we come to the question of our own relationship with God through the merits of our Lord Jesus Christ, we come to one of those areas which in a supreme degree is truly a matter of life and death.

This is so desperately a matter of importance for every human being who comes into the world that I first become indignant, and then I become sad, when I try to give spiritual counsel to a person who looks me in the eye and tells me: "Well, I am trying to make up my mind if I should accept Christ or not."

Such a person gives absolutely no indication that he realizes he is talking about the most important decision he can make in his lifetime—a decision to get right with God, to believe in the eternal Son, the Savior, to become a disciple, an obedient witness to Jesus Christ as Lord. CES144-145

Holy Son of God, thank You for making me right with the Father and granting me peace. May I be a faithful and obedient disciple. Amen.

MARCH 6

Your Cross, Not Christ's

Those who belong to Christ Jesus have crucified the flesh with its passions and desires.
—GALATIANS 5:24

An earnest Christian woman long ago sought help from Henry Suso concerning her spiritual life. She had been imposing austerities upon herself in an effort to feel the sufferings that Christ had felt on the cross. Things were not going so well with her and Suso knew why.

The old saint wrote his spiritual daughter and reminded her that our Lord had not said, "If any man will come after me let him deny himself, and take up MY cross." He had said, "Let him . . . take up his cross." There is a difference of only one small pronoun; but that difference is vast and important.

Crosses are all alike, but no two are identical. Never before nor since has there been a cross experience just like that endured by the Saviour. The whole dreadful work of dying which Christ suffered was something unique in the experience of mankind. It had to be so if the cross was to mean life for the world. The sin-bearing, the darkness, the rejection by the Father were agonies peculiar to the Person of the holy sacrifice. For anyone to claim that experience of Christ would be sacrilege.

Every cross was and is an instrument of death, but no man could die on the cross of another; hence Jesus said, "Let him . . . take up his cross, and follow me!" EWT126

Lord Jesus, give me strength and grace to take up my cross today and follow You, that my sinful flesh may be crucified and I may walk in newness of life. Amen.

MARCH 7

Promised to Receive Us

For it is with your heart that you believe and are justified, and it is with your mouth that you profess your faith and are saved.
—ROMANS 10:10

Doesn't that proud human know that the Christ he is putting off is the Christ of God, the eternal Son who holds the worlds in His hands? Does he not know that Christ is the eternal Word, the Jesus who made the heavens and the earth and all things that are therein?

Why, this One who patiently waits for our human judgment is the One who holds the stars in His hands. He is the Savior and Lord and head over all things to the church. It will be at His word that the graves shall give up their dead, and the dead shall come forth, alive forevermore. At His word, the fire shall burst loose and burn up the earth and the heavens and the stars and planets shall be swept away like a garment.

He is the One, the Mighty One!

And yet there He stands, while we animated clothespins—that's what we look like and that's what we are—decide whether we will accept Him or not. How grotesque can it be?

The question ought not to be whether I will accept Him; the question ought to be whether He will accept me!

But He does not make that a question. He has already told us that we do not have to worry or disturb our minds about that. "And him that cometh to me I will in no wise cast out" (John 6:37). He has promised to receive us, poor and sinful though we be. CES146-147

Jesus, You are Lord of the universe and head of the church, in charge of everything. May I not waiver in following You this day. Amen.

MARCH 8

A Saving Relationship

I have been crucified with Christ and I no longer live, but Christ lives in me. The life I now live in the body, I live by faith in the Son of God, who loved me and gave himself for me.
—GALATIANS 2:20

The average person with even a minimum of instruction in church or Sunday school will generally take two things for granted, without argument.

The first is that Jesus Christ came into the world to save sinners. That is declared specifically in the Bible, and it is declared in other words adding up to the same thing all through the New Testament.

If we have been reared in gospel churches, we also generally will take for granted the second fact: that we are saved by faith in Christ alone, without our works and without our merit.

I am discussing these two basic things with you here because too many individuals take them for granted, believe them to be true; and still they are asking, "How do I know that I have come into a saving relationship with Jesus Christ?" We had better find the answer because this is the matter of life or death. . . .

Oh, that lost men and women would get concerned to the point of asking and finding out how they may come into a saving relationship with thc Savior, Jcsus Christ! CES147-149

Lord Christ, You came to save sinners, yet so many do not recognize You or receive You. Give me the strength and boldness to proclaim the gospel and the ability to demonstrate it with my life, that many would be drawn to You. Amen.

MARCH 9

The Cross We Bear

For it has been granted to you on behalf of Christ not only to believe in him, but also to suffer for him.
—PHILIPPIANS 1:29

The Christian as a member of the body of Christ is crucified along with his divine Head. Before God every true believer is reckoned to have died when Christ died. All subsequent experience of personal crucifixion is based upon this identification with Christ on the cross.

But in the practical, everyday outworking of the believer's crucifixion, his own cross is brought into play. "Let him . . . take up his cross." That is obviously not the cross of Christ. Rather, it is the believer's own personal cross by means of which the cross of Christ is made effective in slaying his evil nature and setting him free from its power.

The believer's own cross is one he has assumed voluntarily. Therein lies the difference between his cross and the cross on which Roman convicts died. They went to the cross against their will; he, because he chooses to do so. No Roman officer ever pointed to a cross and said, "If any man will, let him!" Only Christ said that, and by so saying He placed the whole matter in the hands of the Christian believer. Each of us, then, should count himself dead indeed with Christ and accept willingly whatever of self-denial, repentance, humility, and humble sacrifice that may be found in the path of obedient daily living. EWT213

Holy Spirit, empower me today to bear my own cross that I would become more like Christ in dying and rising with Him. Amen.

MARCH 10

Our Sovereign Lord

However, the Most High does not live in houses made by human hands. As the prophet says: "'Heaven is my throne, and the earth is my footstool.'"

—ACTS 7:48–49

How can you be a Christian and not be aware of the sovereignty of the God who has loved us to the death?

To be sovereign, God must be the absolute, infinite, unqualified ruler in all realms in heaven and earth and sea. To be Lord over all the creation, He must be omnipotent. He must be omniscient. He must be omnipresent.

With all that is within me, I believe that the crucified and risen and glorified Savior, Jesus Christ, is the sovereign Lord. He takes no orders from anyone. He has no counselors and no advisers. He has no secretary to the throne. He knows in the one effortless act all that can be known and He has already lived out our tomorrows and holds the world in the palm of His hand.

That is the Lord I serve! I gladly own that I am His; glory to God! The Christ we know and serve is infinitely beyond all men and all angels and all archangels, above all principalities and powers and dominions, visible and invisible—for He is the origin of them all! MWT196

Lord, to begin to understand Your attributes is totally overwhelming. That such an Almighty God would care so much for His creation is truly humbling. Amen.

MARCH 11

Worthy—Or Unworthy?

And to know this love [of Christ] that surpasses all knowledge.
—EPHESIANS 3:19

The love of Jesus is so inclusive that it knows no boundaries. At the point where we stop loving and caring, Jesus is still there—loving and caring!

The question may be asked: "How does the living Christ feel today about the sinful men and women who walk our streets?"

There is only one answer: He loves them!

We may be righteously indignant about the things they do. We may be disgusted with their actions and their ways. We are often ready to condemn and turn away from them.

But Jesus keeps on loving them! It is His unchanging nature to love and seek the lost. He said many times when He was on earth, "I have come to help the needy. The well do not need a doctor—but the sick need attention and love."

We are prone to look at the needy and measure them: "Let us determine if they are worthy of our help." During all of His ministry, I do not think Jesus ever helped a "worthy" person. He only asked, "What is your need? Do you need My help?" MWT345

Dear Lord Jesus, thank You for Your unconditional love for all mankind. I pray that lost men and women everywhere will acknowledge their sin problem and give their hearts to Jesus. Amen.

MARCH 12

Everyone Put Jesus on the Cross

For Christ also suffered once for sins, the righteous for the unrighteous, to bring you to God. He was put to death in the body, but made alive in the Spirit.

—1 PETER 3:18

There is a strange conspiracy of silence in the world today—even in religious circles—about man's responsibility for sin, the reality of judgment, and about an outraged God and the necessity for a crucified Saviour. But still there lies a great shadow upon every man and every woman—the fact that our Lord was bruised and wounded and crucified for the entire human race! This is the basic human responsibility that men are trying to push off and evade.

Let us not eloquently blame Judas nor Pilate. Let us not curl our lips at Judas and accuse: "He sold Him for money!"

Oh, they were guilty, certainly! But they were our accomplices in crime. They and we put Him on the cross, not they alone. That rising malice and anger that burns so hotly in your breast today put Him there! The evil, the hatred, the suspicion, the jealousy, the lying tongue, the cheating, the carnality, the fleshly love of pleasure—all of these in natural man joined in putting Him on the cross!

There is a powerful movement swirling throughout the world designed to give people peace of mind in relieving them of any historical responsibility for the trial and crucifixion of Jesus Christ. But we may as well admit it. Every one of us in Adam's race had a share in putting Him on the cross! EWT114

Heavenly Father, I acknowledge that my sin put Jesus on the cross. Thank You for forgiving me in Christ and making me a new creation. Amen.

MARCH 13

He Is Our Passover

He took bread . . . Then their eyes were opened and they recognized him.

—LUKE 24:30–31

What a sweet comfort to us that our Lord Jesus Christ was once known in the breaking of the bread. In earlier Christian times, believers called Communion "the medicine of immortality," and God gave them the desire to pray:

Be known to us in breaking bread,
But do not then depart;
Savior, abide with us and spread
Thy table in our heart.

Some churches have a teaching that you will find God only at their table—and that you leave God there when you leave. I am so glad that God has given us light. We may take the Presence of the table with us.

Then sup with us in love divine,
Thy body and Thy blood;
That living bread and heavenly wine
Be our immortal food!

In approaching the table of our Lord, we dare not forget the cost to our elder Brother, the Man who was from heaven. He is our Savior; He is our Passover! MWT370

Lord, just as You promised Moses that Your "Presence" would go with him (see Ex. 33:14), I pray that Your Presence will go with me wherever You lead. I will not go without You, dear Lord. Amen.

MARCH 14

An Exclusive Attachment

But now that you know God—or rather are known by God—how is it that you are turning back to those weak and miserable forces?
—GALATIANS 4:9

I am not in the business of trying to downgrade any other believer's efforts to win souls. I am just of the opinion that we are often too casual and there are too many tricks that can be used to make soul-winning encounters completely "painless" and at "no cost" and without any "inconvenience."

Some of the unsaved with whom we deal on the "quick and easy" basis have such little preparation and are so ignorant of the plan of salvation that they would be willing to bow their heads and "accept" Buddha or Zoroaster if they thought they could get rid of us in that way.

To "accept Christ" in anything like a saving relationship is to have an attachment to the Person of Christ that is revolutionary, complete, and exclusive!

It is more than joining some group that you like. It is more than having enjoyable social fellowship with other nice people. You give your heart and life and soul to Jesus Christ—and He becomes the center of your transformed life! MWT143

Lord, as Your followers share the gospel around the world today, I pray that each hearer will have a clear understanding of the consequences of the decision they will make to either accept or reject Jesus. Amen.

MARCH 15

Never Change Christ's Words

By the resurrection of Jesus Christ, who has gone into heaven . . . with angels, and authorities and powers in submission to him.

—1 PETER 3:21, 22

As believers, we should be warned that any appeal to the public in the name of Christ that rises no higher than an invitation to tranquility must be recognized as mere humanism with a few words of Jesus thrown in to make it appear Christian! . . .

Christ calls men to carry a cross; we call them to have fun in His name!

He calls them to forsake the world; we assure them that if they but accept Jesus, the world is their oyster!

He calls them to suffer; we call them to enjoy all the bourgeois comforts modern civilization affords!

He calls them to self-abnegation and death; we call them to spread themselves like green bay trees or perchance even to become stars in a pitiful fifth-rate religious zodiac!

He calls them to holiness; we call them to a cheap and tawdry happiness that would have been rejected with scorn by the least of the Stoic philosophers!

Only that is truly Christian which accords with the spirit and teachings of Christ. Whatever is foreign to the Spirit of the Man of Sorrows and contrary to the teachings and practice of His apostles is un-Christian or anti-Christian, no matter whence it emanates! EWT292

Lord Christ, forgive me for the times in which I have changed Your words. May I acknowledge Your call for what it is and answer You faithfully with my life. Amen.

MARCH 16

The Wonder of the Atonement

"He himself bore our sins" in his body on the cross, so that we might die to sins and live for righteousness; "by his wounds you have been healed."

—1 PETER 2:24

But oh, the mystery and wonder of the atonement! The soul that avails itself of that atonement, that throws itself out on that atonement, the moral situation has changed. God has not changed! Jesus Christ did not die to change God; Jesus Christ died to change a moral situation. When God's justice confronts an unprotected sinner, that justice sentences him to die. And all of God concurs in the sentence! But when Christ, who is God, went onto the tree and died there in infinite agony, in a plethora of suffering, this great God suffered more than they suffer in hell. He suffered all that they could suffer in hell. He suffered with the agony of God, for everything that God does, He does with all that He is. When God suffered for you, my friend, God suffered to change your moral situation. . . .

When God looks at an atoned-for sinner He doesn't see the same moral situation that He sees when He looks at a sinner who still loves his sin. When God looks at a sinner who still loves his sin and rejects the mystery of the atonement, justice condemns him to die. When God looks at a sinner who has accepted the blood of the everlasting covenant, justice sentences him to live. And God is just in doing both things. AOG070

I praise You for Your atoning work, Lord Christ, for reconciling me to the Father. May I grow into deeper union with Him now that You have made a way back to Him. Amen.

MARCH 17

He Is the Host

Everyone is but a breath . . . Surely everyone goes around like a mere phantom.

—PSALM 39:5–6

Brethren, I am not ashamed of this world God created—I am only ashamed of man's sin! If you could take all of man's sin out of this world, there would be nothing to be ashamed of and nothing to be afraid of.

Our apologies must be for humanity—and for our sins. I keep repeating that we have no business making excuses for God.

It is popular now to talk about Christ being a guest here. I dare to tell people that they should stop patronizing Jesus Christ!

He is not the guest here—He is the Host!

We have apologists who write books and give lectures—apologizing for the person of Christ, trying to "explain" to our generation that the Bible does not really mean "exactly" what it says. But God has revealed Himself in Jesus Christ and thus we know where we stand, believing that all things were made by Him and "without him was not any thing made that was made" (John 1:3). MWT168

Lord, in my own personal life I relinquish control to Your Spirit within me. Slay my vanity, Lord. Amen.

MARCH 18

Power of the Cross

The cross of our Lord Jesus Christ, through which the world has been crucified to me, and I to the world.

—GALATIANS 6:14

Only a person with a perfect knowledge of mankind could have dared to set forth the terms of discipleship that our Lord Jesus Christ expects of His followers.

Only the Lord of men could have risked the effect of such rigorous demands: "Let him deny himself" (Matt. 16:24).

Can the Lord lay down such severe rules at the door of His kingdom? He can—and He does!

If He is to save the man, He must save him from himself. It is the "himself" which has enslaved and corrupted the man. Deliverance comes only by denial of that self.

No man in his own strength can shed the chains with which self has bound him, but in the next breath the Lord reveals the source of the power which is to set the soul free: "Let him take up his cross."

The cross was an instrument of death—slaying a man was its only function. "Let him take his cross," said Jesus, and thus he will know deliverance from himself! MWT105

Dear Lord, I have much to learn about denying myself and bearing my cross daily—especially in the midst of so many mundane activities. Have Your way with me, Lord. Amen.

MARCH 19

Justice on Our Side

But if we walk in the light, as he is in the light, we have fellowship with one another, and the blood of Jesus, his Son, purifies us from all sin.

—1 JOHN 1:7

Now here's something you may have never noticed: "He is faithful *and just* to forgive us our sins, and to cleanse us from all unrighteousness." God promised He would forgive and He is faithful to do so. But it says He is faithful *and just* to forgive. *Justice* is on our side now! Instead of justice being against us and grace being for us, the blood of Jesus Christ works such an amazing wonder before the throne of God and before the presence of man that now justice has come over on the side of the returning sinner. And when the sinner comes home, there isn't a thing standing between him and the very heart of God. It's all been swept away by the blood of the Lamb.

So if any old memories back in your mind, or the devil or some preacher tells you that justice is against you, remember that the Scriptures say, "He is faithful *and just* to forgive." Justice has come over on the side of the Christian, because Jesus Christ is on the side of the Christian. So if you confess your sins, God will put them away and you will be delivered. AOGII187

Lord, I confess to You my sins today, knowing that You are faithful and just to forgive and cleanse me. Renew me and make me more like You. Amen.

MARCH 20

We Can Afford to Die

For here we do not have an enduring city, but we are looking for the city that is to come.
—HEBREWS 13:14

Brethren, it is a fact indeed that we will never fully realize in our earthly life what it means to be coheirs with Christ!

The apostles have made it quite plain that all of the eternal implications of our heavenly inheritance will not be known to us until we see Christ face-to-face in a future time.

I have said that only a Christian has the right and can afford to die! But if we believers were as spiritual as we ought to be, we might be looking to our "home going" with a great deal more pleasure and anticipation than we do.

I say also that if we are true believers in the second advent of our Savior, we will be anticipating His return with yearning. Common sense, the perspective of history, the testimony of the saints, reason, and the Bible—all agree with one voice that He may come before we die.

The Christian believer whose faith and hope are in Jesus Christ alone knows that he may die before the Lord comes. If he dies, he is better off, for Paul said, "It is far better that I go to be with the Lord" (see Phil. 1:23). MWT252

You've placed eternity in our hearts, Lord. Therefore, You've created us with a built-in desire to live with You in heaven. I pray that all my family members will come to know You before it's too late. Amen.

MARCH 21

Flee It or Die Upon It

Jesus said to his disciples, "Whoever wants to be my disciple must deny themselves and take up their cross and follow me."
—MATTHEW 16:24

We must do something about the cross, and one of two things only we can do—flee it or die upon it. And if we should be so foolhardy as to flee, we shall by that act put away the faith of our fathers and make of Christianity something other than it is. Then we shall have left only the empty language of salvation; the power will depart with our departure from the true cross.

If we are wise, we will do what Jesus did: endure the cross and despise its shame for the joy that is set before us. To do this is to submit the whole pattern of our lives to be destroyed and built again in the power of an endless life. And we shall find that it is more than poetry, more than sweet hymnody and elevated feeling. The cross will cut into our lives where it hurts worst, sparing neither us nor our carefully cultivated reputations. It will defeat us and bring our selfish lives to an end. Only then can we rise in fullness of life to establish a pattern of living wholly new and free and full of good works. TRC015-016

Lord Jesus, You did not flee the cross but embraced it and died on it. Grant me strength today to carry my cross, that my old self would be mortified and that I would be raised to new life with You. Amen.

MARCH 22

Resurrection: A Fact

[You] are firmly established in the truth you now have . . . For we did not follow cleverly devised stories.

—2 PETER 1:12, 16

The resurrection of Christ and the fact of the empty tomb are not a part of this world's complex and continuing mythologies. This is not a Santa Claus tale—it is history and it is a reality!

The true Church of Jesus Christ is necessarily founded upon the belief and the truth that there was a real death, a real tomb, and a real stone!

But, thank God, there was a sovereign Father in heaven, an angel sent to roll the stone away, and a living Savior in a resurrected and glorified body, able to proclaim to His disciples, "All power is given unto me in heaven and in earth!" (Matt. 28:18).

Brethren, He died for us, but ever since the hour of the Resurrection, He has been the mighty Jesus, the mighty Christ, the mighty Lord!

Our business is to thank God with tearful reverence for the cross, but to go on to a right understanding of what the Resurrection meant both to God and to men. We understand and acknowledge that the Resurrection has placed a glorious crown upon all of Christ's sufferings! MWT115

Lord, I praise You that the resurrection of Jesus Christ is a fact and not a fable. Because He lives, I have real purpose in this life and I can look forward to the life hereafter. Amen.

MARCH 23

Easter without Good Friday

For it has been granted to you on behalf of Christ not only to believe in him, but also to suffer for him.

—PHILIPPIANS 1:29

God will crucify without pity those whom He desires to raise without measure! . . .

God wants to crucify us from head to foot—making our own powers ridiculous and useless—in the desire to raise us without measure for His glory and for our eternal good. . . .

Willingness to suffer for Jesus' sake—this is what we have lost from the Christian church. We want our Easter to come without the necessity of a Good Friday. We forget that before the Redeemer could rise and sing among His brethren. He must first bow His head and suffer among His brethren!

We forget so easily that in the spiritual life there must be the darkness of the night before there can be the radiance of the dawn. Before the life of resurrection can be known, there must be the death that ends the dominion of self. It is a serious but a blessed decision, this willingness to say, "I will follow Him no matter what the cost. I will take the cross no matter how it comes!" ITB096-099

Lord, I come before You on my knees to say, "I will follow You no matter what the cost. I will take the cross no matter how it comes!" Amen.

MARCH 24

Hold No Grudges

Jesus said, "Father, forgive them, for they do not know what they are doing."
—LUKE 23:34

Jesus Christ left us an example for our daily conduct and from it there can be no appeal. He felt no bitter resentment and He held no grudge against anyone!

Even those who crucified Him were forgiven while they were in the act. Not a word did He utter against them nor against the ones who stirred them up to destroy Him.

How evil they all were He knew better than any other man, but He maintained a charitable attitude toward them. They were only doing their duty, and even those who ordered them to their grisly task were unaware of the meaning of their act.

To Pilate, Jesus said: "Thou couldest have no power at all against me, except it were given thee from above."

So He referred everything back to the will of God and rose above the swampland of personalities.

The person with the resentful heart takes just the opposite course, however. He grows every day harder and more acrimonious as he defends his reputation, his rights, his ministry, against his imagined foes! . . .

As he pushes on toward his selfish goal, his very prayers will be surly accusations against the Almighty and his whole relationship toward other Christians will be one of suspicion and distrust! EWT259

Heavenly Father, grant me grace and strength to love all people, even my enemies, as Christ has loved all people. Amen.

MARCH 25

Alone

Going a little farther, he fell with his face to the ground and prayed, "My Father, if it is possible, may this cup be taken from me. Yet not as I will, but as you will."

—MATTHEW 26:39

Most revealing of all is the sight of that One of whom Moses and all the prophets did write, treading His lonely way to the cross, His deep loneliness unrelieved by the presence of the multitudes.

'Tis midnight, and on Olive's brow
  The star is dimmed that lately shone.
'Tis midnight; in the garden now
  The suffering Savior prays alone.
'Tis midnight, and from all removed,
  The Savior wrestles lone with fears;
E'en that disciple whom He loved
  Heeds not his Master's grief and tears.
—William B. Tappan

He died alone in the darkness, hidden from the sight of mortal man, and no one saw Him when He arose triumphant and walked out of the tomb, though many saw Him afterward and bore witness to what they saw. TRC039

Sweet Savior, You died all alone so that I might be one with You. Thank You for Your amazing sacrifice. Amen.

MARCH 26

Making Christ Wait

If anyone . . . does not agree to the sound instruction of our Lord Jesus Christ and to godly teaching . . . they are conceited and understand nothing.

—1 TIMOTHY 6:3–4

First I become indignant and then I become sad when a person to whom I am trying to give spiritual counsel tells me: "Well, I am trying to make up my mind whether or not I should accept Christ."

This scene is taking place in our society over and over again, as proud Adamic sinners argue within themselves: "I don't know whether I should accept Christ or not." So, in this view, our poor Lord Christ stands hat in hand, shifting from one foot to the other, looking for a job—wondering whether He will be accepted!

Is it possible that we proud humans do not know that the Christ we are putting off is the eternal Son, the Lord who made the heavens and the earth and all things that are therein? He is indeed the One, the Mighty One!

Thankfully, He has promised to receive us, poor and sinful though we be. But the idea that we can make Him stand while we render the verdict of whether He is worthy is a frightful calumny—and we ought to get rid of it!

Dear Lord, thank You for Your wonderful promise to receive us just as we are—warts and all. You are entirely trustworthy, Lord. Amen.

MARCH 27

The Cross and the Rod

Fixing our eyes on Jesus, the pioneer and perfecter of faith. For the joy set before him he endured the cross, scorning its shame, and sat down at the right hand of the throne of God.
—HEBREWS 12:2

For the Christian, cross carrying and chastisement are alike but not identical. They differ in a number of important ways. The two ideas are usually considered to be the same and the words embodying the ideas are used interchangeably. There is, however, a sharp distinction between them. . . .

The cross and the rod occur close together in the Holy Scriptures, but they are not the same thing. The rod is imposed without the consent of the one who suffers it. The cross cannot be imposed by another. Even Christ bore the cross by His own free choice. He said of the life He poured out on the cross, "No man taketh it from me, but I lay it down of myself." (John 10:18). He had every opportunity to escape the cross but He set His face like a flint to go to Jerusalem to die. The only compulsion He knew was the compulsion of love.

Chastisement is an act of God; cross carrying an act of the Christian. TRC053-54

O Jesus, give me strength today to willingly and joyfully pick up my cross and follow You, that I might be a faithful disciple and honor You in all my ways. Amen.

MARCH 28

Obedience

Blessed are you when people insult you, persecute you and falsely say all kinds of evil against you because of me.
—MATTHEW 5:11

But what is the cross for the Christian? Obviously it is not the wooden instrument the Romans used to execute the sentence of death upon persons guilty of capital crimes. The cross is the suffering the Christian endures as a consequence of his following Christ in perfect obedience. Christ chose the cross by choosing the path that led to it; and it is so with His followers. In the way of obedience stands the cross, and we take the cross when we enter that way.

As the cross stands in the way of obedience, so chastisement is found in the way of disobedience. God never chastens a perfectly obedient child. Consider the fathers of our flesh; they never punished us for obedience, only for disobedience.

When we feel the sting of the rod we may be sure we are temporarily out of the right way. Conversely, the pain of the cross means that we are in the way. But the Father's love is not more or less, wherever we may be. God chastens us not that He may love us but because He loves us. TRC054-055

Lord, I long to be an obedient disciple, one who pleases You in word and deed. Empower me by Your Spirit to obey Your commands today. Amen.

MARCH 29

Sent to Die

For God so loved the world that he gave his one and only Son, that whoever believes in him shall not perish but have eternal life.

—JOHN 3:16

We remember, too, that without the cross on which the Savior died there could be no Scriptures, no revelation, no redemptive message, nothing! But here He gave us a loving proclamation—He sent His Son; He gave His Son! Then later it develops that in giving His Son, He gave Him to die!

I have said that this must be a personal word for every man and every woman. Like a prodigal son in that most moving of all stories, each one of us must come to grips with our own personal need and to decide and act as he did: "I am hungry. I will perish here. But I will get up. I will go to my father. I remember his house and his provision" (see Luke 15:17–20). He said, "I will go"—so he got up and went to his father.

You must think of yourself—for God sent His Son into the world to save you! TRC064-065

Father, thank You for sending Your only Son to save me, a poor sinner! How great is Your love! Amen.

MARCH 30

His Cross Daily

For whoever wants to save their life will lose it, but whoever loses their life for me will save it.

—LUKE 9:24

Now there is a real sense in which the cross of Christ embraces all crosses and the death of Christ encompasses all deaths. "For the love of Christ constraineth us; because we thus judge, that if one died for all, then were all dead" (2 Cor. 5:14). "I am crucified with Christ" (Gal. 2:20). "Save in the cross of our Lord Jesus Christ, by whom the world is crucified unto me, and I unto the world" (6:14). This is in the judicial working of God in redemption. The Christian as a member of the Body of Christ is crucified along with his divine Head. Before God, every true believer is reckoned to have died when Christ died. All subsequent experience of personal crucifixion is based upon this identification with Christ on the cross.

But in the practical, everyday outworking of the believer's crucifixion his own cross is brought into play. "He must . . . take up his cross daily" (Luke 9:23). That is obviously not the cross of Christ. Rather it is the believer's own personal cross by means of which the cross of Christ is made effective in slaying his evil nature and setting him free from its power. TRC068

Lord, I know that the cross You bore was unique and can never be picked up by a mere human. Grant me strength to pick up my own cross today, that I would become a faithful disciple. Amen.

MARCH 31

Walking a Tightrope between Two Kingdoms?

For I always do what pleases him.
—JOHN 8:29

We who follow Christ are aware of the fact that we inhabit at once two worlds, the spiritual and the natural. As children of Adam we do live our lives on earth subject to the limitations of the flesh and the weaknesses and ills to which human nature is heir.

In sharp contrast to this is our life in the Spirit. There we enjoy a higher kind of life; we are children of God. We possess heavenly status and enjoy intimate fellowship with Christ!

This tends to divide our total life into two departments, as we unconsciously recognize two sets of actions, the so-called secular acts and the sacred. This is, of course, the old "sacred-secular" antithesis and most Christians are caught in its trap. Walking the tightrope between two kingdoms they find no peace in either. Actually, the sacred-secular dilemma has no foundation in the New Testament. Without doubt a more perfect understanding of Christian truth will deliver us from it.

The Lord Jesus Christ Himself is our perfect example and He lived no divided life. God accepted the offering of His total life and made no distinction between act and act. "I do always the things that please Him" was His brief summary of His own life as related to the Father. We are called upon to exercise an aggressive faith, in which we offer all our acts to God and believe that He accepts them. Let us believe that God is in all our simple deeds and learn to find Him there! EWT032

Heavenly Father, enable me by Your Spirit to live as Christ did, that my deeds may be acceptable to You. Amen.

APRIL

APRIL 1

Not the Strong Fists

By his wounds we are healed.
—ISAIAH 53:5

God redeemed lost mankind not by the strong fists of Jesus but by His nail-pierced hands. We do not sing about the power of the clenched fist; we sing with thanksgiving that we "shall know Him by the print of the nails in His hands." This gospel of Jesus Christ is unique. There is nothing within it that brings glory or credit to our human means or methods. Our redemption was not by muscle, but by love. It was not wrought by vengeance, but by forgiveness. It was not by sword, but by sacrifice.

We are Christians because Jesus destroyed His enemies by dying for them. He conquered death by letting death conquer Him, and then He turned death inside out as He burst forth from the tomb as Victor! This whole work of redemption had to be accomplished in the way things are done in heaven. That is why I say that as Christians, we have learned that whatever Christ the Lion will do in bringing the world into submission, He will do because of what He has already done as the Lamb of God. JIV068-069

Lord, thank You for saving me not by physical force but by humility and sacrifice. May I humbly present myself as a living sacrifice to You today. Amen.

APRIL 2

Ready

If we are faithless, he remains faithful, for he cannot disown himself.

—2 TIMOTHY 2:13

He was ready first for His labors on earth, the work with the plow. And He was ready for the altar of sacrifice—the cross. With no side interests, He moved with steady purpose—almost with precision—toward the cross. He would not be distracted or turned aside. He was completely devoted to the cross, completely devoted to the rescue of mankind, because He was completely devoted to His Father's will.

Even "if we believe not," as the ancient hymn puts it (see 2 Tim. 2:13), Jesus' faithful devotion is unchanged. He has not changed. And He will not change. He is as devoted now as He was then. He came to earth to be a Devoted One, for the word *devoted* actually is a religious term referring usually to an animal, often a lamb, that was selected and marked for sacrifice to a god. So, our Lord Jesus Christ, the Lamb of God, was devoted—completely devoted—to be the Infinite Sacrifice for sin. TRC072-073

Lord Christ, Your devotion while on earth never changed, and You never change! Grant today that I would be single-minded in my devotion to You. Amen.

APRIL 3

Separation From

Such a high priest truly meets our need—one who is holy, blameless, pure, set apart from sinners, exalted above the heavens.
—HEBREWS 7:26

There are many ways in which our Lord deliberately separated Himself from those around Him. We might say He separated Himself from people for people. Jesus did not separate Himself from people because He was weary of them, or because He disliked them. Rather, it was because He loved them. It was a separation in order that He might do for them what they could not do for themselves. He was the only One who could rescue them. . . .

The separation of Jesus Christ from people was the result of love. He separated Himself from them for them. It was for them He came—and died. It was for them that He arose and ascended. For them He intercedes at the right hand of God.

"Separation from" is a phrase that marked Jesus. He not only kept Himself separated from sinners in the sense that He did not partake of their sins, but He was separated from the snare of trivialities.

TRC073-074

Lord Christ, may I separate myself from sin and the sinful ways of the world so that I would become more like You and honor the Father by the power of the Spirit. Amen.

APRIL 4

Waves of Glory: Now Few and Far Between

Ask and you will receive, and your joy will be complete.
—JOHN 16:24

There seems to be a chilling and paralyzing fear of holy enthusiasm among the people of God in our day. We try to tell how happy we are—but we remain so well controlled that there are very few waves of glory among us!

Some go to the ball game and come back whispering because they are hoarse from shouting and cheering. But no one in our day ever goes home from church with a voice hoarse from shouts brought about by a manifestation of the glory of God among us.

Actually, our apathy about praise in worship is like an inward chill in our beings. We are under a shadow and we are still wearing the grave clothes. You can sense this in much of our singing in the contemporary church. Perhaps you will agree that in most cases it is a kind of plodding along, without the inward lift of blessing and victory, resurrection joy and overcoming in Jesus' name.

Why is this?

It is largely because we are looking at what we are, rather than responding to who Jesus Christ is! . . .

Brethren, human activity and human sweat and tears work not the victory of Christ! It took the sweat and tears and blood of the Lord Jesus Christ. It took the painful dying and the victorious resurrection and ascension to bring us the victory. Jesus Christ is our Overcomer! EWT382

Forgive me, gracious Lord, for looking at what I am rather than looking to You and what You have done for me. May I ever look to You and glorify You in my life. Amen.

APRIL 5

Symbol of Death

For as in Adam all die, so in Christ all will be made alive.
—1 CORINTHIANS 15:22

The old cross is a symbol of death. It stands for the abrupt, violent end of a human being. The man in Roman times who took up his cross and started down the road had already said good-bye to his friends. He was not coming back. He was going out to have it ended. The cross made no compromise, modified nothing, spared nothing; it slew all of the man, completely and for good. It did not try to keep on good terms with its victim. It struck cruel and hard, and when it had finished its work, the man was no more.

The race of Adam is under death sentence. There is no commutation and no escape. God cannot approve any of the fruits of sin, however innocent they may appear or beautiful to the eyes of men. God salvages the individual by liquidating him and then raising him again to newness of life. TRC079

My God and Savior, thank You for putting an end to death by Your death on the cross. May I walk in newness of life this day. Amen.

APRIL 6

Christ Before All

If anyone comes to me and does not hate father and mother, wife and children, brothers and sisters—yes, even their own life—such a person cannot be my disciple. And whoever does not carry their cross and follow me cannot be my disciple.

—LUKE 14:26–27

All fleshly relationships will be dissolved in the glory of the resurrection, including the relationship between husband and wife. For this reason our Lord said plainly that for some people it would be necessary to break family ties if they would follow Him. . . .

What Christ is saying here is that faith in Him immediately introduces another and a higher loyalty into the life. He demands and must have first place. For the true disciple it is Christ before family, Christ before country, Christ before life itself. The flesh must always be sacrificed to the spirit and the heavenly placed ahead of the earthly, and that at any cost. When we take up the cross, we become expendable, along with all natural friendships and all previous loyalties, and Christ becomes all in all.

In these days of sweet and easy Christianity, it requires inward illumination to see this truth and real faith to accept it. We had better pray for both before time runs out on us. TRC086-88

Lord Jesus, forgive me for the ways in which I have placed other things and people ahead of You in my life. May You be first! Amen.

APRIL 7

Cross of Obedience

Submit yourselves, then, to God. Resist the devil, and he will flee from you. Come near to God and he will come near to you.
—JAMES 4:7-8

When we are willing to consider the active will of God for our lives, we come immediately to a personal knowledge of the cross because the will of God is the place of blessed, painful, fruitful trouble!

The Apostle Paul knew about that. He called it "the fellowship of Christ's sufferings." It is my conviction that one of the reasons we exhibit very little spiritual power is because we are unwilling to accept and experience the fellowship of the Savior's sufferings, which means acceptance of His cross.

How can we have and know the blessed intimacy of the Lord Jesus if we are unwilling to take the route which He has demonstrated? We do not have it because we refuse to relate the will of God to the cross.

All of the great saints have been acquainted with the cross—even those who lived before the time of Christ. They were acquainted with the cross in essence because their obedience brought it to them.

All Christians living in full obedience will experience the cross and find themselves exercised in spirit very frequently. If they know their own hearts, they will be prepared to wrestle with the cross when it comes. TRC101-102

Lamb of God, give me strength and grace today to willingly follow You by taking up my cross. May Your spirit empower me to live in full obedience to You. Amen.

APRIL 8

Demands of Justice

God presented Christ as a sacrifice of atonement, through the shedding of his blood—to be received by faith. He did this to demonstrate his righteousness, because in his forbearance he had left the sins committed beforehand unpunished—he did it to demonstrate his righteousness at the present time, so as to be just and the one who justifies those who have faith in Jesus.

—ROMANS 3:25–26

The cross of Christ has altered somewhat the position of certain persons before the judgment of God. Toward those who embrace the provisions of mercy that center around the death and resurrection of Christ, one phase of judgment is no longer operative. "He that heareth my word, and believeth on him that sent me, hath everlasting life, and shall not come into condemnation; but is passed from death unto life." (John 5:24).

That is the way our Lord stated this truth, and we have only to know that the word *condemned* as it occurs here is actually "judgment" to see that for believers the consequences of sinful deeds have, in at least one aspect, been remitted.

When Christ died in the darkness for us men, He made it possible for God to remit the penalty of the broken law, re-establish repentant sinners in His favor exactly as if they had never sinned, and do the whole thing without relaxing the severity of the law or compromising the high demands of justice (see Rom. 3:24–26). TRC114-115

Lord Jesus, thank You for paying the price of salvation, that I might be forgiven and reunited with the Father. What a great price You paid! Amen.

APRIL 9

Lord of Our Living

He died for us so that, whether we are awake or asleep, we may live together with him.

—1 THESSALONIANS 5:10

I have studied the New Testament enough to know that our Lord Jesus Christ never made the sharp distinctions between "secular" and "sacred" that we do!

I think it is wrong to place our physical necessities on one side, and put praying and singing and giving and Bible reading and testifying on the other.

When we are living for the Lord and living to please and honor Him, eating our breakfast can be just as spiritual as having our family prayers. There is no reason for a committed Christian to apologize: "Lord, I am awfully sorry but you know I have to eat now. I will be with you again just as soon as I am through."

Well, we have a better way than that in our living for God, and we see as we consider His feeding of the 5,000 the meaning of His lordship. Jesus Christ is Lord—Lord of our bread and Lord of our eating and Lord of our sleeping and Lord of our working!

Brethren, our Lord is with us, sanctifying everything we do, provided it is honest and good. MWT200

Lord, today I want to be especially aware that You are the Lord of whatever I am doing. Thank You for Your all-encompassing presence in my life. Amen.

APRIL 10

Men May Now Be One with God

Through these he has given us his very great and precious promises, so that through them you may participate in the divine nature, having escaped the corruption in the world caused by evil desires.

—2 PETER 1:4

Deity indwelling men! That is Christianity in its fullest effectuation, and even those greater glories of the world to come will be in essence but a greater and more perfect experience of the soul's union with God. Deity indwelling men! That, I say, is Christianity and no man has experienced rightly the power of Christian belief until he has known this for himself as a living reality.

Everything else is preliminary to this! Incarnation, atonement, justification, regeneration; what are these but acts of God preparatory to the work of invading and the act of indwelling the redeemed human soul? Man who moved out of the heart of God now moves back into the heart of God by redemption!

God who moved out of the heart of man because of sin now enters again His ancient dwelling to drive out His enemies and once more make the place of His feet glorious!

That visible fire on the day of Pentecost had for the church a deep and tender significance, for it told to all ages that they upon whose heads it sat were men and women apart. The mark of the fire was the sign of divinity; they who received it were forever a peculiar people, sons and daughters of the Flame. EWT399

Loving Father, thank You that by Your Son's incarnation, death, and resurrection, I may be one with You. Grant that I would commune more deeply with You today. Amen.

APRIL 11

More than Pardon

Godly sorrow brings repentance that leads to salvation and leaves no regret, but worldly sorrow brings death.
—2 CORINTHIANS 7:10

It is a fact that the New Testament message of good news, "Christ died for our sins according to the scriptures" (1 Cor. 15:3), embraces a great deal more than an offer of free pardon.

Surely it is a message of pardon—and for that may God be praised—but it is also a message of repentance!

It is a message of atonement—but it is also a message of temperance and righteousness and godliness in this present world!

It tells us that we must accept a Savior—but it tells us also that we must deny ungodliness and worldly lusts!

The gospel message includes the idea of amendment—of separation from the world, of cross carrying and loyalty to the kingdom of God even unto death!

These are all corollaries of the gospel and not the gospel itself; but they are part and parcel of the total message which we are commissioned to declare. No man has authority to divide the truth and preach only a part of it. To do so is to weaken it and render it without effect! MWT380

Lord, I pray for You to anoint every believer with a "holy boldness" to proclaim Your gospel and all of its implications. It may not be an attractive message, but it will be the Truth for those with ears to hear. Amen.

APRIL 12

A Personal Matter

But he was pierced for our transgressions, he was crushed for our iniquities.

—ISAIAH 53:5

There is no expression in the English language which can convey the full weight and force of terror inherent in the words *transgression* and *iniquity.* But in man's fall and transgression against the created order and authority of God we recognize perversion and twistedness and deformity and crookedness and rebellion. These are all there, and, undeniably, they reflect the reason and the necessity for the death of Jesus Christ on the cross.

The word *iniquity* is not a good word—and God knows how we hate it! But the consequences of iniquity cannot be escaped.

The prophet reminds us clearly that the Savior was crushed for "our iniquities."

We deny it and say, "No!" But the fingerprints of all mankind are plain evidence against us. The authorities have no trouble finding and apprehending the awkward burglar who leaves his fingerprints on tables and doorknobs, for they have his record. So, the fingerprints of man are found in every dark cellar and in every alley and in every dimly lighted evil place throughout the world—every man's fingerprints are recorded and God knows man from man. It is impossible to escape our guilt and place our moral responsibilities upon someone else. It is a highly personal matter—"our iniquities."
TRC126-127

Thank You, Father, for sending Your Son to pay the price for my transgressions and iniquities. May I be ever grateful for Your gift of salvation. Amen.

APRIL 13

Bruised and Wounded

The punishment that brought us peace was on him.
—ISAIAH 53:5

For our iniquities and our transgressions He was bruised and wounded. I do not even like to tell you of the implications of His wounding. It really means that He was profaned and broken, stained and defiled. He was Jesus Christ when men took Him into their evil hands. Soon He was humiliated and profaned. They plucked out His beard. He was stained with His own blood, defiled with earth's grime. Yet He accused no one and He cursed no one. He was Jesus Christ, the wounded One.

Israel's great burden and amazing blunder was her judgment that this wounded One on the hillside beyond Jerusalem was being punished for His own sin. . . .

He was profaned for our sakes. He who is the second person of the Godhead was not only wounded for us, but He was profaned by ignorant and unworthy men.

How few there are who realize that it is this peace—the health and prosperity and welfare and safety of the individual—which restores us to God. A chastisement fell upon Him so that we as individual humans could experience peace with God if we so desired. TRC127-128

O wounded One, I praise and thank You today for taking my place so that I might be joined to God. May I faithfully proclaim Your goodness today. Amen.

APRIL 14

Corrective Suffering

By his wounds we are healed.
—ISAIAH 53:5

I speak for myself as a forgiven and justified sinner, and I think I speak for a great host of forgiven and born-again men and women, when I say that in our repentance we sensed just a fraction and just a token of the wounding and chastisement which fell upon Jesus Christ as He stood in our place and in our behalf. A truly penitent man who has realized the enormity of his sin and rebellion against God senses a violent revulsion against himself—he does not feel that he can actually dare to ask God to let him off. But peace has been established, for the blows have fallen on Jesus Christ. He was publicly humiliated and disgraced as a common thief, wounded and bruised and bleeding under the lash for sins He did not commit, for rebellions in which He had no part, for iniquity in the human stream that was an outrage to a loving God and Creator. TRC129

Lord Jesus, I praise You for making peace between me and the Father. You have forgiven me of my sins and given me new life. May I walk in that newness of life and so become more like You, the perfect One. Amen.

APRIL 15

Cleansing Wounds

Have mercy on me, O God, according to your unfailing love;
according to your great compassion blot out my transgressions.
—PSALM 51:1

What is our repentance? I discover that repentance is mainly remorse for the share we had in the revolt that wounded Jesus Christ, our Lord. Further, I have discovered that truly repentant men never quite get over it, for repentance is not a state of mind and spirit that takes its leave as soon as God has given forgiveness and as soon as cleansing is realized.

That painful and acute conviction that accompanies repentance may well subside and a sense of peace and cleansing come, but even the holiest of justified men will think back over his part in the wounding and the chastisement of the Lamb of God. A sense of shock will still come over him. A sense of wonder will remain—wonder that the Lamb that was wounded should turn His wounds into the cleansing and forgiveness of one who wounded Him. . . .

The believing Christian, the child of God, should have a holy longing and desire for the pure heart and clean hands that are a delight to his Lord. It was for this that Jesus Christ allowed Himself to be humiliated, maltreated, lacerated. He was bruised, wounded, and chastised so that the people of God could be a cleansed and spiritual people—in order that our minds might be pure and our thoughts pure. This provision all began in His suffering and ends in our cleansing. TRC130-131

Lord, may I truly repent of my sins and not just be remorseful! Grant me the ability to turn away from that which dishonors You so that You would be glorified in my life. Amen.

APRIL 16

Two Basic Facts

But he was pierced for our transgressions, he was crushed for our iniquities; the punishment that brought us peace was on him, and by his wounds we are healed.
—ISAIAH 53:5

Those who compose the body of Christ, His church, must be inwardly aware of two basic facts if we are to be joyfully effective for our Lord.

We must have the positive knowledge that we are clean through His wounds, with God's peace realized through His stripes. This is how God assures us that we may be all right inside. In this spiritual condition, we will treasure the purity of His cleansing and we will not excuse any evil or wrongdoing.

Also, we must keep upon us a joyful and compelling sense of gratitude for the bruised and wounded One, our Lord Jesus Christ. Oh, what a mystery of redemption—that the bruises of One healed the bruises of many; that the wounds of One healed the wounds of millions; that the stripes of One healed the stripes of many.

The wounds and bruises that should have fallen upon us fell upon Him, and we are saved for His sake! TRC133

O bruised and wounded One, thank You for cleansing me and giving me peace with the Father. Increase my joy in the mystery of redemption. Amen.

APRIL 17

The Easter Triumph

Why do you look for the living among the dead? He is not here; he has risen!

—LUKE 24:5–6

I do not mind telling you that within me I find the Easter message and the reality of the Resurrection more beautiful and glorious than the Christmas scene.

Christmas tells us that Jesus was born—that He was born for the humiliation of suffering and death and atonement.

But Easter is the radiant and glory-filled celebration of Christ's mighty triumph over the grave and death and hell!

When Easter comes, our voices are raised in the triumphant chorus:

The three sad days had quickly sped;
He rises glorious from the dead!

There is the real beauty! This is more than the beauty of color; more than the beauty of outline or form; more than the beauty of physical proportion.

In the living Christ is the perfection of all beauty; and because He lives, we too shall live in the presence of His beauty and the beauties of heaven forever! MWT113

Risen Lord, what a privilege it is to call You my Savior and King! That You triumphed over death is both wonderful and incomprehensible. Amen.

APRIL 18

The Just Died for the Unjust

He did it to demonstrate his righteousness at the present time, so as to be just and the one who justifies those who have faith in Jesus.

—ROMANS 3:26

The whole question of right and wrong, of moral responsibility, of justice and judgment and reward and punishment, is sharply accented for us by the fact that we are members of a fallen race, occupying a position halfway between heaven and hell, with the knowledge of good and evil inherent within our intricate natures, along with ability to turn toward good and an inborn propensity to turn toward evil.

The cross of Christ has altered somewhat the position of certain persons before the judgment of God. Toward those who embrace the provisions of mercy that center around the death and resurrection of Christ, one phase of judgment is no longer operative. Our Lord stated this truth in this way: "He that heareth my word, and believeth on him that sent me, hath everlasting life, and shall not come into condemnation; but is passed from death unto life" (John 5:24).

When Christ died in the darkness for us men, He made it possible for God to remit the penalty of the broken law, reestablish repentant sinners in His favor exactly as if they had never sinned, and do the whole thing without relaxing the severity of the law or compromising the high demands of justice (Rom. 3:24–26). The Just died for the unjust. Thanks be to God for His unspeakable gift! EWT221

Gracious Lord, I do not deserve what You have done for me. I bow down before You in gratitude today and bask in the wonderful gift You have given me. Amen.

APRIL 19

What Easter Is About

For as Jonah was three days and three nights in the belly of a huge fish, so the Son of Man will be three days and three nights in the heart of the earth.
—MATTHEW 12:40

The Man called Jesus is alive after having been publicly put to death by crucifixion. The Roman soldiers nailed Him to the cross and watched Him till the life had gone from Him. Then a responsible company of persons, headed by one Joseph of Arimathea, took the body down from the cross and laid it in a tomb, after which the Roman authorities sealed the tomb and set a watch before it to make sure the body would not be stolen away by zealous but misguided disciples. This last precaution was the brain child of the priests and the Pharisees, and how it backfired on them is known to the ages, for it went far to confirm the fact that the body was completely dead and that it could have gotten out of the tomb only by some miracle.

In spite of the tomb and the watch and the seal, in spite of death itself, the Man who had been laid in the place of death walked out alive after three days. That is the simple historical fact attested by more than 500 trustworthy persons, among them being a man who is said by some scholars to have had one of the mightiest intellects of all time. That man of course was Saul, who later became a disciple of Jesus and was known as Paul the apostle. This is what the Church has believed and celebrated throughout the centuries. This is what the Church celebrates today. TRC160-161

Resurrected Lord, I celebrate Your victory today, knowing that You have conquered sin and death! May You be glorified by my sacrifice of thanksgiving. Amen.

APRIL 20

The Glory of the Cross

Surely he took up our pain and bore our suffering, yet we considered him punished by God, stricken by him, and afflicted.
—ISAIAH 53:4

Never make any mistake about this—the suffering of Jesus Christ on the cross was not punitive! It was not for Himself and not for punishment of anything that He Himself had done.

The suffering of Jesus was corrective. He was willing to suffer in order that He might correct us and perfect us.

Brethren, that is the glory of the cross! That is the glory of the kind of sacrifice that was for so long in the heart of God! That is the glory of the kind of atonement that allows a repentant sinner to come into peaceful and gracious fellowship with his God and Creator!

It began in His wounds and ended in our purification!

It began in His bruises and ended in our cleansing!

That painful and acute conviction that accompanies repentance may well subside and a sense of peace and cleansing come, but even the holiest of justified men will think back over his part in the wounding and chastisement of the Lamb of God.

A sense of shock will still come over him!

A sense of wonder will remain—wonder that the Lamb that was wounded should turn his wounds into the cleansing and forgiveness of one who wounded Him! EWT253

Lord Christ, I praise You for making a way by your cross for me to enjoy peaceful and gracious fellowship with the Father! Amen.

APRIL 21

Joy Unspeakable

Though you have not seen him, you love him; and even though you do not see him now, you believe in him and are filled with an inexpressible and glorious joy, for you are receiving the end result of your faith, the salvation of your souls.

—1 PETER 1:8–9

His joyful resurrection followed hard upon His joyless crucifixion. But the first had to come before the second. The life that halts short of the cross is but a fugitive and condemned thing, doomed at last to be lost beyond recovery. That life which goes to the cross and loses itself there to rise again with Christ is a divine and deathless treasure. Over it death hath no more dominion. Whoever refuses to bring his old life to the cross is but trying to cheat death, and no matter how hard we may struggle against it, he is nevertheless fated to lose his life at last. The man who takes his cross and follows Christ will soon find that his direction is *away* from the sepulcher. Death is behind him and a joyous and increasing life before. His days will be marked henceforth not by ecclesiastical gloom, the churchyard, the hollow tone, the black robe (which are all but the cerements of a dead church), but by "joy unspeakable and full of glory" (1 Peter 1:8).

Heavenly Father, thank You for the unspeakable joy You offer as a result of Your Son's resurrection. Increase my joy today. Amen.

APRIL 22

Resurrection Power

Then Jesus came to them and said, "All authority in heaven and on earth has been given to me."
—MATTHEW 28:18

Let us be confident, Christian brethren, that our power does not lie in the manger at Bethlehem nor in the relics of the cross. True spiritual power resides in the victory of the mighty, resurrected Lord of glory, who could pronounce after spoiling death: "All power is given me in heaven and in earth."

The power of the Christian believer lies in the Savior's triumph of eternal glory!

Christ's resurrection brought about a startling change of direction for the believers. Sadness and fear and mourning marked the direction of their religion before they knew that Jesus was raised from the dead—their direction was towards the grave. When they heard the angelic witness, "He is risen, as He said," the direction immediately shifted away from the tomb—"He is risen, indeed!" If this is not the meaning of Easter, the Christian church is involved only in a shallow one-day festival each year.

Thankfully, the resurrection morning was only the beginning of a great, vast outreach that has never ended—and will not end until our Lord Jesus Christ comes back again! MWT114

Dear Heavenly Father, speed the triumphant resurrection message into areas not yet reached by the gospel. Strengthen, encourage, and equip Your servants for this awesome task. Amen.

APRIL 23

Christ's Victory Belongs to Us

For this reason he had to be made like them, fully human in every way.
—HEBREWS 2:17

I cannot assure you whether Christians should know discouragement or not: I can only tell you that they all do! Inwardly, they are often heavyhearted, defeated, unhappy, and a little bit frightened—yet they are Christians!

What we need, brethren, is to get the true scriptural vision of our victorious Lord, our victorious human brother. Paul wrote to the Philippians about Jesus Christ humbling Himself and becoming obedient even unto the death of the cross, and then: "Wherefore, God also hath highly exalted him and given him a name which is above every name" and "every tongue should confess that Jesus Christ is Lord, to the glory of God, the Father" (2:9–11).

Now, that is our victorious Lord, our victorious human brother.

Someone may say: "It is no great news to say that God is victorious."

But what we read in the New Testament is that God has joined His nature to the nature of man and has made a Man victorious, so that men might be victorious and overcoming in that Man!

God has made Him to be Head of the Church and He meanwhile waits for the time of His returning, guiding and keeping and instructing His Church. This He does by the Holy Spirit through the Word of God! EWT047

Father, thank You for the victory of Your Son, my Lord and Savior. May I walk in His victory today. Amen.

APRIL 24

The Daunting Task

For I am not ashamed of the gospel, because it is the power of God that brings salvation to everyone who believes: first to the Jew, then to the Gentile.

—ROMANS 1:16

The greatest event in history was the coming of Jesus Christ into the world to live and to die for mankind. The next greatest event was the going forth of the Church to embody the life of Christ and to spread the knowledge of His salvation throughout the earth.

It was not an easy task which the Church faced when she came down from that upper room. . . . Left to herself the Church must have perished as a thousand abortive sects had done before her, and have left nothing for a future generation to remember.

That the Church did not so perish was due entirely to the miraculous element within her. That element was supplied by the Holy Spirit who came at Pentecost to empower her for her task. For the Church was not an organization merely, not a movement, but a walking incarnation of spiritual energy. And she accomplished within a few brief years such prodigies of moral conquest as to leave us wholly without an explanation—apart from God. PTP007-008

Empower us for our work, Holy Spirit, even as You empowered the early Church. Amen.

APRIL 25

The Soul in the Body

But in fact God has placed the parts in the body, every one of them, just as he wanted them to be.
—1 CORINTHIANS 12:18

Let us review something here that we probably know: the doctrine of the life and operation of Christian believers on earth—starting with the fact that the Christian church is the body of Christ, Jesus Himself being the Headship of that body. Every true Christian, no matter where he or she lives, is a part of that body, and the Holy Spirit is to the church what our own souls are to our physical bodies. Through the operation of the Holy Spirit, Christ becomes the life, the unity, and the consciousness of the body, which is the church. Let the soul leave the physical body and all the parts of the body cease to function. Let the Spirit be denied His place in the spiritual body, and the church ceases to function as God intended. . . .

According to the Bible, the whole body exists for its members and the members exist for the whole body. And that, of course, is the reason God gives gifts, so that the body may profit spiritually and maintain spiritual health and prosperity in its service for Jesus Christ in an unfriendly world. TRA014-016

Lord, I pray today that we in our church might be aware of Your presence, that we might be faithfully exercising the gifts You have given, and that we might be a healthy body that pleases You. Amen.

APRIL 26

Weak in Discipleship

Let us, then, go to him outside the camp, bearing the disgrace he bore.

—HEBREWS 13:13

The absence of the concept of discipleship from present-day Christianity leaves a vacuum which men and women instinctively try to fill with a variety of substitutes.

One is a kind of pietism—an enjoyable feeling of affection for the person of our Lord, which is valued for itself and is wholly unrelated to cross bearing.

Another substitute is literalism—which manifests itself among us by insisting on keeping the letter of the Word while ignoring its spirit. It habitually fails to apprehend the inward meaning of Christ's words and contents itself with external compliance with the text.

A third substitute surely is zealous religious activity. "Working for Christ" has today been accepted as the ultimate test of godliness among all but a few evangelical Christians. Christ has become a project to be promoted or a cause to be served, instead of a Lord to be obeyed! To avoid the snare of unauthorized substitution, I recommend careful and prayerful study of the lordship of Christ and the discipleship of the believer! MWT280

Dear Lord, I pray that there will be a growing interest in our churches to implement training strategies that will help believers take their relationship with Christ to a new, higher level. Amen.

APRIL 27

Faith Rests Upon the Character of God

So that now was always Christ will be exalted in my body, whether by life or by death. For to me, to live is Christ and to die is gain.
—PHILIPPIANS 1:20, 21

The power of Christianity appears in its antipathy toward, never in its agreement with, the ways of fallen men. At the heart of the Christian system lies the cross of Christ with its divine paradox and the truth of the cross is revealed in its contradictions.

The cross stands in bold opposition to the natural man. Its philosophy runs contrary to the processes of the unregenerate mind, so that Paul could say bluntly that the preaching of the cross is to them that perish foolishness. To try to find a common ground between the message of the cross and man's fallen reason can only result in an impaired reason, a meaningless cross and a powerless Christianity!

Note this also about the cross-carrying Christian: when he looks at the cross he is a pessimist, for he knows that the same judgment that fell on the Lord of glory condemns in that one act all nature and all the world of men. He rejects every human hope out of Christ because he knows that man's noblest effort is only dust building on dust.

Yet he is calmly, restfully optimistic, for the resurrection of Christ guarantees the ultimate triumph of good throughout the universe. Through Christ, all will be well at last and the Christian waits the consummation! EWT033

Lord Christ, thank You for Your cross and what it means for me today. Enable me to carry my cross and to proclaim the cross, that I may share in Your resurrection and lead others to You. Amen.

APRIL 28

Whole Life Prayer

If you remain in me and my words remain in you, ask whatever you wish, and it will be done for you.

—JOHN 15:7

Prayer at its best is the expression of the total life. . . .

All things else being equal, our prayers are only as powerful as our lives. In the long pull we pray only as well as we live. . . .

Most of us in moments of stress have wished that we had lived so that prayer would not be so unnatural to us and have regretted that we had not cultivated prayer to the point where it would be as easy and as natural as breathing. . . .

Undoubtedly the redemption in Christ Jesus has sufficient moral power to enable us to live in a state of purity and love where our whole life will be a prayer. Individual acts of prayer that spring out of that kind of total living will have about them a wondrous power not known to the careless or the worldly Christian. ROR081-083

Lord, the real key here is that there is "sufficient moral power" available. In my own strength I fail, but thank You for Your enabling power. Amen.

APRIL 29

A Sense of Inadequacy

But we have this treasure in jars of clay to show that this all-surpassing power is from God and not from us.
—2 CORINTHIANS 4:7

I believe I had anticipated that it was going to be a pleasure to expound this beautiful and high-soaring Gospel of John. However, I must confess that in my preparation and study a sense of inadequacy has come over me—a feeling of inadequacy so stunning, so almost paralyzing that I am not at this juncture able to call it a pleasure to preach.

Perhaps this will be God's way of reducing the flesh to a minimum and giving the Holy Spirit the best possible opportunity to do His eternal work. I fear that sometimes our own eloquence and our own concepts may get in the way, for the unlimited ability to talk endlessly about religion is a questionable blessing. . . .

None of us can approach a serious study and consideration of the eternal nature and person of Jesus Christ without sensing and confessing our complete inadequacy in the face of the divine revelation.

CES003, 009

Lord, I've so often been at that place of total inadequacy. I've learned that that is so healthy because then I step aside, I quit relying on my own "eloquence," and I allow the Holy Spirit to take over and do what only He can do anyway! Use me today in my weakness. Amen.

APRIL 30

Easter—and Missions

I want to know Christ—yes, to know the power of his resurrection.
—PHILIPPIANS 3:10

Do we really believe that the resurrection of Jesus Christ is something more than making us the "happiest fellows in the Easter parade"?

Are we just to listen to the bright cantata and join in singing, "Up from the Grave He Arose," smell the flowers, and go home and forget it?

No, certainly not!

It is truth and a promise with a specific moral application. The Resurrection certainly commands us with all the authority of sovereign obligation—the missionary obligation!

I cannot give in to the devil's principal, deceitful tactic which makes so many Christians satisfied with an "Easter celebration" instead of experiencing the power of Christ's resurrection. It is the devil's business to keep Christians mourning and weeping with pity beside the cross instead of demonstrating that Jesus Christ is risen indeed.

When will the Christian church rise up, depending on His promise and power, and get on the offensive for the risen and ascended Savior? MWT116

Lord, Your resurrection is a call to action. No other religion can claim the power You displayed on that first Easter morning. You are the one, true God! Give me opportunities to tell others about Your saving power. Amen.

MAY

MAY 1

Restoration of the Divine Image

Now may the Lord of peace himself give you peace at all times and in every way.

—2 THESSALONIANS 3:16

If redemption is a moral restoration to the divine image (and it must be that ultimately), then we may expect one of the first acts of God in the Christian's life to be a kind of moral tuning-up, a bringing into harmony the discordant elements within the personality, an adjustment of the soul to itself and to God. And that He does just this is the testimony of everyone who has been truly converted!

The new believer may state it in other language and the emotional lift he enjoys may be so great as to prevent calm analysis, but the gist of his testimony will be that he has found peace, a peace he can actually feel! The twists and tensions within his heart have corrected themselves as a result of his new orientation to Christ.

He can then sing, "Now rest, my long-divided heart; Fixed on this blissful center rest." EWT286

Jesus my Lord, thank You for reorienting me to the Father by Your death and resurrection! May the divine image in me be increasingly restored to the glory of Your name. Amen.

Common People

Brothers and sisters, think of what you were when you were called. Not many of you were wise by human standards; not many were influential; not many were of noble birth. But God chose the foolish things of the world to shame the wise; God chose the weak things of the world to shame the strong.
—1 CORINTHIANS 1:26–27

Christian believers and Christian congregations must be thoroughly consecrated to Christ's glory alone. This means absolutely turning their backs on the contemporary insistence on human glory and recognition. I have done everything I can to keep "performers" out of my pulpit. I was not called to recognize "performers." I am confident our Lord never meant for the Christian church to provide a kind of religious stage where performers proudly take their bows, seeking personal recognition. That is not God's way to an eternal work. He has never indicated that proclamation of the gospel is to be dependent on human performances.

Instead, it is important to note how much the Bible has to say about the common people—the plain people. The Word of God speaks with such appreciation of the common people that I am inclined to believe they are especially dear to Him. Jesus was always surrounded by the common people. He had a few "stars," but largely His helpers were from the common people—the good people and, surely, not always the most brilliant. TRA005

In our church, Lord, help us to treat all alike as Your servants. Amen.

MAY 3

Christ's Picture Everywhere

You are worthy, our Lord and God, to receive glory and honor and power.

—REVELATION 4:11

We try to sympathize with the writer John as he attempts to describe heavenly creatures in human terms in the book of Revelation. He knew and we know that it was impossible for God to fully reveal Himself and the heavenly glories to a man.

John tries to describe for us the four "living creatures" in Revelation 4. The first was like a lion; the second was like an ox; the third had the face of a man; the fourth was like a soaring eagle. Did you know that for centuries Christians have seen those same "faces" in the four gospels of the New Testament?

God has put Jesus Christ's picture everywhere! Matthew's is the gospel of the King. Mark's, the gospel of the suffering Servant. Luke's, the gospel of the Son of Man. John's, the gospel of the Son of God. Four loving, adoring, worshiping beings, faithfully and forever devoted to praising God!

Make no mistake about it: The imagery is plainly the gospel of Christ. He is what Christianity is all about! MWT400

Lord, You are truly what this world is all about: You created it, You hold it together, and You have redeemed it! You are worthy to be praised every moment of every day! Amen.

Sovereign Obligation

I am obligated both to Greeks and non-Greeks, both to the wise and the foolish. That is why I am so eager to preach the gospel also to you who are in Rome.

—ROMANS 1:14–15

The resurrection of Jesus Christ is something more than making us the happiest people in the Easter parade. Are we to listen to a cantata, join in singing "Up from the Grave He Arose," smell the lilies, and go home and forget it? No, certainly not!

The resurrection of Jesus Christ lays hold on us with all the authority of sovereign obligation. It says that the Christian church is to go and make disciples—to go and make disciples of all nations. The moral obligation of the resurrection of Christ is the missionary obligation—the responsibility and privilege of personally carrying the message, of interceding for those who go, of being involved financially in the cause of world evangelization. TRA090

Stimulate me, Lord, with that sense of sovereign obligation. Then lead me to the right person with whom I could share Your grace. Amen.

MAY 5

Free to Be a Servant

Understand what the Lord's will is.
—EPHESIANS 5:17

Every man in a free society must decide whether he will exploit his liberty or curtail it for intelligent and moral ends. He may take upon him the responsibility of a business and a family, . . . or he may shun all obligations and end on skid row. The tramp is freer than president or king, but his freedom is his undoing. While he lives, he remains socially sterile; and when he dies, he leaves nothing . . . to make the world glad he lived.

The Christian cannot escape the peril of too much liberty. He is indeed free, but his very freedom may prove a source of real temptation to him. He is free from the chains of sin, free from the moral consequences of evil acts now forgiven, free from the curse of the law and the displeasure of God. . . .

The ideal Christian is one who knows he is free to do as he will and wills to be a servant. This is the path Christ took; blessed is the man who follows Him. MWT209

Thank You, Lord, for the freedom I have through Christ. I am not bound by sin or fear. Help me to use my freedom to serve You with unfettered boldness. Amen.

MAY 6

Just a Small Church Upcountry

How precious to me are your thoughts, God! How vast is the sum of them! Were I to count them, they would outnumber the grains of sand—when I awake, I am still with you.

—PSALM 139:17–18

No matter how insignificant he may have been before, a man becomes significant the moment he has had an encounter with the Son of God. When the Lord lays His hand upon a man, that man ceases at once to be ordinary. He immediately becomes extraordinary, and his life takes on cosmic significance. The angels in heaven take notice of him and go forth to become his ministers (Heb. 1:14). Though the man had before been only one of the faceless multitude, a mere cipher in the universe, an invisible dust grain blown across endless wastes—now he gets a face and a name and a place in the scheme of meaningful things. Christ knows His own sheep "by name."

A young preacher introduced himself to the pastor of a great metropolitan church with the words, "I am just the pastor of a small church upcountry." "Son," replied the wise minister, "there are no small churches." And there are no unknown Christians, no insignificant sons of God. Each one signifies, each is a "sign" drawing the attention of the Triune God day and night upon him. The faceless man has a face, the nameless man a name, when Jesus picks him out of the multitude and calls him to Himself. WTA019

Lord, I pray for the pastors of small churches. Let them see how much You care for them, and how significant You see their ministry to be. Amen.

MAY 7

For Jesus' Sake

But God demonstrates his own love for us in this: While we were still sinners, Christ died for us.

—ROMANS 5:8

God loves sinners for that which He sees in them of His lost and fallen image, for God can never love any thing but Himself, directly. He loves everything else for His own sake. So, you are loved of God—but you are loved of God for Jesus' sake! God loves lost men, not because He is careless or morally lax, but because He once stood and said: "Let us make man in our image."

Man was made in the image of God, and while sin has ruined him and condemned him to death forever unless he be redeemed through the blood of Jesus Christ, mankind is a being only one degree removed from the angels.

But sin, God knows, is like a cancer in the very being of man. Although once made in the image of God, he is now a dying man, sick unto spiritual death, because of the poison of sin. But extract and take out that sin and you have the image of God again! And Jesus Christ was the image of God because He was a man without sin.

God sees in Jesus Christ what you would have been! He sees that in His perfect humanity, not His deity—for you and I could never be divine in that sense. When Jesus Christ came to us, He was incarnated in the body of a man without embarrassment and without change, because man was an image of the God who made him. EWT046

I praise You, Father, for loving me on account of Jesus Christ, the image of the invisible God. May I ever grow in awe and appreciation for what You have done in Him. Amen.

Christ's Primary Work

It is because of him that you are in Christ Jesus, who has become for us wisdom from God—that is, our righteousness, holiness and redemption.
—1 CORINTHIANS 1:30

We can know our present properly only as we know our past, and in that past there occurred something disgraceful and tragic, namely, the loss of our moral character and rebellion against our Creator. That we also lost our happiness is of secondary importance, since it is but a result of our alienation from God and not a part of that alienation.

The primary work of Christ in redemption is to justify, sanctify, and ultimately to glorify a company of persons salvaged from the ruin of the human race. For the convenience of any who may not be familiar with the words used here, I would explain that justify means to declare righteous before God, sanctify means to make holy, and glorify means in effect to remake the entire personality after the image of Christ. This will fit us to dwell eternally in that heaven about which the Bible speaks and which is both a state of being and a location. In that heaven, the ransomed will experience unclouded communion with the Triune God; and that will itself assure unalloyed blessedness.
BAM165-166

Lord Jesus, I praise You for saving me, for justifying me, sanctifying me, and promising to glorify me. Complete the good work You have begun in me. Amen.

MAY 9

Just Plain Faithful

The things that you have heard . . . entrust to reliable people who will also be qualified to teach others.

—2 TIMOTHY 2:2

I realize that faithfulness is not a very dramatic subject and that many among us in the Christian faith would like to do something with more dash and more flair than just being faithful. While some are just concerned about getting their picture in the paper, I thank God for every loyal and faithful Christian who has only one recognition in mind, and that is to hear their Lord say in that Great Day to come: "Well done, thou good and faithful servant . . . enter thou into the joy of thy lord" (Matt. 25:21).

It is plain truth that faithfulness and goodness are at the root of much of the consistent fruit bearing among the witnessing children of God! Throughout the Bible the Lord has always placed a great premium on the faithfulness of those who love Him and serve Him.

Noah was faithful in his day. Abraham was faithful in his day. Moses was faithful in his day. And what do we need to say about the faithfulness of our Savior, Jesus Christ? The devil was there with his lies. The world threatened Him all around. But Christ was faithful to His Father and to us!

Are we willing to learn from the Holy Spirit how to be faithful and loving, unselfish and Christlike? MWT241

Lord, great is Your faithfulness! I pray that You will enable me to be marked by faithfulness in my walk with You—just like Noah, Abraham, and Moses. Amen.

MAY 10

The Ministry of the Night

For his anger lasts only a moment, but his favor lasts a lifetime; weeping may stay for the night, but rejoicing comes in the morning.

—PSALM 30:5

But there is a limit to man's ability to live without joy. Even Christ could endure the cross only because of the joy set before Him. The strongest steel breaks if kept too long under unrelieved tension. God knows exactly how much pressure each one of us can take. He knows how long we can endure the night, so He gives the soul relief, first by welcome glimpses of the morning star and then by the fuller light that harbingers the morning.

Slowly you will discover God's love in your suffering. Your heart will begin to approve the whole thing. You will learn from yourself what all the schools in the world could not teach you—the healing action of faith without supporting pleasure. You will feel and understand the ministry of the night; its power to purify, to detach, to humble, to destroy the fear of death and, what is more important to you at the moment, the fear of life. And you will learn that sometimes pain can do what even joy cannot, such as exposing the vanity of earth's trifles and filling your heart with longing for the peace of heaven. TIC123-124

Thank You, Father, for the ministry of the night, for the lessons of pain. And thank You that we're not alone in the night, for Christ has gone before us. Thank You for the morning star and the glimpse of the light of morning. Amen.

MAY 11

The Meaning of Pentecost

Therefore let all Israel be assured of this: God has made this Jesus, whom you crucified, both Lord and Messiah.

—ACTS 2:36

When you give yourself to prayerful study of the opening chapters of the book of Acts, you will discover a truth that is often overlooked—the thought that wherever Jesus is glorified, the Holy Spirit comes!

Contrary to what most people unintentionally assume, the important thing was that Jesus had been exalted. The emphasis upon the coming of the Spirit was possible because Christ's work was accomplished and He was glorified at the Father's right hand.

Jesus Himself had said on that last great day of the feast in Jerusalem, recorded in John 7:38–39: "He that believeth on me, as the scriptures hath said, out of his belly shall flow rivers of living water. (But this spake he of the Spirit, which they that believe on him should receive: for the Holy Ghost was not yet given; because Jesus was not yet glorified.)"

It is plain that the glorification of Jesus brought the Holy Spirit, and we ought to be able to get hold of that thought instantly. So, we repeat: Where Jesus is glorified, the Holy Spirit comes. He does not have to be begged. When Christ the Savior is truly honored and exalted, the Spirit comes! EWT167

Lord Christ, may You be exalted in my life today, that I would be filled with Your Spirit and Your greatness would be known throughout the earth. Amen.

MAY 12

Less of Me, More of Him

Filled with the fruit of righteousness that comes through Jesus Christ—to the glory and praise of God.
—PHILIPPIANS 1:11

Jesus Christ Himself is the deeper life and as I plunge on into the knowledge of the triune God, my heart moves on into the blessedness of His fellowship.

This means that there is less of me and more of God. Thus my spiritual life deepens, and I am strengthened in the knowledge of His will.

I think this is what Paul meant when he penned that great desire, "That I may know Him!" He was expressing more than the desire for acquaintance—he was yearning to be drawn into the full knowledge of fellowship with God which has been provided in the plan of redemption.

God originally created man in His own image so that man could know companionship with God in a unique sense and to a degree which is impossible for any other creature.

Because of his sin, man lost this knowledge, this daily partnership with God, and his heart has been darkened. But God has given sinful man another opportunity in salvation through the merits of a Redeemer, only because he was made in the image of God, and God has expressed His own everlasting love for man through the giving of His Son. EWT036

Holy Father, grant by Your Spirit that Jesus Christ would increase in my life today and that I could decrease, that I might know You more intimately. Amen.

MAY 13

The Utilitarian Christ

My ears had heard of you but now my eyes have seen you. Therefore I despise myself and repent in dust and ashes.

—JOB 42:5–6

Within the past few years, for instance, Christ has been popularized by some so-called evangelicals as one who, if a proper amount of prayer were made, would help the pious prize fighter to knock another fighter unconscious in the ring. Christ is also said to help the big league pitcher to get the proper hook on his curve. In another instance He assists an athletically-minded person to win the high jump, and still another not only to come in first in a track meet but to set a new record in the bargain. He is said also to have helped a praying businessman to beat out a competitor in a deal, to underbid a rival and to secure a coveted contract to the discomfiture of someone else who was trying to get it. He is even thought to lend succor to a praying movie actress while she plays a role so lewd as to bring the blood to the face of a professional prostitute.

Thus our Lord becomes the Christ of utility, a kind of Aladdin's lamp to do minor miracles in behalf of anyone who summons Him to do his bidding. ROR024

Lord, help me not to demean the person of Christ or the sovereignty of God with this cheap sham of prayer. Amen.

MAY 14

Heavenly Minded Christians

Father, I want those you have given me to be with me where I am, and to see my glory, the glory you have given me because you loved me before the creation of the world.

—JOHN 17:24

Our Lord is looking for heavenly minded Christians, for His Word encourages us to trust Him with such a singleness of purpose that He is able to deliver us from the fear of death and the uncertainties of tomorrow!

If we had actually reached a place of such spiritual commitment that the wonders of heaven were so close that we longed for the illuminating Presence of our Lord, we would not go into such a fearful and frantic performance every time we find something wrong with our physical frame.

I do not think that a genuine, committed Christian ever ought to be afraid to die. We do not have to fear because Jesus promised—that He would prepare a proper place for all of those who shall be born again, raised up out of the agony and stress of this world through the blood of the everlasting covenant into that bright and gracious world above.

Notice that Jesus said, "In my Father's house are many mansions." If it is His Father's house, it is also our Father's house because the Lord Jesus is our elder brother. Jesus also said, "I go to my Father and your Father—my God and your God."

If the Father's house is the house of Jesus, it is also the house of all of His other sons and daughters! And we Christians are much better off than we really know! EWT269

Lord Christ, enable me to set my mind on things above, where You are seated at the right hand of the Father, and not on things on the earth. For I know I will be there with You someday! Amen.

MAY 15

It Requires Obedience

Why do you call me, "Lord, Lord," and do not do what I say?
—LUKE 6:46

It is my conviction that much, very much, prayer for and talk about revival these days is wasted energy. Ignoring the confusion of figures, I might say that it is hunger that appears to have no object; it is dreamy wishing that is too weak to produce moral action. It is fanaticism on a high level for, according to John Wesley, "a fanatic is one who seeks desired ends while ignoring the constituted means to reach those ends." . . .

The correction of this error is extremely difficult for it entails more than a mere adjustment of our doctrinal beliefs; it strikes at the whole Adam-life and requires self-abnegation, humility, and cross-carrying. In short, it requires obedience. And that we will do anything to escape.

It is almost unbelievable how far we will go to avoid obeying God. We call Jesus "Lord" and beg Him to rejuvenate our souls, but we are careful to do not the things He says. When faced with a sin, a confession, or a moral alteration in our life, we find it much easier to pray half a night than to obey God. SIZ018-020

May this never be true of my life, Lord! I see the futility; I'm convinced of the need. Now enable me by Your Spirit to live in obedience to Your Son and not just call Him Lord. Amen.

MAY 16

The Abomination of Self-Righteousness

But grow in the grace and knowledge of our Lord and Savior Jesus Christ. To him be glory both now and forever! Amen.
—2 PETER 3:18

Self-righteousness is terrible among God's people. If we feel that we are what we ought to be, then we will remain what we are. We will not look for any change or improvement in our lives. This will quite naturally lead us to judge everyone by what we are. This is the judgment of which we must be careful. To judge others by ourselves is to create havoc in the local assembly.

Self-righteousness also leads to complacency. Complacency is a great sin. . . . Some have the attitude, "Lord, I'm satisfied with my spiritual condition. I hope one of these days You will come, I will be taken up to meet You in the air and I will rule over five cities." These people cannot rule over their own houses and families, but they expect to rule over five cities. They pray spottily and sparsely, rarely attending prayer meeting, but they read their Bibles and expect to go zooming off into the blue yonder and join the Lord in the triumph of the victorious saints. RRR010-011

Lord, keep me from the curse of self-righteousness and grant that I would always trust in the perfect righteousness of Christ. Amen.

MAY 17

Salvation Apart from Obedience

For we are God's handiwork, created in Christ Jesus to do good works, which God prepared in advance for us to do.
—EPHESIANS 2:10

Therefore, I must be frank in my feeling that a notable heresy has come into being throughout our evangelical Christian circles—the widely accepted concept that we humans can choose to accept Christ only because we need Him as Savior and we have the right to postpone our obedience to Him as Lord as long as we want to! . . .

I think the following is a fair statement of what I was taught in my early Christian experience and it certainly needs a lot of modifying and a great many qualifiers to save us from being in error.

"We are saved by accepting Christ as our Savior; we are sanctified by accepting Christ as our Lord; we may do the first without doing the second!"

The truth is that salvation apart from obedience is unknown in the sacred Scriptures. Peter makes it plain that we are "elect according to the foreknowledge of God the Father, through sanctification of the Spirit, unto obedience" (1 Peter 1:2). ICH001-002

Lord, as I rejoice in the free gift of salvation, by grace through faith, remind me regularly that it is a salvation unto good works, that we're saved to serve. Amen.

MAY 18

Christ Died for All

Salvation is found in no one else, for there is no other name under heaven given to mankind by which we must be saved.
—ACTS 4:12

Our Lord Jesus Christ came and demonstrated the vast difference between being charitable and being tolerant! He was so charitable that in His great heart He took in all the people in the world and was willing to die even for those who hated Him!

But even with that kind of love and charity crowning His being, Jesus was completely frank and open when He taught: "If you are not on My side, you are against Me!" There is no "twilight zone" in the teachings of Jesus—no place in between.

So, charity is one thing, but tolerance is quite another matter.

Suppose we take the position of compromise that many want us to take: "Everyone come, and be saved if you want to. But if you do not want to be saved, maybe there is some other way that we can find for you. We want you to believe in the Lord Jesus Christ if you will, but if you do not want to, there may be a possibility that God will find some other way for you because there are those who say that there are many ways to God."

To take that position would not be a spirit of tolerance on our part—it would be downright cowardice! We would be guilty with so many others of a spirit of compromise that so easily becomes an anti-God attitude. Tolerance easily becomes a matter of cowardice if spiritual principles are involved, if the teachings of God's Word are ignored and forgotten! EWT087

Lord Christ, teach me to love all people, even my enemies, just as You did. Amen.

MAY 19

Trying to Decide

For he says, "In the time of my favor I heard you, and in the day of salvation I helped you." I tell you, now is the time of God's favor, now is the day of salvation.

—2 CORINTHIANS 6:2

This is so desperately a matter of importance for every human being who comes into the world that I first become indignant, and then I become sad, when I try to give spiritual counsel to a person who looks me in the eye and tells me: "Well, I am trying to make up my mind if I should accept Christ or not."

Such a person gives absolutely no indication that he realizes he is talking about the most important decision he can make in his lifetime—a decision to get right with God, to believe in the eternal Son, the Savior, to become a disciple, an obedient witness to Jesus Christ as Lord.

How can any man or woman, lost and undone, sinful and wretched, alienated from God, stand there and intimate that the death and resurrection of Jesus Christ and God's revealed plan of salvation do not take priority over some of life's other decisions? CES156

Lord, give us boldness to share this vital message with anyone with whom we come in contact who may be facing a Christless eternity. Amen.

MAY 20

A Joyful People

But whoever drinks the water I give them will never thirst. Indeed, the water I give them will become in them a spring of water welling up to eternal life.

—JOHN 4:14

We do have many professing Christians in our day who are not joyful, but they spend time trying to work it up. Now, brethren, I say that when we give God His place in the Church, when we recognize Christ as Lord high and lifted up, when we give the Holy Spirit His place, there will be joy that doesn't have to be worked up. It will be a joy that springs like a fountain. Jesus said that it should be a fountain, an artesian well, that springs up from within. That's one characteristic of a Spirit-filled congregation. They will be a joyful people, and it will be easy to distinguish them from the children of the world.

I wonder what the apostle Paul would say if he came down right now and looked us over in our congregations. What if he walked up and down the aisles of our churches, then went to a theater and looked them over, then on to a hockey game, on to the crowds at the shopping center, and into the crowded streets? Then when he came back and looked us over again, I wonder if he would see very much difference? COU008

Father, I need that artesian well of joy today. The burdens and busyness of leadership sometimes really sap my strength and kill the joy. Help me today to demonstrate that real Spirit-inspired joy that You have given me in Your Son. Amen.

MAY 21

A Shell Here and a Shell There

The Word became flesh and made his dwelling among us. We have seen his glory, the glory of the one and only Son, who came from the Father, full of grace and truth.

—JOHN 1:14

None of us can approach a serious study and consideration of the eternal nature and person of Jesus Christ without sensing and confessing our complete inadequacy in the face of the divine revelation. . . .

Now, I have said all of this because my best faith and my loftiest expectation do not allow me to believe that I can do justice to a text that begins: "And the Word was made flesh, and dwelt among us" (John 1:14) and concludes: "No man hath seen God at any time, the only begotten Son, which is in the bosom of the Father, he hath declared him" (1:18).

This is what we will attempt to do: we will walk along the broad seashore of God and pick up a shell here and a shell there, holding each up to the light to admire its beauty. While we may ultimately have a small store of shells to take with us, they can but remind us of the truth and the fact that there stretches the vastness of the seashore around the great lips of the oceans—and that still buried there is far more than we can ever hope to find or see! CES009, 011

Lord, I glory in the shells I'm looking at this day—and revel in the vastness of the seashore around me and grow in my love for and awe of Your Son, Jesus Christ! Amen.

MAY 22

God's Saving Grace

But Noah found favor in the eyes of the LORD.
—GENESIS 6:8

Grace is the goodness of God confronting human demerit. So, grace is what God is—unchanging, infinite, eternal!

This throws light on God's dealings with men and women throughout the Old Testament dispensations and history. It is certainly the truth, and a proper concept for us to hold, that no one was ever saved, no one is now saved, and no one will ever be saved except by the grace of God.

Before Moses came with the Law, men were saved only by grace. During the time of Moses, no one was saved except by grace. After Moses, before the cross, and after the cross, and during all of the dispensations, anywhere, anytime, no one was ever saved by anything but the grace of God!

We can say this with assurance because God dealt in grace with mankind looking forward to the Incarnation and the atoning death of Christ.

If God had not always operated in grace, He would have swept the sinning human race away. This, then, is the good news: God is gracious all the time, and when His grace becomes operative through our faith in Jesus Christ, then there is the new birth from above! MWT217

Thank You, Father, that by Your grace—that is, the death and resurrection of Your Son Jesus Christ—we are saved and restored to a right relationship with You. Amen.

MAY 23

Yearn to Be More Like Jesus

Surely the righteous will praise your name, and the upright will live in your presence.

—PSALM 140:13

There should be a holy quality, a mysterious and holy Presence within the fellowship of Christian believers! If we are what we ought to be in Christ and by His Spirit, if the whole sum of our lives beginning with the inner life is becoming more Godlike and Christ-like, I believe something of God's divine and mysterious quality and Presence will be upon us!

I have met a few of God's saints who appeared to have this holy brightness upon them, but they did not know it because of their humility and gentleness of spirit. I do not hesitate to confess that my fellowship with them has meant more to me than all of the teaching I have ever received. I do stand deeply indebted to every Bible teacher I have had through the years, but they did little but instruct my head. The brethren I have known who had this strange and mysterious quality and awareness of God's Person and Presence instructed my heart!

Do we understand what a gracious thing it is to be able to say of a man, a brother in the Lord, "He is truly a man of God"? He does not have to tell us that, but he lives quietly and confidently day by day with the sense of this awe-inspiring Presence that comes down on some people and means more than all the glib tongues in the world!

Oh, that we might yearn for the knowledge and Presence of God in our lives from moment to moment! EWT387

Heavenly Father, I repent for my weak desire to be more like Your Son, Jesus. Grant by Your Spirit that I would be conformed more to His likeness today. Amen.

MAY 24

The Passion

We have been made holy through the sacrifice of the body of Jesus Christ once for all.

—HEBREWS 10:10

That Holy One suffered, and His suffering in His own blood for us was three things. It was infinite, almighty, and perfect.

Infinite means without bound and without limit, shoreless, bottomless, topless, forever and ever, without any possible measure or limitation. And so the suffering of Jesus and the atonement He made on that cross under that darkening sky was infinite in its power.

It was not only infinite but *almighty*. It's possible for good men to "almost" do something or to "almost" be something. That is the fix people get in because they are people. But Almighty God is never "almost" anything. God is always exactly what He is. He is the Almighty One. Isaac Watts said about His dying on the cross, "God the mighty Maker died for man the creature's sin." And when God the Almighty Maker died, all the power there is was in that atonement. You never can overstate the efficaciousness of the atonement. You never can exaggerate the power of the cross.

And God is not only infinite and almighty but *perfect*. The atonement in Jesus Christ's blood is perfect; there isn't anything that can be added to it. It is spotless, impeccable, flawless. It is perfect as God is perfect. So the question, "How dost Thou spare the wicked if Thou art just?" is answered from the effect of Christ's passion. That holy suffering there on the cross and that resurrection from the dead cancels our sins and abrogates our sentence. AOG067-068

Dear Lord, thank You for your infinite, almighty, and perfect sacrifice on the cross. May I be ever grateful for what You have done and may I ever live in a manner that reflects Your glory. Amen.

MAY 25

Our Charter Is from God

On this rock I will build my church, and the gates of Hades will not overcome it.
—MATTHEW 16:18

While we are right to thank God in appreciation for all of the great and good men in the history of the Christian church, we actually "follow" none of them. Our charter goes farther back and is from a higher source. They were rightly looked upon as leaders, but they were all servants of God, even as you and I are.

Luther sowed. Wesley watered. Finney reaped—but they were only servants of the living God.

In our local assemblies, we are part of the church founded by the Lord Jesus Christ and perpetuated by the mystery of the new birth. Therefore, our assembly is that of Christian believers gathered unto a Name to worship and adore the Presence. So, in that sense, the strain is gone. The strain and pressure to abide by traditional religious forms all begin to pale in importance as we function in faith as the people of God who glorify His Name and honor His Presence!

If all of this is true—and everything within me witnesses that it is—we may insist that God is able to do for us all that He did in the days of the apostles. There has been no revocation of our charter!
MWT013

Dear Lord, thank You for the people in my life who have helped to shape me spiritually. And thank You that You alone are still the Source of new life. Amen

MAY 26

Riches of Grace

In these last days [God] has spoken to us by his Son, whom he appointed heir of all things, and through whom also he made the universe.

—HEBREWS 1:1–2

Would it startle you if I dared to say that the living God has never done anything in His universe apart from Jesus Christ?

Christians seem to be woefully unaware of the full meaning and measure of the grace of God. Why should we question God's provision when the Holy Spirit tells us through the Apostle John that the Word who became flesh is "full of grace and truth"? Brethren, the stars in their courses, the frogs that croak beside the lake, the angels in heaven above, and men and women on earth below—all came out of the channel we call the eternal Word!

In the book of Revelation, John bears record of the whole universe joining to give praise to the Lamb that was slain. Under the earth and on the earth and above the earth, John heard creatures praising Jesus Christ, all joining in a great chorus: "Worthy is the Lamb that was slain to receive power, and riches, and wisdom, and strength, and honour, and glory, and blessing" (5:12).

Yes, surely the entire universe is beneficiary of God's rich grace in Jesus Christ! MWT015

Lord Jesus, I praise Your name. You alone are worthy of all my adoration. Help me to walk uprightly today as a testimony to Your presence in my life. Amen.

MAY 27

United with Christ

We are in him who is true by being in his Son Jesus Christ.
—1 JOHN 5:20

The Spirit of God has impelled me to preach and write much about the believer's conscious union with Christ—a union that must be felt and experienced. I will never be through talking about the union of the soul with the Savior, the conscious union of the believer's heart with Jesus.

Remember, I am not talking about a "theological union" only. I am speaking also of a conscious union, a union that is felt and experienced.

I have never been ashamed to tell my congregations that I believe in feelings. I surely believe in what Jonathan Edwards termed "religious affections." That is man's perspective. I am aware also that from God's perspective there are qualities in the Divine Being that can only be known by the heart; never by the intellect!

Long ago John wrote: "Hereby perceive we the love of God, because he laid down his life for us" (1 John 3:16). So it is best for us to confess that as humans we have difficulty in understanding what God has said when He says that He loves us! MWT019

Heavenly Father, help me to be conscious of Your presence in my life today in Christ. And I pray that others will see You through me. Amen.

MAY 28

The Wonder of Redemption

For in Christ all the fullness of the Deity lives in bodily form.
—COLOSSIANS 2:9

My brethren in the Christian faith, stand with me in defense of this basic doctrine: The living God did not degrade Himself in the Incarnation. When the Word was made flesh, there was no compromise on God's part! It is plain in the ancient Athanasian Creed that the early church fathers were cautious at this point of doctrine. They would not allow us to believe that God, in the Incarnation, became flesh by a coming down of the Deity into flesh, but rather by the taking of mankind into God. That is the wonder of redemption!

In the past the mythical gods of the nations were not strangers to compromise. But the holy God who is God, our heavenly Father, could never compromise Himself!

He remained ever God, and everything else remained not God. That gulf still existed even after Jesus Christ had become man and dwelt among us. This much, then, we can know about the acts of God—He will never back out of His bargain. This amazing union of man with God is effected unto perpetuity! MWT022

Heavenly Father, thank You for making it possible for mankind to become redeemed. Praise to the most high God for sending Your Son to become one of us and save us! Amen.

MAY 29

Faith and Obedience

For, "Everyone who calls on the name of the Lord will be saved."
—ROMANS 10:13

What is our answer to the many confused persons who keep asking: "How can we know that we have come into a saving relationship with Jesus Christ?"

First, we stand together on the basic truth that Christ Jesus came into the world to save sinners. A second fact is that men and women are saved by faith in Christ alone, without works and without our merit.

However, the fact that Christ came to save sinners is not enough—that fact in itself cannot save us. Now in our day, the issues of believing faith and the gift of eternal life are clouded and confused by an "easy acceptance" that has been fatal to millions who may have stopped short in matters of faith and obedience.

Faith is believing and receiving, as in Acts 16:31: "Believe on the Lord Jesus Christ, and thou shalt be saved"; and as in John 1:12: "But as many as received him, to them gave he power to become the sons of God, even to them that believe on his name." MWT026

I praise You, Lord, for accomplishing the mission for which You came to this earth. I pray today for my family members and coworkers who have not put their faith in You. Bring them to Yourself, Father. Amen.

MAY 30

Benefits of Grace

But now in Christ Jesus you who once were far away have been brought near by the blood of Christ.

EPHESIANS 2:13

Only a believing Christian can testify, "I am a sinner—saved by the grace of God!" But that is not the whole story. All that we have is cut of His grace. Jesus Christ, the eternal Word who became flesh and dwelt among us, is the open channel through whom God moves to provide all the benefits He gives, both to saints and to sinners—yes, even to sinners!

Even though you may still be unconverted and going your own way, you have received much out of the ocean of His fullness. You have received the pulsing life that beats in your bosom.

You have received the brilliant mind and the brain without which you could not function. You have received a memory that strings the events you cherish as a jeweler strings pearls into a necklace.

When we say to an unbelieving man, "Believe on the Lord Jesus Christ," we are actually saying to him: "Believe on the One who sustains you and upholds you and who has given you life. Believe in the One who pities you and spares you and keeps you. Believe on the One out of whom you came!" MWT016

Lord, You are such a merciful God! Your offer of salvation in Christ is available to all. You send Your rain on both the just and the unjust. Lord, open my eyes to those in my sphere of influence who don't know You. Amen.

MAY 31

Christ as He Really Is

Someone like a son of man . . . out of his mouth was a sharp, double-edged sword.

REVELATION 1:13, 16

The Christian message has ceased to be a pronouncement and has become instead a proposition. Scarcely anyone catches the imperious note in the words spoken by Jesus Christ.

The invitational element of the Christian message has been pressed far out of proportion in the total scriptural scene. Christ with His lantern, His apologetic stance, and His weak pleading face has taken the place of the true Son of Man whom John saw—His eyes as a flame of fire, His feet like burnished brass, and His voice as the sound of many waters.

Only the Holy Spirit can reveal our Lord as He really is, and He does not paint in oils. He manifests Christ to the human spirit, not to our physical eyes.

These are strenuous times, and men and women are being recruited to devote themselves to one or another master. But anything short of complete devotion to Christ is inadequate and must end in futility and loss. MWT029

Lord, help me to see You as You truly are—mighty, righteous, just, and holy. Amen.

JUNE

JUNE 1

Our Life Is in Christ

Thanks be to God, who always leads us as captives in Christ's triumphal procession.
—2 CORINTHIANS 2:14

Certainly not all of the mystery of the Godhead can be known by man—but just as certainly, all that men can know of God in this life is revealed in Jesus Christ!

When the Apostle Paul said with yearning, "That I may know him" (Phil. 3:10), he was not speaking of intellectual knowledge. Paul was speaking of the reality of an experience of knowing God personally and consciously, spirit touching spirit and heart touching heart.

We know that people spend a lot of time talking about a deeper Christian life—but few seem to want to know and love God for Himself.

The precious fact is that God is the deeper life! Jesus Christ Himself is the deeper life, and as I plunge on into the knowledge of the triune God, my heart moves on into the blessedness of His fellowship. This means that there is less of me and more of God—thus my spiritual life deepens and I am strengthened in the knowledge of His will! MWT023

Dear Lord, may there be more and more of You and less and less of me. Amen.

JUNE 2

Majesty—and Meekness

They speak of the glorious splendor of your majesty—and I will meditate on your wonderful works.

—PSALM 145:5

When the prophets try to describe for me the attributes, the graces, the worthiness of the God who appeared to them and dealt with them, I feel that I can kneel down and follow their admonition: "He is thy Lord—worship thou Him!" They described Him as radiantly beautiful and fair.

They said that He was royal and that He was gracious. They described Him as a mysterious being, and yet they noted His meekness.

The meekness was His humanity. The majesty was His deity. You find them everlastingly united in Him. So meek that He nursed at His mother's breast, cried like any baby, and needed all the human care that every child needs.

But He was also God, and in His majesty He stood before Herod and before Pilate. When He returns, coming down from the sky, it will be in His majesty, the majesty of God; yet it will be in the majesty of the Man who is God!

This is our Lord Jesus Christ. Before His foes He stands in majesty. Before His friends, He stands in meekness! MWT031

Lord Christ, You are both my King and my Friend. Lead me through this day, O King, and pick me up when I stumble, dear Friend. Amen.

JUNE 3

Spiritual Readiness

The end of all things is near. Therefore be alert and of sober mind so that you may pray.

—1 PETER 4:7

When the Bible says that God is calling a special people out of the nations to bear the name of His eternal Son, I believe it—and His name is Jesus!

Our pious forefathers believed in spiritual preparation, and they said so. They saw themselves as a bride being prepared to meet the Bridegroom. They regarded this earth as the dressing room to outfit themselves for heaven.

The evangelical church has come through a period when nearly everyone has believed that there is just one prerequisite to readiness: being born again. We have made being born again almost like receiving a pass to a special event—when Jesus returns, we whip out the pass to prove our readiness.

Frankly, I do not think it will be like that. I do not believe that all professed believers are automatically ready to meet the Lord. Our Savior Himself was joined by Peter and John and Paul in warning and pleading that we should live and watch and pray, so to be ready for Jesus' coming. MWT033

Jesus my Lord, help me to "act out" my faith today with seriousness and passion. Enable me to give spiritual guidance or encouragement to someone who is hurting. Amen.

JUNE 4

The Grace of God Cannot Be Extinguished

The grace of our Lord was poured out on me abundantly, along with the faith and love that are in Christ Jesus.

—1 TIMOTHY 1:14

Brethren, we should be keenly aware that the living God can no more hide His grace than the sun can hide its brightness!

We must keep in mind also that the grace of God is infinite and eternal. Being an attribute of God, it is as boundless as infinitude!

The Old Testament is indeed a book of law, but not of law only. Before the great flood Noah "found grace in the eyes of the Lord" (Gen. 6:8) and after the law was given God said to Moses, "Thou hast found grace in My sight" (Ex. 33:17).

There never was a time when the law did not represent the will of God for mankind nor a time when the violation of it did not bring its own penalty, though God was patient and sometimes "winked" at wrongdoing because of the ignorance of the people.

The great source and spring of Christian morality is the love of Christ Himself, not the law of Moses; nevertheless there has been no abrogation of the principles of morality contained in the law. The grace of God made sainthood possible in Old Testament days just as it does today! EWT024

Father, thank You for the grace You offer me in Jesus Christ. May Your grace empower me to follow Your Son today to the glory of Your name. Amen.

JUNE 5

All That the Godhead Is

It is because of him that you are in Christ Jesus, who has become for us wisdom from God—that is, our righteousness, holiness and redemption.
—1 CORINTHIANS 1:30

I advise you not to listen to those who spend their time demeaning the person of Christ. I advise you to look beyond the cloudiness of modern terms used by those who themselves are not sure who Jesus Christ was in reality.

You cannot trust the man who can only say, "I believe that God revealed Himself through Christ." Find out what he really believes about the person of the incarnate Son of God!

You cannot trust the man who will only say that Christ reflected more of God than other men do. Neither can you trust those who teach that Jesus Christ was the supreme religious genius, having the ability to catch and reflect more of God than any other man.

All of these approaches are insults to the Person of Jesus Christ. He was and is and can never cease to be God, and when we find Him and know Him, we are back at the ancient fountain again.

Christ is all that the Godhead is!

This is the wonder, the great miracle—that by one swift, decisive, considered act of faith and prayer, our souls go back to the ancient fountain of our being, and we start over again!

It is in Jesus Christ Himself that we find our source, our satisfaction. I think this is what John Newton perceived in the miracle of the new birth, causing him to sing, "Now rest my long-divided heart, fixed on this blissful center—rest!" EWT010

Lord Christ, I stand in awe of who You are and praise You this day. Fill me with greater gratitude and love for You. Amen.

JUNE 6

The Means for Receiving Christ's Benefits

Now faith is confidence in what we hope for and assurance about what we do not see.

—HEBREWS 11:1

Without dealing in pinpoint definitions, we know that faith as demonstrated in the Word of God is complete confidence and trust in God and in His plan of salvation through Christ.

Let us agree further that faith is a gift of God to every penitent, trusting person. Beyond that, faith is a miracle, for God gives lost men and women the blessed ability to trust and serve Jesus Christ as Savior and Lord.

The Bible assures us that faith in God is the plain gateway to forgiveness, to cleansing, to regeneration, to restoration. The Bible declares that where there is no faith there are no answers to fervent prayers. The Bible makes clear that every spiritual benefit flowing from the atonement of Christ is given to faith and is received by faith. All of this is common evangelical doctrine and is accepted wherever the cross of Christ is rightly understood. JAF003-004

Father, thank You for the benefits You offer me in Your Son, Jesus Christ. He has accomplished so great a salvation for me, and I long to possess every gift He wants to give me. Increase my faith that I may do so. Amen.

JUNE 7

Everywhere in the Bible

For us there is but one God, the Father, from whom all things came and for whom we live; and there is but one Lord, Jesus Christ, through whom all things came and through whom we live.
—1 CORINTHIANS 8:6

I do not mind telling you that I have always found Jesus Christ beckoning to me throughout the Scriptures. I am convinced that it was God's design that we should find the divine Creator, Redeemer, and Lord whenever we search the Scriptures.

The Son of God is described by almost every fair and worthy name in the creation. He is called the Sun of Righteousness with healing in His wings. He is called the Star that shone on Jacob. He is described as coming forth with His bride, clear as the moon. His Presence is likened unto the rain coming down upon the earth, bringing beauty and fruitfulness. He is pictured as the great sea and as the towering rock. He is likened to the strong cedars. A figure is used of Him as of a great eagle, going literally over the earth.

Where the person of Jesus Christ does not stand out tall and beautiful and commanding, as a pine tree against the sky, you will find Him behind the lattice, but stretching forth His hand. If He does not appear as the sun shining in His strength, He may be discerned in the reviving by the promised gentle rains.

Our Lord Jesus Christ was that One divinely commissioned to set forth the mystery and the majesty and the wonder and the glory of the Godhead throughout the universe. It is more than an accident that both the Old and New Testaments comb heaven and earth for figures of speech or simile to set forth the wonder and glory of God! EWT080

Holy Spirit, open my eyes that I would see Christ more clearly throughout Scripture, that I would know and love Him more. Amen.

JUNE 8

Creator and Sustainer

Through him all things were made; without him nothing was made that has been made.
—JOHN 1:3

Many years ago Alexander Patterson wrote a great and compelling book titled *The Greater Life and Work of Christ.* I think it has been out of print for some years but it deserves to be reprinted. In his volume, this great preacher attempts to go back into the basic foundation of things and to encourage Christians to believe and trust and exalt Jesus Christ for being much more than the Redeemer of mankind.

I agree with him completely that Christ Jesus is not only Redeemer, but the Sustainer, the Creator, the Upholder, the One who holds all things together, the adhesive quality of the universe. To those who believe, Christ Jesus is the medium through whom God dispenses grace to all of His creatures, including those to be redeemed and those who do not need to be redeemed. CES017-018

Lord, the Incarnation is a mystery to me. I cannot fully comprehend how You could remain fully God, Creator and Sustainer of all things, and be fully man. But I believe what You have revealed, and I rejoice in it. Give me greater wisdom and revelation. Amen.

JUNE 9

God's Highest Will

Then he said, "Here I am, I have come to do your will."
—HEBREWS 10:9

Let us consider three simple things reinforced in the Word of God for those who would discern God's highest will.

First, be willing to put away known sin!

Second, separate yourself from all of the attractions of the world, the flesh, and the devil!

Finally, offer yourself to your God and Savior in believing faith!

God has never yet turned away an honest, sincere person who has come to know the eternal value of the atonement and the peace that is promised through the death and resurrection of our Lord Jesus Christ.

The only person who will never be cleansed and made whole is the one who insists he or she needs no remedy. The person who comes in faith to God and confesses, "I am unclean; I am sin sick; I am blind," will find mercy and righteousness and life.

Our Lord Jesus Christ is the Savior, the Cleanser. He is the Purifier, the Healer. He is the Sight Giver and the Life Giver. He alone is the Way, the Truth, and the Life! MWT061

Dear Lord, truth seems to be in short supply in our postmodern world today. Help me to be bold but loving in my presentation of Your truth. Amen.

JUNE 10

Learn the Truth about the Enemy of Your Soul

In order that Satan might not outwit us. For we are not unaware of his schemes.

—2 CORINTHIANS 2:11

We should learn the truth about the enemy, but we must stand bravely against every superstitious notion he would introduce about himself. The truth will set us free but superstition will enslave us!

The scriptural way to see things is to set the Lord always before us, put Christ in the center of our vision; and if Satan is lurking around he will appear on the margin only and be seen as but a shadow on the edge of the brightness. It is always wrong to invert this—to set Satan in the focus of our vision and push God out to the margin. Nothing but tragedy can come from such inversion!

The best way to keep the enemy out is to keep Christ in! The sheep need not be terrified by the wolf; they have but to stay close to the shepherd. The instructed Christian whose faculties have been developed by the Word and the Spirit will practice the presence of God moment by moment! EWT314

Holy Spirit, give me wisdom and discernment that I might recognize the tactics of the devil and give me strength to place Christ in the center of my life always. Amen.

JUNE 11

Believe the Right Things

You are from below; I am from above. You are of this world; I am not of this world. I told you that you would die in your sins; if you do not believe that I am he, you will indeed die in your sins.
—JOHN 8:23–24

Because the heart of the Christian life is admittedly faith in a person, Jesus Christ the Lord, it has been relatively easy for some to press this truth out of all proportion and teach that faith in the person of Christ is all that matters. Who Jesus is matters not, who His Father was, whether Jesus is God or man or both, whether or not He accepted the superstitions and errors of His time as true, whether He actually rose again after His passion or was only thought to have done so by His devoted followers—these things are not important, say the no-creed advocates. What is vital is that we believe on Him and try to follow His teachings.

What is overlooked here is that the conflict of Christ with the Pharisees was over the question of *who He was*. His claim to be God stirred the Pharisees to fury. He could have cooled the fire of their anger by backing away from His claim to equality with God, but He refused to do it. And He further taught that faith in Him embraced a belief that He is very God, and that apart from this there could be no salvation for anyone. . . .

To believe on Christ savingly means to believe the right things about Christ. There is no escaping this. TIC015-016

Jesus, don't let me ever back down from this vital truth of Who You are. Amen.

JUNE 12

Our Lord, the Object of Faith for Salvation

Announcing the good news of peace through Jesus Christ, who is Lord of all.
—ACTS 10:36

It is altogether doubtful whether any man can be saved who comes to Christ for His help but with no intention of obeying Him, for Christ's saviorhood is forever united to His lordship.

Look at the apostle's instruction and admonition:

> If thou shalt confess with thy mouth the Lord Jesus, and shalt believe in thine heart that God hath raised him from the dead, thou shalt be saved . . . for the same Lord over all is rich unto all that call upon him. For whosoever shall call upon the name of the Lord shall be saved. (Rom. 10:9, 12–13)

There the Lord is the object of faith for salvation! And when the Philippian jailer asked the way to be saved, Paul replied, "Believe on the Lord Jesus Christ, and thou shalt be saved" (Acts 16:31).

Paul did not tell him to believe on the Savior with the thought that he could later take up the matter of His lordship and settle it at his own convenience. To Paul there could be no division of offices. Christ must be Lord or He will not be Savior! EWT031

Jesus, You are Lord of my life! Today may I grow in the knowledge of You as Lord, the loving and exalted one. Amen.

JUNE 13

Obedient Daily Living

What good is it for someone to gain the whole world, and yet lose or forfeit their very self? Whoever is ashamed of me and my words, the Son of Man will be ashamed of them when he comes in his glory and in the glory of the Father and of the holy angels.

—LUKE 9:25–26

The believer's own cross is one he has assumed voluntarily. Therein lies the difference between his cross and the cross on which Roman convicts died. They went to the cross against their will; he, because he chooses to do so. No Roman officer ever pointed to a cross and said, "If any man will, let him." Only Christ said that, and by so saying He placed the whole matter in the hands of the Christian. He can refuse to take his cross, or he can stoop and take it up and start for the dark hill. The difference between great sainthood and spiritual mediocrity depends upon which choice he makes.

To go along with Christ step by step and point by point in identical suffering of Roman crucifixion is not possible for any of us and certainly is not intended by our Lord. What He does intend is that each of us should count himself dead indeed with Christ and then accept willingly whatever of self-denial, repentance, humility and humble sacrifice that may be found in the path of obedient daily living. That is *his* cross, and it is the only one the Lord has invited him to bear. TRC069

Lord, You invite and call me to follow You. I know that the only way to follow You is to carry my own cross. Give me strength to do that today. Amen.

JUNE 14

Burning with an Inward Fire

Even though you do not see him now, you believe in him and are filled with an inexpressible and glorious joy.

—1 PETER 1:8

If there is any reality within the whole sphere of human experience that is by its very nature worthy to challenge the mind, charm the heart, and bring the total life to a burning focus, it is the reality that revolves around the Person of Christ!

If He is who and what the Christian message declares Him to be, then the thought of Him should be the most stimulating to enter the human mind.

God dwells in a state of perpetual enthusiasm. He is delighted with all that is good and lovingly concerned about all that is wrong. No wonder the Spirit came at Pentecost as the sound of a rushing mighty wind and sat in tongues of fire on every forehead. In so doing, He was acting as one of the Persons of the blessed Godhead.

Whatever else happened at Pentecost, one thing that cannot be missed was the sudden upsurging of moral enthusiasm. Those first disciples burned with a steady, inward fire. They were enthusiastic to the point of complete abandon!

But what do we find in our day? We find the contradictory situation of noisy, headlong religious activity carried on without moral energy or spiritual fervor! . . . We look in vain among the professed followers of Christ for the flush and excitement of the soul in love with God.

The low level of moral enthusiasm among us may have a significance far deeper than we are willing to believe! EWT067

Father, fill me with Your Spirit and with such enthusiasm for Your Son that I would proclaim His greatness to those around me. Amen.

JUNE 15

Doctrine Enfleshed

The Word became flesh and made his dwelling among us.
—JOHN 1:14

I have been impressed by a statement on Christian doctrine made by Martin Lloyd-Jones, the English preacher and writer, in a published article. The gist of his message was this: It is perilously close to being sinful for any person to learn doctrine for doctrine's sake. I agree with his conclusion that doctrine is always best when it is incarnated—when it is seen fleshed out in the lives of godly men and women.

Doctrine merely stated has no arms or legs, no tongue and no teeth. Standing alone, it has no purpose, no intentions, and it certainly carries no moral imperative.

Our God Himself appeared at His very best in the Incarnation, when He came into our world and lived in our flesh. What He had been trying to say to mortal man about Himself, He was now able to demonstrate in the person and life of Jesus, the Son of Man. JAF031

Heavenly Father, thank You for revealing Yourself fully in Your Son, Jesus Christ, that I might know You and serve You. Amen.

JUNE 16

If Jesus Came Today

We don't want this man to be our king.
—LUKE 19:14

People have asked me if our present generation would gladly accept Jesus if He came at this time, instead of 2,000 years ago. I have to believe that history does repeat itself!

In our own day, many who want to follow the Christian traditions still balk and reject a thoroughgoing spiritual house-cleaning within their own lives.

When Jesus came, many realized that it would mean probable financial loss for them to step out and follow Christ. Also, many of those men and women who considered the claims of Christ in His day knew that following Him would call for abrupt and drastic changes in their patterns of living. The proud and selfish aspects of their lives would have been disturbed.

Beyond that, there was an almost complete disdain for the inward spiritual life which Jesus taught as a necessity for mankind—that it is the pure in heart who will see God!

I am afraid that humanity's choice would still be the same today. People are still more in love with money and pride and pleasure than they are with God and His salvation! MWT393

Thank You, Lord, for coming to earth at just the right time according to Your eternal plan. You have revealed God's character to us in a most graphic way. Help us to be faithful to Your "Great Commission" (see Matt. 28:19–20) until You return as You promised. Amen.

JUNE 17

Status Symbols

I turned around to see the voice that was speaking to me. And when I turned I saw seven golden lampstands, and among the lampstands was someone like a son of man, dressed in a robe reaching down to his feet and with a golden sash around his chest.

—REVELATION 1:12–13

In our time we have all kinds of status symbols in the Christian church—membership, attendance, pastoral staff, missionary offerings. But there is only one status symbol that should make a Christian congregation genuinely glad. That is to know that our Lord is present, walking in our midst! . . .

No matter the size of the assembly or its other attributes, our Lord wants it to be known by His presence in the midst. I would rather have His presence in the church than anything else in all the wide world. . . .

The Christian church dares not settle for anything less than the illumination of the Holy Spirit and the presence of our divine Prophet, Priest, and King in our midst. Let us never be led into the mistake that so many are making—sighing and saying, "Oh, if we only had bigger, wiser men in our pulpits! Oh, if we only had more important men in places of Christian leadership!" JIV059-060, 063

Lord, I pray that I might never deviate from that significant thought: "I would rather have His presence in the church than anything else in all the wide world." Amen.

JUNE 18

The Flock of God: Safe in Jesus Christ

Be shepherds of God's flock that is under your care . . . And when the Chief Shepherd appears, you will receive the crown of glory that will never fade away.

—1 PETER 5:2, 4

The people who want to know God and walk with God, those who have learned to recognize the voice of the good Shepherd, will always be at home in a Spirit-filled congregation.

It is sad indeed that some have never heard the voice of the Shepherd. His voice is as tender as a lullaby and as strong as the wind and as mighty as the sound of many waters. The people who have learned to hear and recognize the voice of Jesus—that healing, musical, solemn, beautiful voice of Jesus in His church—are always at home where everything centers around Him. The true Christian church can be a conglomeration of everything under the sun. That is, we may have Calvinists and Arminians and Methodists and Baptists and all sorts of others, and yet we are all together on one thing—Jesus Christ is wisdom, righteousness, sanctification, and redemption! He is All in all, and the people of the Lord who have learned to hear the voice of the Shepherd gravitate towards that kind of church! . . .

Do you find your own heart sensitive to the Lord's presence or are you among those who are "samplers" and "nibblers"? God help you if you are, for the child of the King is a sheep who loves his Shepherd and he stays close to Him! That's the only safe place for a sheep. Stay close to Jesus and all of the wolves in the world cannot get a tooth in you! EWT015

O Good Shepherd, grant by Your Spirit that I would stay close to You this day and remain safe, never drifting away. Amen.

JUNE 19

Justice on Our Side

Blessed is the one whose transgressions are forgiven,
whose sins are covered.
—PSALM 32:1

When God justifies a sinner, everything in God is on the sinner's side. All the attributes of God are on the sinner's side. It isn't that mercy is pleading for the sinner and justice is trying to beat him to death, as we preachers sometimes make it sound. All of God does all that God does. When God looks at a sinner and sees him there unatoned for (he won't accept the atonement; he thinks it doesn't apply to him), the moral situation is such that justice says he must die. And when God looks at the atoned-for sinner, who in faith knows he's atoned for and has accepted it, justice says he must live! The unjust sinner can no more go to heaven than the justified sinner can go to hell. Oh friends, why are we so still? Why are we so quiet? We ought to rejoice and thank God with all our might!

I say it again: Justice is on the side of the returning sinner. First John 1:9 says, "If we confess our sins, he is faithful and just to forgive us our sins, and to cleanse us from all unrighteousness." Justice is over on our side now because the mystery of the agony of God on the cross has changed our moral situation. So justice looks and sees equality, not inequity, and we are justified. That's what justification means. TRC021

Heavenly Father, I thank You that You are on my side and that Your justice is on my side. May I ever trust in You when circumstances in life seem unjust. Amen.

JUNE 20

"Now It is the Lord"

In Christ Jesus, who has become for us . . . holiness.
—1 CORINTHIANS 1:30

Is it possible to become so enamored of God's good gifts that we fail to worship Him, the Giver?

Dr. Albert B. Simpson, the founder of The Christian and Missionary Alliance, invited to preach in a Bible conference in England, discovered on his arrival that he was to follow two other Bible teachers. All three had been given the same topic, "Sanctification."

From the pulpit, the first speaker made clear his position that sanctification means eradication—the old carnal nature is removed. The second, a suppressionist, advised: "Sit on the lid and keep the old nature down!"

Dr. Simpson in his turn quietly told his audience that he could only present Jesus Christ Himself as God's answer.

"Jesus Christ is your Sanctifier, your all and in all! God wants you to get your eyes away from the gifts. He wants your gaze to be on the Giver—Christ Himself," he said.

This is a wonderful word for those who would worship rightly:

Once it was the blessing;
Now it is the Lord! MWT067

Father, this morning I praise You for Your holy presence in my life and for giving me Your Son. May He be my focus today. Amen.

JUNE 21

Christ Opens Our Hearts

Then he opened their minds so they could understand the Scriptures.

—LUKE 24:45

The disciples of Jesus were instructed in the Scriptures. Christ Himself had taught them out of the Law of Moses and the Prophets and the Psalms; yet it took a specific act of inward "opening" before they could grasp the truth!

The apostle Paul discovered very early in his ministry that, as he put it, "not all men have faith." And he knew why: "But if our gospel be hid, it is hid to them that are lost: In whom the god of this world hath blinded the minds of them which believe not, lest the light of the glorious gospel of Christ, who is the image of God, should shine unto them" (2 Cor. 4:3–4). . . .

The intellect of the hearer may grasp saving knowledge while yet the heart makes no moral response to it.

A classic example of this is seen in the meeting of Benjamin Franklin and George Whitefield. In his autobiography, Franklin recounts how he listened to the mighty preaching of the great evangelist. Whitefield talked with Franklin personally about his need of Christ and promised to pray for him. Years later Franklin wrote rather sadly that the evangelist's prayers must not have done any good, for he was still unconverted.

Why? Franklin had light without sight. To see the Light of the World requires an act of inward enlightenment wrought by the Spirit. We must pit our prayer against that dark spirit who blinds the hearts of men! EWT346

Lord Christ, open my heart today that I may more firmly grasp Your truth and live in accordance with it. Amen.

JUNE 22

The Mystery in Worship

Though the bush was on fire it did not burn up.
—EXODUS 3:2

Consider the experience of Moses in the desert as he beheld the fire that burned in the bush without consuming it. Moses had no hesitation in kneeling before the bush and worshiping God. Moses was not worshiping a bush; it was God and His glory dwelling in the bush whom Moses worshiped!

This is an imperfect illustration, for when the fire departed from that bush, it was a bush again.

But this Man, Christ Jesus, is eternally the Son. In the fullness of this mystery, there has never been any departure, except for that awful moment when Jesus cried, "My God, my God, why hast thou forsaken me?" (Matt. 27:46). The Father turned His back for a moment when the Son took on Himself that putrefying mass of sin and guilt, dying on the cross not for His own sin, but for ours.

The deity and the humanity never parted, and to this day, they remain united in that one Man.

When we kneel before Him and say, "My Lord and my God, Thy throne, O God, is forever and ever," we are talking to God! MWT190

Lord, I may not have seen You in a burning bush like Moses did, but I still kneel before You and worship You as my King. Amen.

JUNE 23

God or an Idiot

I and the Father are one.
—JOHN 10:30

Now the words of the Lord Jesus Christ were words so lofty and so astounding and so filled with authority that no other religious teacher in history could ever match His teachings . . . Frankly, the claims that He made brand Him immediately as being God—or an idiot! . . . Of His own body He said, "Destroy this temple, and in three days I will raise it up" (John 2:19).

He told His hearers, "I beheld Satan as lightning fall from heaven" (Luke 10:18). He declared with authority, "Before Abraham was, I am" (John 8:58). He predicted that "when the Son of man shall come in his glory, and all the holy angels with him, then shall he sit upon the throne of his glory: And before him shall be gathered all nations: and he shall separate them one from another, as a shepherd divideth his sheep from the goats" (Matt. 25:31–32).

No one else has ever been able to say, "Marvel not at this: for the hour is coming, in the which all that are in the graves shall hear his voice, and shall come forth" (John 5:28–29).

No one else has ever talked like that! EFE022-023

Lord, I know that You are God and I see the authority in Your words. Help me to share You faithfully with those around me who still do not believe. Amen.

JUNE 24

The Lordship of Christ in Control

You were marked in him with a seal, the promised Holy Spirit, who is a deposit guaranteeing our inheritance until the redemption of those who are God's possession—to the praise of his glory.

—EPHESIANS 1:13–14

The nervous compulsion to get things done is found everywhere among us and right here is where the pragmatic philosophy comes into its own.

It asks no embarrassing questions about the wisdom of what we are doing or even about the morality of it.

It accepts our chosen ends as right and good and casts about for efficient means and ways to get them accomplished. When it discovers something that works, it soon finds a text to justify it, "consecrates" it to the Lord, and plunges ahead. Next a magazine article is written about it, then a book, and finally the inventor is granted an honorary degree. After that, any question about the scripturalness of things or even the moral validity of them is completely swept away.

You cannot argue with success. The method works; ergo, it must be good!

The whole religious atmosphere around us is largely geared to pragmatic methodology. What shall we do to break its power over us?

The answer is simple. We must acknowledge the right of Jesus Christ to control the activities of His Church. The New Testament contains full instructions, not only about what we are to believe but what we are to do and how we are to go about doing it. Any deviation from those instructions is a denial of the Lordship of Christ! EWT332

Take control of Your church, Lord Jesus, that we may follow Your lead and not human methods and so accomplish Your will. Amen.

JUNE 25

What Is True Religion?

If anyone does not speak according to this word, they have no light of dawn.

—ISAIAH 8:20

To the convicted Christian there can be but one true religion. The self-converted may shy away from the bigotry and intolerance which he fears lie in an exclusive devotion to Christianity, but the wholly converted will have no such apprehensions. To him Christ is all in all, and the faith of Christ is God's last word to mankind. To him there is but one God the Father, one Lord and Savior, one faith, one baptism, one body, one Spirit, one fold, and one Shepherd. To him there is none other name under heaven given among men whereby we must be saved. For him Christ is the only way, the only truth, and the only life. For him Christ is the only wisdom, the only righteousness, the only sanctification, and the only redemption.

When, therefore, I ask the question, "Are we having a revival of true religion?" I have only one religion in mind. I mean the faith of the New Testament as held and experienced by the fathers. I mean religion of which Moses and all the prophets did write, that religion which originated in the heart of God the Father, was made effectual through the dying and resurrection of God the Son, and is vitalized by God the Holy Spirit. Of this religion the Hebrew and Christian Scriptures are the source book, the first and last word, to which we dare add nothing and from which we dare take nothing away. MWT071

Lord, You are my All in all, my righteousness. I pray that I will not be caught up with religious accoutrements but that my focus will always be on the Father, the Son, and the Holy Spirit. Amen.

JUNE 26

A Good Husbandman

Father, I want those you have given me to be with me where I am, and to see my glory, the glory you have given me because you loved me before the creation of the world.

—JOHN 17:24

I believe that a pastor who is content with a vineyard that is not at its best is not a good husbandman. It is my prayer that we may be a healthy and fruitful vineyard and that we may be an honor to the Well Beloved, Jesus Christ the Lord, that He might go before the Father and say, "These are mine for whom I pray, and they have heard the Word and have believed on Me." I pray that we might fit into the high priestly prayer of John 17, that we would be a church after Christ's own heart so that in us He might see the travail of His soul and be satisfied. . . .

The church should be a healthy, fruitful vineyard that will bring honor to Christ, a church after Christ's own heart where He can look at the travail of His soul and be satisfied. RRR112, 119

Lord, I long that Jesus Christ might indeed be satisfied with my own life and the lives of those whom He has called me to lead. Help me to be a faithful husbandman in whatever vineyard You place me. Amen.

JUNE 27

The Zeal and the Humility of Christ

Who, being in very nature God, did not consider equality with God something to be used to his own advantage; rather, he made himself nothing by taking the very nature of a servant, being made in human likeness. And being found in appearance as a man, he humbled himself by becoming obedient to death—even death on a cross!

—PHILIPPIANS 2:6–8

Think of the zeal of Jesus. "The zeal of thine house hath eaten me up" (Ps. 69:9). Think of the zeal of God. "The zeal of the LORD of hosts will perform this" (Isa. 9:7). The most zealous thing I know is fire. Wherever fire burns, it burns with hot zeal. And the heart of Jesus was like that. But think of the lukewarm Christian, of Christians who haven't been to a prayer meeting in years, of the careless and torpid Christian—the torpor that lies over the Church of God.

Then there is the humility of Jesus. Though He was the highest, He came down and acted like the lowest. And though we are the lowest, we sometimes act the proudest and the most arrogant. How completely unlike Jesus, how unlike God. AOG150

Father, forgive me for being lukewarm at times, not being zealous for Your Son. May I pursue Him wholeheartedly today and experience more of Your kingdom. Amen.

JUNE 28

Our Identification Is with Jesus

All these people were still living by faith when they died. They did not receive the things promised; they only saw them and welcomed them from a distance, admitting that they were foreigners and strangers on earth.

—HEBREWS 11:13

We who are involved in the upward gaze of this long-range faith identify ourselves with Jesus Christ forever! We are satisfied that God is at work. We are satisfied to be misunderstood for Christ's sake. We are willing to be treated as the minority, for the people of God are always in the minority in this earthly context.

Our true identity is with Jesus Christ, our Savior and Lord. We have taken His cause as our cause. We have taken His way as our way. We have taken His place as our place. We have taken His future as our future. We have taken His life as our life. We have taken the long look of faith to the day of His triumph, and we know it will be our triumph as well. . . .

By faith we have the assurance of God's favor and welcome in that wonderful hour when Jesus returns. It will be a glad day for the pilgrims—the pilgrims of eternity—their eyes fixed on heaven above.

That is the long-range kind of faith. Let us humbly, confidently ask God for it! JAF063-064

I identify with You, Lord Christ! Increase my faith in You and what You have done, O Savior and King, that I may be ready for Your victorious return. Amen.

JUNE 29

Be Prepared

He said to them, "Go into all the world and preach the gospel to all creation."

—MARK 16:15

Recall what happened when Jesus said to the disciples, "Go ye into all the world, and preach the gospel to every creature" (Mark 16:15).

Peter jumped up right away, grabbed his hat, and would have been on his way, but Jesus stopped him, and said, "Not yet, Peter! Don't go like that. Tarry until you are endued with power from on high, and then go!"

I believe that our Lord wants us to learn more of Him in worship before we become busy for Him. He wants us to have a gift of the Spirit, an inner experience of the heart, as our first service, and out of that will grow the profound and deep and divine activities which are necessary. ITB139

Quiet our hearts, Lord, that our evangelistic efforts might spring from a heart of worship. Amen.

JUNE 30

Journey of the Heart

They replied, "Believe in the Lord Jesus, and you will be saved."
—ACTS 16:31

I object to the charge that "Tozer preaches experience." I preach Christ, the Savior—that is my calling! But I am positive about the validity, the reality, and the value of genuine Christian experience. We can talk to Jesus just as we talk to our other friends.

As a boy, I was not a Christian. I did not have the privilege of growing up in a home where Christ was known and loved. God spoke to me through a street preacher who quoted the words of Jesus, "Come unto me, all ye that labour and are heavy laden, and I will give you rest" (Matt. 11:28).

That invitation let me know that Jesus is still calling "Come now!" I went home and up into the attic. There in earnest prayer I gave my heart and life to Jesus Christ. My feet had taken me home and into the attic. But it was my heart that went to Jesus! Within my heart I consented to go to Jesus. I have been a Christian ever since that moment. MWT034

Dear Jesus, I want to thank You for saving me through Your difficult journey to the cross. Give me grace and strength to honor Your sacrifice through my life this week. Amen.

JULY

JULY 1

Mysteries

As the heavens are higher than the earth, so are my ways higher than your ways and my thoughts than your thoughts.

—ISAIAH 55:9

With effortless power, God did and is doing His redeeming work. We stand in awe and speak in hushed tones of His incarnation. How could it be that the great God Almighty could be conceived in the womb of a virgin? I don't know how it could be, but I know that the Great God who is omnipotent, the Great God Almighty, could do it if He wanted to. The incarnation was easy for God. It may be hard for us to understand—a mystery of godliness—but it is not hard for God.

And what about the atonement? Jesus died in the darkness on that cross to save the whole world. Don't try to understand it—you can't. I know no more about how the blood of Jesus Christ can atone for sin than I know what God's nature is like. I only know it does. I only know that I'm reconciled to God through the blood of the Lamb. That's all I know, and that's enough. AOGII92

Lord, I am amazed at the world of redemption You have accomplished by Your atoning sacrifice on the cross! May I stand ever in awe of what You have done. Amen.

JULY 2

Obedience: The Final Test of Love for Christ

Whoever has my commands and keeps them is the one who loves me. The one who loves me will be loved by my Father, and I too will love them and show myself to them.

—JOHN 14:21

The final test of love is obedience, not sweet emotions, not willingness to sacrifice, not zeal, but obedience to the commandments of Christ!

Our Lord drew a line plain and tight for everyone to see. On one side He placed those who keep His commandments and said, "These love Me." On the other side He put those who keep not His sayings, and said, "These love Me not."

The commandments of Christ occupy in the New Testament a place of importance that they do not have in current evangelical thought. The idea that our relation to Christ is revealed by our attitude to His commandments is now considered legalistic by many influential Bible teachers, and the plain words of our Lord are rejected outright or interpreted in a manner to make them conform to religious theories ostensibly based upon the epistles of Paul.

The Christian cannot be certain of the reality and depth of his love until he comes face-to-face with the commandments of Christ and is forced to decide what to do about them. Then he will know! . . .

Love for Christ is a love of willing, as well as a love of feeling, and it is psychologically impossible to love Him adequately unless we will to obey His words! EWT026

Holy Father, give me the desire and strength to obey Your blessed Son, that I may show Him my love. Amen.

JULY 3

God's Validation

Our gospel came to you not simply with words but also with power, with the Holy Spirit and deep conviction.
—1 THESSALONIANS 1:5

One marked characteristic of modern evangelicalism is its lack of assurance, resulting in a pathetic search for external evidence to corroborate its faith. It sets out bravely to declare its trust in Christ but is shortly overawed by the counter declarations of science and philosophy and before long it is looking about for some collateral evidence to restore its confidence.

The faith of the Christian must rest upon Christ Himself. He is the mystery of godliness, a miracle, and emergence of the Deity into time and space for a reason and a purpose. He is complete in Himself and gains nothing from any human philosophy.

The New Testament points to Christ and says God now commands all men everywhere to repent: because He has appointed a day in which He will judge the world in righteousness by that Man He has ordained! Our assurance is the fact that He raised Him from the dead. In that, God validated forever the claims of Christ. He is who He said He was and what He said He was. So, Christ is enough! To have Him and nothing else is to be rich beyond all conceiving. MWT285

Lord, it seems that mankind always wants to make something more complex than it really is. Help us to be satisfied with simple faith in Jesus only! Amen.

JULY 4

His Highest Will

I want to know Christ—yes, to know the power of his resurrection and participation in his sufferings, becoming like him in his death, and so, somehow, attaining to the resurrection from the dead.

—PHILIPPIANS 3:10–11

People will pray and ask God to be filled—but all the while there is that strange ingenuity, that contradiction within which prevents our wills from stirring to the point of letting God have His way. . . .

Those who live in this state of perpetual contradiction cannot be happy Christians. A man who is always on the cross, just piece after piece, cannot be happy in that process. But when that man takes his place on the cross with Jesus Christ once and for all, and commends his spirit to God, lets go of everything and ceases to defend himself—sure, he has died, but there is a resurrection that follows!

If we are willing to go this route of victory with Jesus Christ, we cannot continue to be mediocre Christians, stopped halfway to the peak. Until we give up our own interests, there will never be enough stirring within our beings to find His highest will. TRC047-048

Lord, I want to be filled with Your Spirit and made more like You. Prevent me from being double-minded or lukewarm, that I may follow zealously after You. Amen.

JULY 5

We See God's Purpose

To bring unity to all things in heaven and on earth under Christ.
—EPHESIANS 1:10

We trust the Word of God—and the inspired revelation makes it plain to the believing Christian that all things in the universe have derived their form from Christ, the eternal Son!

We are assured that even as an architect builder gathers the necessary materials needed to fashion the structure he has designed, so God will ultimately gather all things together under one head, even Christ (see Eph. 1:9–10).

Everything in the universe has received its meaning by the power of His Word; each has maintained its place and order through Him.

Jesus Christ is God creating!

Jesus Christ is God redeeming!

Jesus Christ is God completing and harmonizing!

Jesus Christ is God bringing together all things after the counsel of His own will!

I can only hope that as we grow and mature and delight in our faith, we are beginning to gain a new appreciation of God's great eternal purpose! MWT058

Father, Your master design of the universe is perfect even though mankind has neglected Your creation and Your desire for fellowship. I pray that by Your Spirit our churches will become "like a mighty army" and help lead many people in the world to faith in Christ. Amen.

JULY 6

Easy Acceptance

Yet to all who did receive him, to those who believed in his name, he gave the right to become children of God.
—JOHN 1:12

You may be surprised, as I was, when I ran this thing down and found that the expression "accept Christ" does not occur in the Bible. It is not found in the New Testament at all. I have looked it up in *Strong's Exhaustive Concordance,* and the old editors worked on that volume so long and so thoroughly that it does not skip a single word.

Strong's concordance shows very definitely that the word "accept" is never used in the Bible in the sense of our accepting God or accepting Jesus as our Savior.

It does seem strange that while we do not find its use anywhere in the Bible, the phrase, "Will you accept Christ?" or "Have you accepted Christ?" have become the catchwords throughout our soul-winning circles.

I am not trying to question our good intentions. I am sure that I have used this same expression many times—but still we have to admit that it does not occur in the Bible at all.

The words "accept" and "acceptance" are used in the Scriptures in a number of ways, but never in connection with believing on Christ or receiving Christ for salvation or being saved.

My concern in this matter is my feeling that "easy acceptance" has been fatal to millions of people who may have stopped short in matters of faith and obedience. CES151-152

Lord Jesus, forgive me for believing and spreading the idea of "easy acceptance." May I see more fully that following You is costly, requiring full denial of myself. And may I lead others to do the same. Amen.

JULY 7

Religious Sinners

Then I will tell them plainly, "I never knew you. Away from me, you evildoers!"
—MATTHEW 7:23

I cannot estimate the number, although I think it is a very large number, of people who have been brought into some kind of religious experience by a fleeting formality of "accepting Christ," and a great, great number of them are still not saved. They have not been brought into a genuine saving relationship with Jesus Christ. We see the results all around us—they generally behave like religious sinners instead of like born-again believers.

That is why there is such a great stirring about the need for revival. That is why so many are asking, "What is the matter with us? We seem so dead, so lifeless, so apathetic about spiritual things!"

I say again that I have come to the conclusion that there are far too many among us who have thought that they accepted Christ—but nothing has come of it within their own lives and desires and habits. Will you just examine this matter a little more closely with me?

This kind of philosophy in soul winning, the idea that it is the easiest thing in the world to "accept Jesus," permits the man or woman to accept Christ by an impulse of the mind, or emotions. It allows us to gulp twice and sense an emotional feeling that may come over us, and then say, "I have accepted Christ."

All of you are aware of some of the very evident examples of the shortcomings in this approach to conversion and the new birth. CES152-153

Lord and Judge, prevent me from embracing the false religion that says accepting You without following You is enough. Amen.

JULY 8

The Pioneer and Perfecter of Our Faith

Let us run with perseverance the race marked out for us, fixing our eyes on Jesus, the pioneer and perfecter of faith.
—HEBREWS 12:1–2

When by faith we have entered this lifelong spiritual course, the Holy Spirit whispers, "Do you truly want to be among the victors in this discipline?" When we breathe our "Yes! Yes!" He whispers of ways that will aid us and carry us to certain victory.

The Spirit tells us to throw off everything that would hinder us in the race. He tells us to be aware of the little sins and errors that could divert us from the will of God as we run. But here is the important thing: He tells us to keep our eyes on Jesus, because He alone is our Pacesetter and victorious Example.

In a very real sense, faith is fixing our eyes on Jesus, keeping Jesus in full view regardless of what others may be doing all around us. This is excellent counsel, because as human beings we know we are not sufficient in ourselves. It is in our nature to look out—to look beyond ourselves for help.

It is also a human trait to look beyond ourselves for assurance. We hope to find someone worthy of trust. We want someone who has made good, someone who has done what we would like to do. The Hebrews writer points us to the perfect and victorious One, our eternal High Priest, seated now at the right hand of God. He is Jesus, the Pioneer and Perfecter of our faith. He has endured the cross and is now the eternal Victor and our Advocate in heaven. JAF078

Lord Jesus, I fix my eyes on You, for You have gone before me and You prepare the way for me. Increase my faith today and bring it to perfection on the day when I see You face to face. Amen.

JULY 9

The Pioneer and Perfecter of the Faith

Let us run with perseverance the race marked out for us, fixing our eyes on Jesus, the pioneer and perfecter of faith.
—HEBREWS 12:1–2

Jesus is more than the Author of just your faith. He is the Author, the Pioneer, the Leader, the Perfecter of the faith subscribed to by our fathers throughout the long centuries. The faith of our fathers rests on the biblical teachings and truths concerning God and the Person of Jesus Christ.

It is truth that God made the heavens and the earth, that God subsists in three persons, that God spoke to men through the prophets. It is truth that God sent His one and only Son into the world in order that whoever believes in Him should not perish. It is truth that to effect our salvation, Christ had to die and to rise again. It is truth that He is now at the right hand of the Father, that He is interceding for His believing people, that He is coming back to take His people to be with Him forever. It is truth that God has promised a new heaven and a new earth, that death will finally be put down, that the enemy of our souls will be destroyed.

This, in brief outline, is the faith of our fathers. Christ Jesus is the Author and Finisher of that faith, regardless of our personal attitudes or whether or not we demonstrate perfect confidence. JAF079-080

Lord Jesus, I praise You for guiding the church, by Your Spirit, to acknowledge and embrace the truth about You. May I always embrace the faith handed down by the apostles and fathers, no matter what my personal attitude may be. Amen.

Into the Arms of God by Faith

For God did not send his Son into the world to condemn the world, but to save the world through him.

—JOHN 3:17

God has never indicated that He is waiting for us to make ourselves morally good. He has indicated, however, that we have a potential that He well knows and He is waiting to make us over to bring glory to Him and to prove the wisdom of His mercy and grace throughout eternity. . . .

Our part is to turn to God in faith, confessing our great need, and thanking Him for revealing His love and concern for us through Jesus Christ, the eternal Son.

Faith cometh by hearing and faith becomes perfect as you pray and talk with God, your heavenly Father. He longs to hear you confide in Him: "Oh God, I do believe I matter to you and I do believe in Jesus Christ as my Savior and Lord."

Perhaps this sounds too simple: frankly, it is simple and easy to come into the arms of God by faith!

Come to Him for the first time as a sinner, for forgiveness and salvation.

Come back to God if you have wandered away. Come back home if you have strayed.

Every one of us must come with full confidence that it is a personal word God has spoken to us in this greatest of all proclamations, that "God so loved the world that he gave his only begotten Son, that whosoever believeth in him should not perish, but have everlasting life."

CES090-091

Lord Jesus, thank You for what You have done in Your work of salvation. Make me over so that I would glorify You! Amen.

JULY 11

Which Cross Do We Carry?

By making peace through his blood, shed on the cross.
—COLOSSIANS 1:20

One of the strange things under the sun is a "crossless" Christianity. The cross of Christendom is a "no cross," an ecclesiastical symbol. The cross of our Lord Jesus Christ is a place of death!

Let each one be careful which cross he carries!

Thousands turn away from Jesus Christ because they will not meet His conditions. He watches them as they go, for He loves them, but He will make no concessions.

Admit one soul into the kingdom by compromise and that kingdom is no longer secure. Christ will be Lord, or He will be Judge. Every man must decide whether he will take Him as Lord now, or face Him as Judge then!

"If any man will . . . let him . . . follow me" (Matt. 16:24). Some will rise and go after Him, but others give no heed to His voice. So the gulf opens between man and man, between those who will and those who will not.

The Man, the kindly Stranger who walked this earth, is His own proof. He will not put Himself again on trial; He will not argue. But the morning of the judgment will confirm what men in the twilight have decided! MWT104

Heavenly Father, thank You for Your patience as You wait for people to repent and turn to You. I pray that this will be a day when many will respond to Your voice calling them to follow You. Amen.

JULY 12

A Radical Thing

Let us run with perseverance the race marked out for us, fixing our eyes on Jesus, the pioneer and perfecter of faith. For the joy set before him he endured the cross, scorning its shame, and sat down at the right hand of the throne of God.

—HEBREWS 12:1–2

The cross of Christ is the most revolutionary thing ever to appear among men. The cross of old Roman times knew no compromise; it never made concessions. It won all its arguments by killing its opponent and silencing him for good. It spared not Christ, but slew Him the same as the rest. He was alive when they hung Him on that cross and completely dead when they took Him down six hours later. That was the cross the first time it appeared in Christian history.

After Christ was risen from the dead the apostles went out to preach His message, and what they preached was the cross. And wherever they went into the wide world they carried the cross, and the same revolutionary power went with them. The radical message of the cross transformed Saul of Tarsus and changed him from a persecutor of Christians to a tender believer and an apostle of the faith. Its power changed bad men into good ones. It shook off the long bondage of paganism and altered completely the whole moral and mental outlook of the Western world. TRC013-014

Jesus, truly Your cross is the most amazing thing in all history! May I stand in great awe of the cross and preach the cross boldly today. Amen.

JULY 13

Trusting the Lifeboat

He then brought them out and asked, "Sirs, what must I do to be saved?" They replied, "Believe in the Lord Jesus, and you will be saved—you and your household."
—ACTS 16:30-31

No man has any hope for eternal salvation apart from trusting completely in Jesus Christ and His atonement for men. Simply stated, our Lord Jesus is the lifeboat and we must fully and truly be committed to trusting the lifeboat.

Again, our Lord and Savior is the rope by which it is possible to escape from the burning building. There is no doubt about it—either we trust that rope or we perish.

He is the wonder drug or medication that heals all ills and sicknesses—and if we refuse it, we die.

He is the bridge from hell to heaven—and we take the bridge and cross over by His grace or we stay in hell.

These are simple illustrations, but they get to the point of the necessity of complete trust in Jesus Christ—absolute trust in Him!
WPJ063-064

Lord, help me to make this clear as I share the gospel. So many seem to persist in wanting to trust Christ plus their own efforts. Thank You for this free gift of salvation. Amen.

JULY 14

The Goal of Doctrine

Listen to my words, LORD, consider my lament . . . For you are not a God who is pleased with wickedness; with you, evil people are not welcome.

—PSALM 5:1, 4

Among Christians of all ages and of varying shades of doctrinal emphasis there has been fairly full agreement on one thing: they all believed that it was important that the Christian with serious spiritual aspirations should learn to meditate long and often on God!

Let a Christian insist upon rising above the poor average of current religious experience and he will soon come up against the need to know God Himself as the ultimate goal of all Christian doctrine.

Let him seek to explore the sacred wonders of the Triune Godhead and he will discover that sustained and intelligently directed meditation on the Person of God is imperative. To know God well he must think on Him unceasingly. Nothing that man has discovered about himself or God has revealed any shortcut to pure spirituality. It is still free, but tremendously costly!

Of course this presupposes at least a fair amount of sound theological knowledge. To seek God apart from His own self-disclosure in the inspired Scriptures is not only futile but dangerous. There must be also a knowledge of and complete trust in Jesus Christ as Lord and Redeemer.

Christ is not one of many ways to approach God, nor is He the best of several ways; He is the only way, "the way, the truth and the life."

To believe otherwise is to be something less than a Christian! EWT035

Triune God, I long to know You more deeply this day! May I approach You more closely through Jesus Christ. Amen.

JULY 15

Not Asking for Anything

I love the LORD, for he heard my voice; he heard my cry for mercy. Because he turned his ear to me, I will call on him as long as I live.

—PSALM 116:1–2

I think that some of the greatest prayer is prayer where you don't say one single word or ask for anything. Now God does answer and He does give us what we ask for. That's plain; nobody can deny that unless he denies the Scriptures. But that's only one aspect of prayer, and it's not even the important aspect. Sometimes I go to God and say, "God, if Thou dost never answer another prayer while I live on this earth, I will still worship Thee as long as I live and in the ages to come for what Thou hast done already." God's already put me so far in debt that if I were to live one million millenniums I couldn't pay Him for what He's done for me.

We go to God as we send a boy to a grocery store with a long written list. "God, give me this, give me this, and give me this," and our gracious God often does give us what we want. But I think God is disappointed because we make Him to be no more than a source of what we want. Even our Lord Jesus is presented too often much as "Someone who will meet your need." That's the throbbing heart of modern evangelism. You're in need and Jesus will meet your need. He's the Need-meeter. Well, He is that indeed; but, ah, He's infinitely more than that. WMJ024-025

Father, forgive me for so often just coming to You with my grocery list. You've been so faithful; You've given me so much; You've blessed so richly. I realize my incredible debt to You, and I simply worship at Your feet. Amen.

JULY 16

Confess Christ's Lordship

So then, just as you received Christ Jesus as Lord,
continue to live your lives in him.
—COLOSSIANS 2:6

I think it is a completely wrong concept in Christian circles to look upon Jesus as a kind of divine nurse to whom we can go when sin has made us sick, and after He has helped us, to say, "Good-bye, Jesus"—and go on our own way.

Suppose I go into a hospital in need of a blood transfusion. After the staff has ministered to me and given their services, do I just slip out with a cheery "good-bye"—as though I owe them nothing and it was kind of them to help me in my time of need?

That may sound far-out to you, but it draws a picture of attitudes among us today.

But the Bible never in any way gives us such a concept of salvation. Nowhere are we ever led to believe that we can use Jesus as a Savior and not own Him as our Lord. He is the Lord and as the Lord He saves us, because He has all of the offices of Savior, Christ, High Priest, and Wisdom and Righteousness and Sanctification and Redemption!

He is all of these—and all of these are embodied in Him as Christ, the Lord! MWT151

Father, You are my Savior and my Lord. My debt to You is huge! I owe You my life. Amen.

JULY 17

Christ Glorified in Us

"What no eye has seen, what no ear has heard" . . . the things God has prepared for those who love him.

—1 CORINTHIANS 2:9

The Bible tells us that eye has not seen nor ear heard, neither has it entered into the heart of men, the things that God has laid up for those who love Him!

That is why the apostle goes on to remind us that God has revealed these mysteries to us by the Holy Spirit.

Oh, if we would only stop trying to make the Holy Spirit our servant and begin to live in His life as the fish lives in the sea, we would enter into the riches of glory about which we know nothing now. Too many of us want the Holy Spirit in order to have some gift—healing or tongues or preaching or prophecy.

Yes, these have their place in that total pattern of the New Testament, but let us never pray that we may be filled with the Spirit for a secondary purpose!

Remember, God wants to fill you with His Spirit as an end in your moral life. God's purpose is that we should know Him first of all, and be lost in Him, and that we should enter into the fullness of the Spirit that the eternal Son, Jesus Christ, may be glorified in us! MWT201

O Lord, I desire to lose my life in Yours today, so that You may be glorified in and through me. Amen.

Personal Resolve

For God so loved the world that he gave his one and only Son, that whoever believes in him shall not perish but have eternal life.
—JOHN 3:16

God lovingly waits for each individual to come with a personal resolve and decision: "I will arise and I will go home to claim the provision in my Father's house." If you will make that personal decision of faith in Jesus Christ, with faith in the fact that it is really you whom God loves and wants to forgive, it will mean something more to you than you have ever known—something beautiful and eternal.

I close by reminding you also as an individual that unbelief always finds three trees behind which to hesitate and hide. Here they are: Somebody Else. Some Other Place. Some Other Time.

We hear someone preaching an invitation sermon on John 3:16 and in effect we run to the garden to hide behind these trees.

"Of course it is true," we say, "but it is for Somebody Else."

If it were only Some Other Place or at Some Other Time you might be willing to come.

Whether you get the right grammar or the proper tense is not important: what our Lord is delighted to hear is your confession that "that means me, Lord! I am the reason, the cause and reason why You came to earth to die." CES107-108

Lord Jesus, keep me from thinking that Your commands and invitations are for someone else in some other place or time. May I see that Your words are living and active, relevant for me today. Amen.

JULY 19

Every Man's Contemporary

Be still, and know that I am God.
—PSALM 46:10

Our fathers had much to say about stillness, and by stillness they meant the absence of motion or the absence of noise, or both. . . .

God can be known in the tumult if His providence has for the time placed us there, but He is known best in the silence. So they held, and so the sacred Scriptures declare. Inward assurance comes out of the stillness. We must be still to know!

There has hardly been another time in the history of the world when stillness was needed more than it is today, and there has surely not been another time when there was so little of it or when it was so hard to find. Christ is every man's contemporary. His presence and His power are offered to us in this time of mad activity and mechanical noises as certainly as to fishermen on the quiet lake of Galilee or to shepherds on the plains of Judea. The only condition is that we get still enough to hear His voice and that we believe and heed what we hear.

As we draw nearer to the ancient Source of our being we find that we are no longer learned or ignorant, modern or old-fashioned, crude or cultured: in that awesome Presence we are just men and women. Artificial distinctions fade away. Thousands of years of education disappear in a moment and we stand again where Adam and Eve stood after the Fall, where Cain stood, and Abel, outside the Garden, frightened and undone and fugitive from the terror of the broken law, desperately in need of a Savior! EWT076

Christ, I recognize that You are with me today. Give me the ability to slow down and embrace silence, that I might hear You and commune with You more intimately. Amen.

JULY 20

Confidence in Him

Now to him who is able to do immeasurably more than all we ask or imagine, according to his power that is at work within us, to him be glory in the church and in Christ Jesus throughout all generations, for ever and ever! Amen.

—EPHESIANS 3:20–21

You can have this confidence in God, and you can have this respect for His will. Do not expect God to perform miracles for you so you can write books about them. Do not ever be caught asking God to send you toys like that to play around with. But if you are in trouble and concerned about your situation and willing to be honest with God, you can have confidence in Him. You can go to Him in the merit of His Son, claiming His promises, and He will not let you down. God will help you, and you will find the way of deliverance. God will move heaven and earth for you if you will trust Him. FBR049

Thank You, Father, for the majesty of this truth. It certainly is only in the merit of Your Son, but in that merit You've given us a powerful promise. Thank You that You never let us down. Amen.

JULY 21

Blessedness to Come

We have a building from God, an eternal house in heaven, not built by human hands.
—2 CORINTHIANS 5:1

A lot of people talk about going to heaven in spite of the feeble hope popular religion affords.

Any valid hope of a state of blessedness beyond the incident of death must be in the goodness of God and in the work of atonement accomplished for us by Jesus Christ on the cross.

The deep, deep love of God is the fountain out of which flows our future beatitude; and the grace of God in Christ is the channel by which it reaches us. The cross of Christ creates a moral situation where every attribute of God is on the side of the returning sinner.

The true Christian may safely look forward to a future state that is as happy as perfect love wills it to be. Because love cannot desire for its object anything less than the fullest possible measure of enjoyment for the longest possible time, it is virtually beyond our power to conceive of a future as consistently delightful as that which Christ is preparing for us.

And who is to say what is possible with God? MWT255

Loving Lord, though we are the objects of Your perfect love, it is a safe guess to say that we are only partially aware of the benefits You desire to bestow upon us. Thank You, Father, for Your unfailing, overflowing love. Amen.

JULY 22

We Died with Christ

I have been crucified with Christ and I no longer live,
but Christ lives in me.
—GALATIANS 2:20

How can there be any question but that our Lord Jesus Christ identified us with Himself? Instead of putting the cross on that hill outside Jerusalem, Jesus puts the cross in our lives, where it belongs!

Evil-minded men hung Jesus on a wooden cross, just as Jesus had told His disciples they would. The salvation of a lost world was at stake. When He died, His body was taken down and laid in a tomb.

When He arose from the dead and ascended to the right hand of God the Father, that wooden cross had no further meaning in the mind of God. None at all! Some Christian churches are very enamored with splinters they say came from the wooden cross on which Jesus died. Apart from such dubious claims, that old wooden cross is no longer in existence. I hope we realize that when we sing "The Old Rugged Cross."

But there remains a very real cross. It is the cross you take and the cross I take as we follow our Lord Jesus who willingly took His cross. That is why I say that our Lord identifies us with Himself. JAF082-083

Holy Lord, help me to see my cross, pick it up, and follow You, that I may be identified with You in every area of my life and become more like You. Amen.

JULY 23

Divine Wisdom Incarnated

Jesus answered, "I am the way and the truth and the life. No one comes to the Father except through me."
—JOHN 14:6

Did you ever notice that our Lord Jesus Christ, when He walked the earth, never apologized? He never got up in the morning and said, "I'm sorry, boys. Yesterday when I was talking I misspoke Myself and I said this, but I meant that." Never! Because He was wisdom divinely incarnated in the voice of a man. And when He spoke, He said it right the first time. He never had to apologize.

I've had to get up and explain myself a few times. I've even had to get up publicly and tell the people I've made a donkey of myself a few times. I'm just a man, you know. But Jesus Christ never once said, "I'm sorry, but I said the wrong thing yesterday; I didn't mean to leave that impression." He always said it right, because He was God. He never apologized, never explained. He said, "This is the way it is," and they either got it or they didn't. And if they didn't get it, He told them a little more but He never backed out on anything that He said, because He is God. AOGII139-140

Lord Jesus, give me the faith to always believe You and Your words, for "you have the words of eternal life" (John 6:68). Amen.

JULY 24

Unclaimed Spiritual Blessings

Praise be to the God and Father of our Lord Jesus Christ, who has blessed us in the heavenly realms with every spiritual blessing in Christ.

—EPHESIANS 1:3

Those spiritual blessings in heavenly places which are ours in Christ may be divided into three classes:

The first is those which come to us immediately upon our believing unto salvation, such as forgiveness, justification, regeneration, sonship to God, and baptism into the Body of Christ. In Christ we possess these even before we know that they are ours!

The second class is those riches which are ours by inheritance but which we cannot enjoy in actuality until our Lord returns. These include ultimate mental and moral perfection, the glorification of our bodies, the completion of the restoration of the divine image in our redeemed personalities and the admission into the very presence of God to experience forever the Beatific Vision. These treasures are as surely ours as if we possessed them now!

The third class consists of spiritual treasures which are ours by blood atonement but which will not come to us unless we make a determined effort to possess them. These are deliverance from the sins of the flesh, victory over self, the constant flow of the Holy Spirit through our personalities, fruitfulness in Christian service, awareness of the Presence of God, growth in grace, an increasing consciousness of union with God, and an unbroken spirit of worship. EWT242

Lord, I long to possess this third class of treasures in Christ. Grant by Your Spirit that I would seek them and possess, that I might grow in my love for and devotion to You. Amen.

JULY 25

Christ Came to Save

For God did not send his Son into the world to condemn the world, but to save the world through him.

—JOHN 3:17

Millions who have rejected the Christian gospel have generally been too busy and too involved to ask themselves a simple question: "What really is God's intention toward me?"

They could have found the plain and simple answer given by the Apostle John: "For God sent not his Son into the world to condemn the world; but that the world through him might be saved" (John 3:17).

This is a gravely significant message from the heart of God Himself! Yet, even in the full light it provides, people are indifferent. Upon our eyes there seems to have fallen a strange dimness; within our ears, a strange dullness. It is a wonder, and a terrible responsibility, that we should have this message in our possession and be so little stirred about it!

I confess that it is very hard for me to accept the fact that it is now very rare for anyone to come into the house of God, silently confessing: "Dear Lord, I am ready and willing to hear what you will speak to me today!" MWT052

Dear Lord, how grateful I am that You do not condemn, but by Your Spirit You do convict. Help me to hear and act upon Your promptings today. Amen.

JULY 26

First and Last and All

Follow God's example, therefore, as dearly loved children and walk in the way of love, just as Christ loved us and gave himself up for us as a fragrant offering and sacrifice to God.

—EPHESIANS 5:1–2

To accept Christ, then, is to attach ourselves to His holy person; to live or die, forever. He must be first and last and all. All of our other relationships are conditioned and determined and colored by our one exclusive relation to Him. . . .

A Christian is one who has accepted Jesus' friends as his friends and Jesus' enemies as his enemies by an exclusive attachment to the person of Christ.

I made up my mind a long time ago. Those who declare themselves enemies of Jesus Christ must look upon me as their enemy—and I ask no quarter from them. And if they are the friends of Jesus Christ they are my friends and I do not care what color they are or what denomination they belong to.

To accept the Lord means to accept His ways as our ways. We have taken His Word and His teachings as the guide in our lives. To accept Christ means that I accept His rejection as my rejection. When I accept Him I knowingly and willingly accept His cross as my cross. I accept His life as my life—back from the dead I come and up into a different kind of life. It means that I accept His future as my future. CES159-161

Lord Jesus, may I be more firmly attached to You today, that I would die with You daily and be raised to newness of life. Amen.

JULY 27

A Birth from Above

You should not be surprised at my saying, "You must be born again."
—JOHN 3:7

This may sound like heresy in some quarters, but I have come to this conclusion—that there are far too many among us who have thought that they accepted Christ, but nothing has come of it within their own lives and desires and habits!

This kind of philosophy in soul winning—the idea that it is "the easiest thing in the world to accept Jesus"—permits the man or woman to accept Christ by an impulse of the mind or of the emotions.

It allows us to gulp twice and sense an emotional feeling that has come over us, and then say, "I have accepted Christ."

These are spiritual matters about which we must be legitimately honest and in which we must seek the discernment of the Holy Spirit. These are things about which we cannot afford to be wrong; to be wrong is still to be lost and far from God.

Let us never forget that the Word of God stresses the importance of conviction and concern and repentance when it comes to conversion, spiritual regeneration, being born from above by the Spirit of God!

MWT144

Lord, I pray that new believers will become firmly discipled in the Word of God and that their lives will reflect the transformation from death to life. Amen.

JULY 28

Prophetic, Not Diplomatic

For Christ did not send me to baptize, but to preach the gospel—not with wisdom and eloquence, lest the cross of Christ be emptied of its power.

—1 CORINTHIANS 1:17

We who witness and proclaim the gospel must not think of ourselves as public relations agents sent to establish goodwill between Christ and the world. . . . We are not diplomats but prophets, and our message is not a compromise but an ultimatum!

God offers life, but not an improved old life. The life He offers is life out of death. It stands always on the far side of the cross. Whoever would possess it must pass under the rod. He must repudiate himself and concur in God's just sentence against him.

What does this mean to the individual, the condemned man who would find life in Christ Jesus? How can this theology be translated into life?

Simply, he must repent and believe. He must forsake his sins and then go on to forsake himself. Let him cover nothing, defend nothing, excuse nothing. Let him not seek to make terms with God, but let him bow his head before the stroke of God's stern displeasure and acknowledge himself worthy to die.

Having done this, let him gaze with simple trust upon the risen Saviour, and from Him will come life and rebirth and cleansing and power. The cross that ended the earthly life of Jesus now puts an end to the sinner; and the power that raised Christ from the dead now raises him to a new life along with Christ! EWT081

Heavenly Father, forgive me of the ways in which I have presented Christ not as He truly is. Grant that I would not compromise on the gospel but be a faithful prophetic voice in this world. Amen.

JULY 29

Three Pillars

With great power the apostles continued to testify to the resurrection of the Lord Jesus. And God's grace was so powerfully at work in them all.

—ACTS 4:33

In the redemptive work of Christ three major epochs may be noted: His birth, His death, and His subsequent elevation to the right hand of God. These are the three main pillars that uphold the temple of Christianity; upon them rest all the hopes of mankind, world without end. All else that He did takes its meaning from these three Godlike deeds. . . .

Christ was born that He might become a man and became a man that He might give His life as ransom for many. Neither the birth nor the dying were ends in themselves. As He was born to die, so did He die that He might atone, and rise that He might justify freely all who take refuge in Him. His birth and His death are history. His appearance at the mercy seat is not history past, but a present, continuing fact, to the instructed Christian the most glorious fact his trusting heart can entertain. . . .

The glory of the Christian faith is that the Christ who died for our sins rose again for our justification. We should joyfully remember His birth and gratefully muse on His dying, but the crown of all our hopes is with Him at the Father's right hand. TRC022-023, 025, 026

Lord Jesus, I believe with all my heart that You died—that You died so I could have forgiveness of sins and new life. Increase my hope today. Amen.

JULY 30

Come to the Throne

Let us then approach God's throne of grace with confidence, so that we may receive mercy and find grace to help us in our time of need.

—HEBREWS 4:16

As long as you remain on this earth, God has not completed His work in you. The Spirit of God will help you discern when the chastening hand of God is upon you. But if it is the devil trying to tamper with your Christian life and testimony, dare to resist him in the victorious power of the living Christ.

This great truth is related to the fact that Jesus is our eternal High Priest, now exalted at the throne of God. He has said to us, "Whatever your need, just come to the throne of grace. Anything you need, you may have!" Why not believe Him and exercise the dominion He has given you?

There is no reason for any of us to hide or to slink about as if we must get permission to exist. As children of God, we need not apologize for walking around in God's earth. Christ has made us a kingdom of believer-priests. This is a fact, a Bible doctrine. We are priests. We have the right as believer-priests to go direct to our great High Priest in the heavens, making our legitimate wants and wishes known to Him. He has promised to intercede for us at the heavenly throne. JIV037-038

O wonderful High Priest, I come to You today for all that I need. Intercede for me that I would remain faithful and live to Your glory. Amen.

JULY 31

Devotion To

I have brought you glory on earth by finishing the work you gave me to do.
—JOHN 17:4

We celebrate Christ's "devotion to" His Father's will. Our Lord Jesus Christ had no secondary aims. His one passion in life was the fulfillment of His Father's will. Of no other human being can this be said in absolute terms. Others have been devoted to God, but never absolutely. Always there has been occasion to mourn the introduction, however brief, of some distraction. But Jesus was never distracted. Never once did He deviate from His Father's will. It was always before Him, and it was to this one thing that He was devoted.

Because it was not the Father's will that any should perish, Jesus was devoted to the rescue of fallen mankind—completely devoted to it. He did not do a dozen other things as avocations. He did that one thing that would permit a Holy God to forgive sin. He was devoted to the altar of sacrifice so that mankind might be rescued from the wages of sin. TRC071-072

Lord Jesus, may I be single-minded like You, aiming only to please the Father. Grant me this by the power of Your Spirit. Amen.

AUGUST

AUGUST 1

Hearing God

This is my Son, whom I love; with him I am well pleased. Listen to him!
MATTHEW 17:5

God has spoken to us in a variety of ways. Our general response has been, "We did not hear His voice. We did not hear any thing!" John recorded in his gospel the reactions of an audience who heard God speak audibly.

When Jesus talked of His coming death, asking God to glorify His name through it, "then came there a voice from heaven, saying, I have both glorified it, and will glorify it again" (John 12:28). And what were the reactions of the bystanders? "The people therefore, that stood by, and heard it, said that it thundered: others said, An angel spake to him" (12:29).

People prefer their logic, their powers of reason. Even when God speaks, they refuse to recognize His voice. They will not confess that God has spoken through Jesus Christ, the eternal Son. When He confronts them with their sin, they consult a psychiatrist and hope they can get their personalities "properly adjusted." But in a coming day, every knee will bow and every tongue will confess that Jesus Christ is Lord of all.

First, however, the trumpets of God will have sounded! JIV098-099

Heavenly Father, grant by Your Spirit that I would listen to Your Son and obey Him. May I not rely on my logic, but solely on You and Your revelation in Jesus Christ. Amen.

AUGUST 2

Total Commitment

He is the atoning sacrifice for our sins, and not only for ours but also for the sins of the whole world.

—1 JOHN 2:2

I believe the gospel of Jesus Christ saved me completely—therefore He asks me for total commitment. He expects me to be a disciple totally dedicated.

Joined to Jesus Christ, how can we be other than what He is? What He does, we do. Where He leads, we go. This is genuine Christianity!

Sin is now an outrage against holy blood. To sin now is to crucify the Son of God afresh. To sin now is to belittle the blood of atonement. For a Christian to sin now is to insult the holy life laid down. I cannot believe that any Christian wants to sin.

All offenses against God will either be forgiven or avenged—we can take our choice. All offenses against God, against ourselves, against humanity, against human life—all offenses will be either forgiven or avenged. There are two voices—one pleading for vengeance, the other pleading for mercy.

What a terrible thing for men and women to get old and have no prospect, no gracious promise for the long eternity before them.

But how beautiful to come up like a ripe shock of corn and know that the Father's house is open, the doors are wide open, and the Father waits to receive His children one after another! TRC118-119

Lord Jesus, You became fully human so that You might redeem all of who I am. May I commit all of myself to You so that You would be fully glorified and I would receive all the blessings You have for me. Amen.

AUGUST 3

Christ Is Not Divided

Jesus replied, "Anyone who loves me will obey my teaching."
—JOHN 14:23

Much of our full gospel literature and much of our preaching tend to perpetuate a misunderstanding of what the Bible says about obedience and Christian discipleship.

I think the following is a fair statement of what I was taught in my early Christian experience and before I began to pray and study and anguish over the whole matter:

> "We are saved by accepting Christ as our Savior."
> "We are sanctified by accepting Christ as our Lord."
> "We may do the first without doing the second."

What a tragedy that in our day we often hear the gospel appeal made in this way:

> "Come to Jesus! You do not have to obey anyone. You do not have to give up anything. Just come to Him and believe in Him as Savior!"

The fact that we hear this everywhere does not make it right! To urge men and women to believe in a divided Christ is bad teaching—for no one can receive a half or a third or a quarter of the divine Person of Christ! MWT049

Heavenly Father, You are a wonderful Savior and Lord, deserving my full obedience to all of Your teachings. Forgive me, Lord, for the times that I've obeyed only a portion of Your Word. Show me the areas in my life in which I am weak. Amen.

AUGUST 4

Judgment Seat of Christ

Each of us will give an account of ourselves to God.
—ROMANS 14:12

Within the household of God among the redeemed and justified there is law as well as grace; not the law of Moses that knew no mercy, but the kindly law of the Father's heart that requires and expects of His children lives lived in conformity to the commandments of Christ.

If these words should startle anyone, so let it be and more also, for our Lord has told us plainly and has risen up early and sent His apostles to tell us that we must all give account of the deeds done in the body. And He has warned us faithfully of the danger that we will have for our reward—only wood, hay, and stubble in the day of Christ (see Rom. 14:7–12; 1 Cor. 3:9–15).

The judgment unto death and hell lies behind the Christian, but the judgment seat of Christ lies ahead. There the question will not be the law of Moses, but how we have lived within the Father's household; our record will be examined for evidence of faithfulness, self-discipline, generosity beyond the demands of the law, courage before our detractors, humility, separation from the world, cross carrying and a thousand little deeds of love that could never occur to the mere legalist or to the unregenerate soul. TRC115-116

Lord, I know that You are both Savior and Judge. May I keep in mind that one day I will stand before You and give account of my life, what I have done with the blessings You have given me. Make me a faithful steward. Amen.

AUGUST 5

Christians Indeed

They are choked by life's worries, riches and pleasures, and they do not mature.
—LUKE 8:14

I believe we are mistaken in Christian life and theology when we try to add the "deeper life" to an imperfect salvation obtained through an imperfect concept of the entire matter.

Under the working of the Spirit of God through men like Finney and Wesley, no one would ever have dared to say, "I am a Christian" if he had not surrendered his whole being, taking Jesus Christ as his Lord and Savior!

Today, we let them say they are saved no matter how imperfect and incomplete the transaction, with the proviso that the deeper Christian life can be "tacked on" at some time in the future.

Brethren, I believe we must put the blame on faulty teaching—teaching that is filled with self-deception.

Let us look unto Jesus our Lord—high and holy, wearing the crown, Lord of lords and King of all, having a perfect right to command full obedience from all of His saved people! MWT214

O Lord, it is a real challenge in today's world to filter out all the worldly "stuff" from our lives. Lord, help me to surrender the things in my life that are hindering the production of fruit for You. Amen.

AUGUST 6

True Wisdom

On hearing it, many of his disciples said, "This is a hard teaching. Who can accept it?"
—JOHN 6:60

In the world of men we find nothing approaching the virtues of which Jesus spoke in the opening words of the famous Sermon on the Mount. Instead of poverty of spirit we find the rankest kind of pride; instead of meekness, arrogance; instead of mourners we find pleasure seekers; instead of hunger after righteousness we hear men saying, "I am rich and increased with goods and have need of nothing"; instead of mercy we find cruelty; instead of purity of heart, corrupt imaginings; instead of peacemakers we find men quarrelsome and resentful; instead of rejoicing in mistreatment we find them fighting back with every weapon at their command!

Into a world like this the sound of Jesus' words comes wonderful and strange, a visitation from above. . . .

Jesus does not offer an opinion for He never uttered opinions. He never guessed; He knew, and He knows! His words are not as Solomon's were, the sum of sound wisdom or the results of keen observation. He spoke out of the fullness of His Godhead, and His words are very Truth itself. He is the only one who could say "blessed" with complete authority for He is the Blessed One come from the world above to confer blessedness upon mankind!

Best of all, His words were supported by deeds mightier than any performed on this earth by another man. It is wisdom for us to listen!

EWT103

Lord Christ, You alone have the words of life. Grant that I would heed Your words today and walk in Your ways. Amen.

AUGUST 7

The Crowd Turns Back

From this time many of his disciples turned back and no longer followed him.

—JOHN 6:66

Our Lord Jesus Christ called men to follow Him, but He plainly taught that "no man can come unto me, except it were given unto him of my Father" (John 6:65).

It is not surprising that many of His early followers, upon hearing these words, went back and walked no more with Him. Such teaching cannot but be deeply disturbing to the natural mind. It takes from sinful men much of the power of self-determination. It cuts the ground out from under their self-help and throws them back upon the sovereign good pleasure of God—and that is precisely where they do not want to be!

These statements by our Lord run contrary to the current assumptions of popular Christianity. Men are willing to be saved by grace, but to preserve their self-esteem, they must hold that the desire to be saved originated with them.

Most Christians today seem afraid to talk about these plain words of Jesus concerning the sovereign operation of God—so they use the simple trick of ignoring them! MWT092

Dear Lord, I do not want to be counted among those who turn their backs on You. I want to follow You, Lord. Guide and empower me by Your Spirit today. Amen.

AUGUST 8

Grace and Forgiveness

And that is what some of you were. But you were washed, you were sanctified, you were justified in the name of the Lord Jesus Christ and by the Spirit of our God.
—1 CORINTHIANS 6:11

I do not know all of the Savior's reasons for choosing the woman at the well. I know that His revelation of Himself to her constituted an everlasting rebuke to human self-righteousness. I know that every smug woman who walks down the street in pride and status ought to be ashamed of herself. I know that every self-righteous man who looks into his mirror each morning to shave what he believes to be an honest face ought to be ashamed of himself. . . .

Jesus was able to see potential in the woman at the well that we could never have sensed. What a gracious thing for us that Jesus Christ never thinks about what we have been! He always thinks about what we are going to be. You and I are slaves to time and space and records and reputations and publicity and the past—all that we call the case history. Jesus Christ cares absolutely nothing about anyone's moral case history. He forgives it and starts from there as though the person had been born one minute before. FBR103-104

Again I worship You today, great God, for Your matchless grace. No matter what my past, thank You, thank You, thank You, that "Jesus Christ cares absolutely nothing about anyone's moral case history." Amen.

AUGUST 9

Present with the Father

This is how we know who the children of God are and who the children of the devil are: Anyone who does not do what is right is not God's child, nor is anyone who does not love their brother and sister.

—1 JOHN 3:10

Many Christians are staking their reputations on church attendance, religious activity, social fellowship, sessions of singing—because in all of these things they are able to lean upon one another. They spend a lot of time serving as religious props for one another in Christian circles!

Let us look at the example of Jesus. When He was here upon earth, the record shows that He had work to do and He also knew the necessity for activity as He preached and healed, taught and answered questions, and blessed the people. He also knew the fellowship of His brethren, those who followed Him and loved Him. But those were the incidental things in Jesus' life compared to His fellowship with and personal knowledge of the Father. When Jesus went into the mountain to pray and to wait on God all night, He was not alone, for He knew the conscious presence of the Father with Him! EWT203

Heavenly Father, may I not prioritize anything else over spending time with You. May I follow the example of Your beloved Son. Amen.

AUGUST 10

More than Creed

You have heard that it was said to the people long ago . . .
But I tell you . . .
—MATTHEW 5:21–22

When Jesus came into our midst and presented Himself as the Messiah, His greatest enemies were the entrenched religious leaders of Israel. Their spiritual principles were drawn not from above, but from below. They used all the tactics of unregenerate men, including bribes, to bring the witness of lies against Jesus. To defend God, they acted like the devil. To claim support from the Scriptures, they defied its true teachings. In the name of a religion of love and mercy, they loosed the reins of blind hate. So fierce was their spirit—the spirit of this world that dominated them—that it never rested until they had put to death the Son of God.

Now, we are evangelicals at a troubled time in history. We face a danger—the danger of taking for granted that because we are evangelicals in theology and creed, we are automatically pleasing in the sight of God. Is it possible that our conservative theology is really a kind of nibbling of God's sweet and precious Word? Do we never allow it to become anything more than the creed and doctrines we say we believe? JIV141-142

Holy and gracious Father, forgive me for the ways in which I have believed human doctrines instead of the truths of Your Son, and embraced the ways of the world rather than His precepts. Grant me strength to follow Him closely today. Amen.

AUGUST 11

Always the Same Lord

Jesus Christ is the same yesterday and today and forever.
—HEBREWS 13:8

Their disappointments must be hard for them to explain. The apostolic method was to provide a foundation of good, sound biblical reasons for following the Savior, for our willingness to let the Spirit of God display the great Christian virtues in our lives. That is why we come in faith and rejoicing to the eternal verity of Hebrews 13:8. Because Jesus Christ is eternal and without change forever and ever, we can trust Him and live for Him!

We hear much discussion about revival and renewal. People talk about spiritual power in the churches. I think this fact—this truth—that Jesus Christ wants to be known in His church as the ever-living, never-changing Lord of all could bring back again the power and the testimony of the early church.

I wonder if you feel like me when I survey much of Christendom in today's world: "They have taken away my Lord and I do not know what they have done with Him!" If we would only seek and welcome our Lord's presence in our midst, we would have the assurance that He is the same Lord He has always been! JAF143-144

Lord Christ, I recognize today that You are the same as You were in the days of the apostles. Fill me with Your Spirit now, that I might see Your power work in my life. Amen.

AUGUST 12

Keys to Greatness

Whoever wants to become great among you must be your servant, whoever wants to be first must be your slave.

—MATTHEW 20:26–27

The essence of Christ's teaching concerning greatness was this: true greatness among humans must be found in character, not in ability or position.

While a few philosophers and religionists of pre-Christian times had noted the fallacy in man's ideas of dominion and status, it was Christ who defined and demonstrated true greatness.

"Let him be your minister: let him be your servant." It is that simple and that easy—and that difficult!

We have but to follow Christ in service to the human race, a selfless service that seeks only to serve, and greatness will be ours! That is all, but it is too much, for it runs counter to all that is Adam in us. Adam still feels the instinct for dominion; he hears deep within him the command, "Replenish the earth and subdue it." Therefore he does not take kindly to the command to serve! Sin must go and Adam must give way to Christ: so says our Lord in effect. By sin men have lost dominion, even their very right to it, until they win it back by humble service.

Though redeemed from death and hell by the vicarious labor of Christ on the cross, still the right to have dominion must be won by each man separately.

After Christ had served (and His service included death), God highly exalted Him and gave Him a name above every name. As a man He served and won His right to have dominion. He knew where true greatness lay—and we do not. EWT065

Lord Christ, give me strength to follow You by humbly serving others in love, that I would know You more. Amen.

AUGUST 13

The Glorified King

Since, then, you have been raised with Christ, set your hearts on things above, where Christ is, seated at the right hand of God.
—COLOSSIANS 3:1

Let this truth penetrate. There is a glorified Human Being at the right hand of God—not a spirit but a Man glorified. He is there interceding for us, representing us. This is why I believe in the security of the saints. How can I help but believe that? If Jesus Christ is at the right hand of God, then He has invested Himself—charged Himself—with full authority, authority given Him by God the Father. My name is on His multistone breastpiece (see Ex. 39:8–14), and I am safe! . . .

Jesus Christ is also Ruler over all the kings of the earth, and we await His day of consummation and triumph when every knee shall bow before Him "of things in heaven, and things in earth, and things under the earth; And that every tongue should confess that Jesus Christ is Lord, to the glory of God the Father" (Phil. 2:10–11). JIV034-035

Lord Christ, I exalt You today! You are the glorious and victorious King who has authority over all things. I long for Your return, the day when I will be fully safe in You. Amen.

AUGUST 14

Same Lord, Same God

I the Lord do not change.

—MALACHI 3:6

The Scriptures are open and plain. Jesus Christ is our Savior and Lord. He is our great High Priest, alive and ministering for us today. His person, His power and His grace are the same, without change, yesterday, today and forever!

He is the same Lord because He is the same God. He is the same, never having changed in substance, in power, in wisdom, in love, in mercy. In His divine person, Jesus Christ has never known correction or change. He feels now as He has always felt about everyone and everything.

Jesus will not yield to those who charge that He is an absentee, that He is far away and unavailable. Our faith tells us that Jesus Christ is close at hand. JAF144-145

Holy Christ, I praise You today for being present with me and for never changing. Thank You for the work You have done for me and for the work You are doing in me. Amen.

AUGUST 15

He Never Stops Caring

While we were still sinners, Christ died for us.

—ROMANS 5:8

Jesus is our Lord and Savior. The best thing we know about Him is that He loves the sinner. He has always loved the outcast—and for that we should be glad, for we, too, were once outcasts. We are descended from that first man and woman who failed God and disobeyed. They were cast out of the garden, and God set in place a flaming sword to keep them from returning.

The greatest encouragement throughout the Bible is God's love for His lost race and the willingness of Christ, the eternal Son, to show forth that love in God's plan of redemption. The love of Jesus is so inclusive that it knows no boundaries. At the point where we stop caring and loving, Jesus is still there, loving and caring! JAF147

Lord Christ, thank You for loving me while I was far from You, sick and lost. I pray today that I would be filled with Your love so that I would act like You in this dark world, showing others how wonderful You are. Amen.

AUGUST 16

The Unselfishness of Christ

For you know the grace of our Lord Jesus Christ, that though he was rich, yet for your sake he became poor, so that you through his poverty might become rich.

—2 CORINTHIANS 8:9

Do you notice that Jesus Christ was completely unselfish and gave Himself? But how self-centered and self-indulgent most Christians are! . . . I'm sick in my own heart, sick about myself, sick about my friends, sick about the preachers and their ministry. How utterly self-centered we can become. We live for self, talk loudly about glorifying God and boast and say, "This is to the glory of God"—and yet we are self-centered. . . .

There's enough money, potentially, in the average congregation not only to keep the church going but to double the missionary offering. There would be enough—if we weren't so self-indulgent. Of course, a perfectly selfless Christ who gave Himself and poured Himself out and had no selfishness can't warm up to the Christian heart that is self-indulgent and self-centered. He loves us; He's our Shepherd; He's our Advocate above, who pleads our cause in heaven. We're His brethren in Christ and God His Father is our Father. But our selfishness prevents us from enjoying the fellowship, the sweetness that changes some people into saints while they walk on earth (and I mean *saint* in more than a technical sense). AOG147-148

Lord, You are completely selfless, and I want to be more like You. I know that true joy is found in giving myself away. Amen.

AUGUST 17

Let Us Move Forward

That you may be filled to the measure of all the fullness of God.
—EPHESIANS 3:19

The Apostle Paul's greatest desire was to always move forward in the knowledge and blessing of God. But some modern Bible teachers now call that kind of hunger and thirsting fanaticism, instead of desire for spiritual maturity.

These teachers assure the new Christian: "You are now complete in Christ. Just relax and be glad that there is nothing more you will ever need."

With great desire Paul wrote: "That I may win Christ" (Phil. 3:8)—and yet he already had Christ! With obvious longing he said: "[That I may] be found in Him" (3:9)—and yet he was already in Him!

Paul humbly and intensely breathed his great desire: "That I may know Him" (3:10)—even though he already knew Him!

Because he did not want to stand still, Paul testified: "I follow after, if that I may apprehend that for which also I am apprehended of Christ Jesus" (see 3:12).

It is very plain that the apostle had no other desire than to be completely available to God. Many of us refuse to follow his example! MWT257

Dear Lord, my prayer this morning is that You will satisfy my hunger to know You more and that You will use me to help advance Your kingdom. Amen.

AUGUST 18

At the Center

Here there is no Gentile or Jew, circumcised or uncircumcised, barbarian, Scythian, slave or free, but Christ is all, and is in all.
—COLOSSIANS 3:11

Jesus Christ is the center of the human race. With Him there are no favored races. We had better come to the point of believing that Jesus Christ is the Son of Man. He is not the Son of the first century nor the twentieth century. He is the Son of Man—not a Son of the Jewish race only. He is the Son of all races no matter what the color or tongue.

When Jesus Christ was incarnated in mortal flesh, He was not incarnated only in the body of the Jew, but in the body of the whole human race.

Go to Tibet or Afghanistan, to the Indians of South America, the Mohammedans of Arabia, the Englishmen of London, or the Scots of Glasgow and preach Jesus. If there is faith and willingness to follow, He will bring them all into His fellowship. They are all in the rim. They are all as near and all as far. That's the reason for the kind of missionary philosophy we hold. We do not first go into a country to educate the people and then preach Christ to them. We know better than that! We know that Jesus Christ is just as near to an uneducated, uncultured native as He is to a polished gentleman from New York or London. Christ is at the center of all cultural levels. TSII392-393

Lord Jesus, thank You for coming near to me. I pray that I would ever seek You and that I would never see myself as more favored than others. Amen.

AUGUST 19

"Born of God!"

He entered the Most Holy Place once for all by his own blood.
—HEBREWS 9:12

I think most of us remember with assurance the words of the Charles Wesley hymn which was his own personal testimony:

His Spirit answers to the blood,
And tells me I am born of God!

Wesley testified here and in many other hymns to an inner illumination!

When I became a Christian, no one had to come to me and tell me what Wesley meant. That is why Jesus taught that whosoever is willing to do His will shall have a revelation in his own heart. He shall have an inward revelation that tells him he is a child of God.

Too many persons try to make Jesus Christ a convenience. They reduce Him simply to a Big Friend who will help us when we are in trouble.

That is not biblical Christianity! Jesus Christ is Lord, and when an individual comes in repentance and faith, the truth flashes in. For the first time he finds himself saying, "I will do the will of the Lord, even if I die for it!" MWT098

Lord, I pray today for friends and family who may be questioning their relationship with You. Draw them to Yourself through Your Son, Heavenly Father. Amen.

AUGUST 20

The Love of Christ

For I am convinced that neither death nor life, neither angels nor demons, neither the present nor the future, nor any powers, neither height nor depth, nor anything else in all creation, will be able to separate us from the love of God that is in Christ Jesus our Lord.

—ROMANS 8:38–39

He so loved that He gave all. But how calculating so many of us are! We say, "Well, I can go to this meeting but I can't go to that one; the doctor has told me not to overdo it." So we have it all figured out. We put our spiritual life on a budget. We won't spend anything for God unless we can justify it in the columns of our budget. What a cheap, carnal way of living, and yet it's true—we do it! How narrow God's people are.

The love of the Lord Jesus Christ was a great, passionate, outpoured thing that caused Him to give Himself completely. It is said, "Christ pleased not himself" (Rom. 15:3). Even our Lord pleased not Himself. But do you know what is wrong with us? We are self-pleasers. We live for ourselves.

There are people who would buy a new car even if it meant their church went broke and had to close its doors. There are women who would dress in the latest style even if the mission cause died and every missionary had to be sent home. Yet we're saints, we're born-again, we're believers—we have our marked New Testament! AOG148-149

Lord Christ, forgive me for the ways in which I have followed You with reservation. Give me the desire and strength to commit all of myself to You, for You deserve nothing less. Amen.

AUGUST 21

Christ Made the World

God . . . has spoken to us by his Son . . .
through whom also he made the universe.
—HEBREWS 1:1–2

Think about the world into which our Lord Jesus Christ came—it is actually Christ's world!

Every section of this earth that we buy and sell and kick around and take by force of arms is a part of Christ's world. He made it all, and He owns it all.

Jesus Christ, the eternal Word, made the world. He made the very atoms of which Mary was made; the atoms of which His own body was made. He made the straw in the manger upon which He was laid as a newborn baby.

Let me digress here. I hear an occasional devotional exercise on the radio, in which the participants ask: "Mary, mother of God, pray for us!" It is only right that we should express our position based on the Word of God, and the truth is that Mary is dead and she is not the "mother of God."

Mary was the mother of that tiny babe, for God in His loving and wise plan of redemption used the body of the virgin Mary as the matrix to give the eternal Son a human body. We join in giving her proper honor when we refer to her as Mary, mother of Christ.
MWT186

Lord, help me and my loved ones make the appropriate choices to be excellent stewards of this world that You created for us to enjoy. Amen.

AUGUST 22

Jesus Knows All About You

Then Jesus came to them and said, "All authority in heaven and on earth has been given to me."
—MATTHEW 28:18

Have you ever heard one of our modern, Christian activists say, "I don't know when I will find a doctrine of the deeper life that is satisfactory to me!"

There is really only one answer to this kind of a quest—turn your eyes upon Jesus and commit yourself fully to Him because He is God and Christ, Redeemer and Lord, "the same yesterday, today and forever!"

In these matters of spiritual blessing and victory, we are not dealing with doctrines—we are dealing with the Lord of all doctrine! We are dealing with a Person who is the Resurrection and the Source from whom flows all doctrine and all truth.

How can we be so ignorant and so dull that we try to find our spiritual answers and the abounding life by looking beyond the only One who has promised that He would never change?

How can we so readily slight the Christ of God who has limitless authority throughout the universe?

How long should it take us to yield completely and without reservation to this One who has been made both Lord and Christ—and yet continues to be the very same Jesus who still loves us with an everlasting love?

The very same Jesus who knows all your troubles and weaknesses and sins, and loves you in spite of everything! EWT100

Lord Christ, I take comfort that You know everything about me. Thank You for Your love and continual care. Amen.

AUGUST 23

Always What We Need

Jesus Christ is the same yesterday and today and forever.
—HEBREWS 13:8

You and I are not always satisfied with the manner in which God deals with us. We would very much like to do something new, something different, something big and dramatic—but we are called back. For everything we need, we are called back to the simplicity of the faith, to the simplicity of Jesus Christ and His unchanging person.

The very same Jesus—a Brother who bears your image at the right hand of the Father, and who knows all your troubles and your weaknesses and sins, and loves you in spite of everything!

The very same Jesus—a Savior and Advocate who stands before the Father taking full responsibility for you and being easier to get along with than the nicest preacher you ever knew and being easier to approach than the humblest friend you ever had.

The very same Jesus—He is the sun that shines upon us, He is the star of our night. He is the giver of our life and the rock of our hope. He is our safety and our future. He is our righteousness, our sanctification, our inheritance. You find that He is all of this in the instant that you move your heart toward Him in faith. This is the journey to Jesus that must be made in the depths of the heart and being. This is a journey where feet do not count. TS626-627

That very same Jesus—who is Lord and Christ—is my Brother, my Savior, my Advocate, my hope, my life. Thank You for that astounding and humbling truth. Amen.

AUGUST 24

The Ethics of Jesus

You will be my witnesses.
—ACTS 1:8

The teachings of Jesus belong to the Church, not to society, for in society is sin, and sin is hostility to God!

Christ did not teach that He would impose His teachings upon the fallen world. He called His disciples to Him and taught them, and everywhere throughout His teachings there is the overt or implied idea that His followers will constitute an unpopular minority group in an actively hostile world.

The divine procedure is to go into the world of fallen men, preach to them the necessity to repent and become disciples of Christ and, after making disciples, to teach them "the ethics of Jesus," which Christ called "all things whatsoever I have commanded you" (Matt. 28:20).

The ethics of Jesus cannot be obeyed or even understood until the life of God has come to the heart of a man or woman in the miracle of the new birth.

The righteousness of the law is fulfilled in those who walk in the Spirit. Christ lives again in His redeemed followers the life He lived in Judea, for righteousness can never be divorced from its source, which is Jesus Christ Himself! MWT146

Lord, pour out Your Spirit upon our society today, that men and women will be convicted of sin and turn their lives over to You. Amen.

AUGUST 25

Our Chief Joy and Delight

Rejoice in the Lord and be glad, you righteous; sing, all you who are upright in heart!
—PSALM 32:11

I must agree with the psalmist, even in our modern day, that the joy of the Lord is still the strength of His people. I do believe that the sad world around us is attracted to spiritual sunshine—the genuine thing, that is! . . .

When the warmth and delight and joy of the Holy Spirit are in a congregation and the folks are just spontaneously joyful and unable to hide the happy grin, the result is a wonderful influence upon others. Conversely, the reason we have to search for so many things to cheer us up is the fact that we are not really joyful and contentedly happy within!

I admit that we live in a gloomy world and that international affairs, nuclear rumors and threats, earthquakes and riots cause people to shake their heads in despair and say, "What's the use?"

But we are Christians and Christians have every right to be the happiest people in the world! We do not have to look to other sources—for we look to the Word of God and discover how we can know the faithful God above and draw from His resources.

Why should the children of the King hang their heads and tote their own burdens, missing the mark about Christian victory? All this time the Holy Spirit has been wanting to make Jesus Christ our chief joy and delight! EWT095

Holy Spirit, make Christ the chief joy of my life! There is none like Him! Amen.

AUGUST 26

What Jesus' Manhood Means to Us

But when Christ came as high priest of the good things that are now already here, he went through the greater and more perfect tabernacle that is not made with human hands, that is to say, is not a part of this creation.

—HEBREWS 9:11

Let me review again what it means to us that Jesus was born into this world and lived among us. I once heard a preacher say that Jesus was man but not a man. I am convinced that Jesus was both man and a man. He had, in the most real sense, that substance and quality that is the essence of mankind. He was a man born of a woman.

Unless we understand this, I do not think we can be fully aware of what it means for Jesus to be representing us—a Man representing us at the right hand of the Majesty in the heavens. Suppose you and I were able right now to go to the presence of the Father. If we could see the Spirit, who is God, and the archangels and seraphim and strange creations out of the fire, we would see them surrounding the throne. But to our delight and amazement, we would see a Man there, human like we are—the Man Christ Jesus Himself! JMI008-009

Lord Christ, I praise You for becoming a man and making a way back to the Father! How amazing You are! Amen.

AUGUST 27

God's Final Word

In the past God spoke to our ancestors through the prophets at many times and in various ways, but in these last days he has spoken to us by his Son, whom he appointed heir of all things, and through whom also he made the universe.

—HEBREWS 1:1–2

We who have admitted Jesus Christ into our lives as Savior and Lord are happy indeed that we did so. In matters of health care, we are familiar with the custom of a "second opinion." If I go to a doctor and he or she advises me to have surgery, I can leave that office and consult with another specialist about my condition. Concerning our decision to receive Jesus Christ, we surely would have been ill-advised to go out and try to get a second opinion! Jesus Christ is God's last word to us. There is no other. God has headed up all of our help and forgiveness and blessing in the person of Jesus Christ, the Son.

In our dark day, God has given us Jesus as the Light of the world. Those who refuse Him give themselves over to the outer darkness that will prevail throughout the eternal ages. JMI022-023

Loving Father, I acknowledge that Your Son is Your final Word, Your fullest revelation. Keep me from looking outside Him for meaning and direction in my life. Amen.

AUGUST 28

We Get Around It

Now that I, your Lord and Teacher, have washed your feet, you also should wash one another's feet.

—JOHN 13:14

The lordship of Jesus is not quite forgotten among Christians, but it has been relegated to our hymnbook, where all responsibility toward it may be comfortably discharged in a glow of pleasant religious emotion.

The idea that the Man Christ Jesus has absolute and final authority over the whole church and over all its members in every detail of their lives is simply not accepted as true by the rank and file of evangelical Christians.

To avoid the necessity of either obeying or rejecting the plain instructions of our Lord in the New Testament, we take refuge in a liberal interpretation of them. We find ways to avoid the sharp point of obedience, comfort carnality and make the words of Christ of none effect. And the essence of it all is that "Christ simply could not have meant what He said." Dare we admit that His teachings are accepted even theoretically only after they have been weakened by "interpretation"? Dare we confess that even in our public worship, the influence of the Lord is very small? We sing of Him and preach about Him, but He must not interfere! MWT035

Dear Lord, I have to admit that there have been times when I have conveniently ignored the clear instructions of Your Word. Help me to give someone a cup of cold water—in Your name—today. Amen.

AUGUST 29

Decision of Action

Then he said to them all: "Whoever wants to be my disciple must deny themselves and take up their cross daily and follow me."
—LUKE 9:23

I think back to that time when God was dealing with the Israelites in bondage in Egypt. Suppose that Moses had said to the Israelites, "Do you accept the blood on the doorpost?"

They would have said, "Yes, of course. We accept the blood."

Moses then would have said, "That's fine. Now goodbye; I will be seeing you."

They would have stayed right in Egypt, slaves for the rest of their lives.

But their acceptance of the blood was a decision of action. Their acceptance of the blood of the Passover meant that they stayed awake all night; girded, ready, shoes on their feet, staffs in their hands, eating the food of the Passover, ready for the moving of God. Then, when the trumpet blasts sang sweet and clear, they all arose and started for the Red Sea. When they got to the Red Sea, having acted in faith, God was there to hold back the sea and they went out, never to return!

Their acceptance had the right kind of feet under it. Their acceptance gave them the guts to do something about it in the demonstration of their faith in God and His word. CES155-156

Lord Jesus, may I never accept You only in theory and not in practice. Give me the desire and ability to truly follow You, putting my faith into action. Amen.

AUGUST 30

The Reason for Hope

We have a building from God, an eternal house in heaven, not built by human hands.
—2 CORINTHIANS 5:1

The true Christian may safely look forward to a future state that is as happy as perfect love wills it to be! No one who has felt the weight of his own sin or heard from Calvary the Savior's mournful cry, "My God, my God, why hast thou forsaken me?" can ever allow his soul to rest on the feeble hope popular religion affords. He will—indeed, he must—insist upon forgiveness and cleansing and the protection the vicarious death of Christ provides.

"God has made him who knew no sin to be sin for us, that we might be made the righteousness of God in him." So wrote Paul, and Luther's great outburst of faith shows what this can mean in a human soul: "O Lord," cried Luther, "Thou art my righteousness, I am Thy sin!"

Any valid hope of a state of righteousness beyond the incident of death must lie in the goodness of God and the work of atonement accomplished for us by Jesus Christ on the cross. The deep, deep love of God is the fountain out of which flows our future beatitude, and the grace of God in Christ is the channel by which it reaches us! EWT053

Heavenly Father, thank You for the hope I have for eternal blessedness because of what Your Son has done. I praise You this day! Amen.

AUGUST 31

Sanctify the Ordinary

It teaches us to say "No" to ungodliness and worldly passions, and to live self-controlled, upright and godly lives in this present age.
—TITUS 2:12

How can we sanctify the ordinary and find true spiritual meaning in the common things of life? The answer has already been suggested. It is to consecrate the whole of life to Christ and begin to do everything in His name and for His sake. . . .

Vacate the throne room of your heart and enthrone Jesus there. Set Him in the focus of your heart's attention and stop wanting to be a hero. Make Him your all in all and try yourself to become less and less. Dedicate your entire life to His honor alone, and shift the motives of your life from self to God. Let the reason back of your daily conduct be Christ and His glory, not yourself, nor your family, nor your country, nor your church. In all things, let Him have the preeminence.

All this seems too simple to be true, but Scripture and experience agree to declare that it is, indeed, the way to sanctify the ordinary. "For Thy sake" will rescue the little, empty things from vanity and give them eternal meaning. The lowly paths of routine living will by these words be elevated to the level of a bright highway. The humdrum of our daily lives will take on the quality of a worship service, and the thousand irksome duties we must perform will become offerings and sacrifices acceptable to God by Christ Jesus. BAM082-084

Lord Christ, be enthroned on my heart today! May I live worthy of my calling as Your disciple. Amen.

SEPTEMBER

SEPTEMBER 1

A Bond of Compassion

Those who sow with tears will reap with songs of joy. Those who go out weeping, carrying seed to sow, will return with songs of joy, carrying sheaves with them.

—PSALM 126:5–6

The testimony of the true follower of Christ might well be something like this: The world's pleasures and the world's treasures henceforth have no appeal for me. I reckon myself crucified to the world and the world crucified to me. But the multitudes that were so dear to Christ shall not be less dear to me. If I cannot prevent their moral suicide, I shall at least baptize them with my human tears. I want no blessing that I cannot share. I seek no spirituality that I must win at the cost of forgetting that men and women are lost and without hope. If in spite of all I can do they will sin against light and bring upon themselves the displeasure of a holy God, then I must not let them go their sad way unwept. I scorn a happiness that I must purchase with ignorance. I reject a heaven that I must enter by shutting my eyes to the sufferings of my fellow men. I choose a broken heart rather than any happiness that ignores the tragedy of human life and human death.

Though I, through the grace of God in Christ, no longer lie under Adam's sin, I would still feel a bond of compassion for all of Adam's tragic race, and I am determined that I shall go down to the grave or up into God's heaven mourning for the lost and the perishing.

And thus and thus will I do as God enables me. Amen. NCA036

Lord Jesus, give me that broken heart as I interact with unsaved people in my ministry today. Amen.

SEPTEMBER 2

The Son Made the Sun

For in him all things were created: things in heaven and on earth, visible and invisible, whether thrones or powers or rulers or authorities; all things have been created through him and for him.
—COLOSSIANS 1:16

Our scientists explain to us how the sun daily gives us light, heat, and health, all the while providing energy and a variety of necessary elements that are absorbed into the earth. Then we dig and probe to release the oil, gas, and coal that the sun has helped to make. We put them in our combustion chambers so that our cars and trains and ships and planes can traverse the world.

John portrays the Man who made it all, the One whose face shines with the brilliance and energy of the sun. "The Man who made it all?" you ask, puzzled. Yes! Hear what the apostle Paul says of Jesus Christ: "[He] is the image of the invisible God, the firstborn of every creature: For by him were all things created, that are in heaven, and that are in earth, visible and invisible, whether they be thrones, or dominions, or principalities, or powers: all things were created by him, and for him" (Col. 1:15–16).

Some may doubt this fact, but for the gospel's sake—and because Scripture clearly states it—we must assert that they are wrong. We must stand up to those who would belittle Jesus Christ. We must take issue with those who question that John saw and tried to describe the eternity, the majesty, the glory, the power, and the final authority of Jesus Christ, our Lord. As for me, I am positive about this revelation God has given to His believing children! JIV042-043

Lord Christ, I believe that You created all things—and for Your glory! Increase my faith in You, and may I not look to the world for validation or wisdom. Amen.

SEPTEMBER 3

The Deeper Life

For whoever wants to save their life will lose it, but whoever loses their life for me will find it.

—MATTHEW 16:25

The deeper life must be understood to mean a life in the Spirit far in advance of the average and nearer to the New Testament norm. . . . To enter upon such a life, seekers must be ready to accept without question the New Testament as the one final authority on spiritual matters. They must be willing to make Christ the one supreme Lord and ruler in their lives. They must surrender their whole being to the destructive power of the cross, to die not only to their sins but to their righteousness as well as to everything in which they formerly prided themselves.

If this should seem like a heavy sacrifice for anyone to make, let it be remembered that Christ is Lord and can make any demands upon us that He chooses, even to the point of requiring that we deny ourselves and bear the cross daily. The mighty anointing of the Holy Spirit that follows will restore to the soul infinitely more than has been taken away. It is a hard way, but a glorious one. Those who have known the sweetness of it will never complain about what they have lost. They will be too well pleased with what they have gained.

TRC028, 030

O wonderful Savior, I want to be filled with Your Spirit! Enable me to fully embrace You and follow You with all my strength, that I may experience more of Your goodness. Amen.

SEPTEMBER 4

Christ's Beauty in Our Lives

To be made new in the attitude of your minds; and to put on the new self, created to be like God in true righteousness and holiness.

—EPHESIANS 4:23–24

God is faithful—He is never going to be done with us in shaping us and fashioning us as dear children of God until the day that we will see Him face-to-face!

Truly, in that gracious day, our rejoicing will not be in the personal knowledge that He saved us from hell, but in the joyful knowledge that He was able to renew us, bringing the old self to an end, and creating within us the new man and the new self in which can be reproduced the beauty of the Son of God!

In the light of that provision, I think it is true that no Christian is where he ought to be spiritually until that beauty of the Lord Jesus Christ is being reproduced in daily Christian life.

I admit that there is necessarily a question of degree in this kind of transformation of life and character.

Certainly there has never been a time in our human existence when we could look into our own being, and say: "Well, thank God, I see it is finished now. The Lord has signed the portrait. I see Jesus in myself!"

Nobody will say that—nobody!

Even though a person has become like Christ, he will not know it, because humility and meekness are also a part of the transformation of true godliness! ETW175

Heavenly Father, thank You for producing the beauty of Christ in my life and promising to complete that work at the resurrection. Amen.

SEPTEMBER 5

Few Lovers of His Cross

You need to persevere so that when you have done the will of God, you will receive what he has promised.
—HEBREWS 10:36

When God needs a person for His service—a good person, an effective person, a humble person—why does He most often turn to a person in deep trouble? Why does He seek out a person deep in the crucible of suffering, a person who is not the jovial, "happy-happy" kind? I can only say that this is the way of God with His human creation. . . .

Ezekiel did not come out of pleasant and favorable circumstances. The light had gone out in his heart. He probably thought that God takes a long time to work out His will.

Does not this same view surface in much of our Christian fellowship? We do not want to take the time to plow and to cultivate. We want the fruit and the harvest right away! We do not want to be engaged in any spiritual battle that takes us into the long night. We want the morning light right now! We do not want to go through the processes of planning and preparation and labor pains. We want the baby this instant! We do not want the cross. We are more interested in the crown.

The condition is not peculiar to our century. Thomas à Kempis wrote long ago, "The Lord has many lovers of His crown but few lovers of His cross." MMG114-115

Lord, make me a lover of Your cross as well as a lover of Your crown. Amen.

SEPTEMBER 6

The Transformed Life

Whoever does not take up their cross . . . is not worthy of me.
—MATTHEW 10:38

Many of the great evangelists who have touched the world for God, including such men as Jonathan Edwards and Charles Finney, have declared that the church is being betrayed by those who insist on Christianity being made "too easy."

Jesus laid down the terms of Christian discipleship, and there are some among us who criticize: "Those words of Jesus sound harsh and cruel."

This is where we stand: Receiving Jesus Christ into your life means that you have made an attachment to the person of Christ that is revolutionary, in that it reverses the life and transforms it completely! It is complete in that it leaves no part of the life unaffected. It exempts no area of the life of the total man.

By faith and through grace, you have now formed an exclusive relationship with your Savior, Jesus Christ. All of your other relationships are now conditioned and determined by your one relationship to your Savior.

To receive Jesus Christ, then, is to attach ourselves in faith to His holy person, to live or die, forever! He must be first and last and all!
MWT120

Lord, Your call upon my life is total. But there are times when I feel pulled in other directions that may not be pleasing to You. Give me grace and strength to keep You in first place in my life. Amen.

SEPTEMBER 7

Jesus Said He Was God

But about the Son he says, "Your throne, O God, will last for ever and ever; a scepter of justice will be the scepter of your kingdom."
—HEBREWS 1:8

The more we study the words of our Lord Jesus Christ when He lived on earth among us, the more certain we are about who He is.

Some critics have scoffed: "Jesus did not claim to be God. He only said He was the Son of Man."

It is true that Jesus used the term "Son of Man" frequently. But He testified boldly, even among those who were His sworn enemies, that He was God. He said with great forcefulness that He had come from the Father in heaven and that He was equal with the Father.

Bible-believing Christians stand together on this. They may differ about the mode of baptism, church polity, or the return of the Lord. But they agree on the deity of the eternal Son. Jesus Christ is of one substance with the Father—begotten, not created (Nicene Creed).

In our defense of this truth, we must be very careful and bold—belligerent, if need be!

Christ is the brightness of God's glory and the express image of God's Person! MWT046

Lord Jesus, the only hope the world has is that You are One with the Father. You are God Almighty! You are our Messiah! I worship You today. Amen.

SEPTEMBER 8

Alone with God

Then Jesus went up on a mountainside and sat down with his disciples.
—JOHN 6:3

Just prior to [His] miraculous multiplying of the bread and fish, Jesus "went up into a mountain, and there he sat with his disciples" (John 6:3). That fact is noteworthy. It seems plain that Jesus withdrew purposely from the great press of people who had been pursuing Him.

There are some things that you and I will never learn when others are present. I believe in church and I love the fellowship of the assembly. There is much we can learn when we come together on Sundays and sit among the saints. But there are certain things that you and I will never learn in the presence of other people.

Unquestionably, part of our failure today is religious activity that is not preceded by aloneness, by inactivity. I mean getting alone with God and waiting in silence and quietness until we are charged with God's Spirit. Then, when we act, our activity really amounts to something because we have been prepared by God for it. . . .

Now, in the case of our Lord, the people came to Him, John reports, and He was ready for them. He had been quiet and silent. . . . Looking upward, He waited until the whole hiatus of divine life moved down from the throne of God into His own soul. FBR130,133

Lord, I come in quietness and silence to wait for You to fill me. Amen.

SEPTEMBER 9

"I Will Not Forsake You!"

Surely I am with you always, to the very end of the age.
—MATTHEW 28:20

Men without God suffer alone and die alone in times of war and in other circumstances of life. All alone!

But it can never be said that any true soldier of the cross of Jesus Christ, no man or woman as missionary or messenger of the Truth has ever gone out to a ministry alone!

There have been many Christian martyrs—but not one of them was on that mission field all alone. Jesus Christ keeps His promise of taking them by the hand and leading them triumphantly through to the world beyond.

We can sum it up by noting that Jesus Christ asks us only to surrender to His lordship and obey His commands. When the Spirit of God deals with our young people about their own missionary responsibility, Christ assures them of His presence and power as they prepare to go: "All power is given unto Me! I am no longer in the grave. I will protect you. I will support you. I will go ahead of you. I will give you effectiveness for your witness and ministry. Go, therefore, and make disciples of all nations—I will never leave you nor forsake you!" MWT117

Thank You, Lord Jesus, that You are very near to me and my loved ones at all times. Amen.

SEPTEMBER 10

Out of His Fullness

Out of his fullness we have all received grace in place of grace already given.

—JOHN 1:16

Out of His fullness we have received. There is no way that it can mean that any of us have received all of His fullness. It means that Jesus Christ, the eternal Son, is the only medium through which God dispenses His benefits to His creation.

Because Jesus Christ is the eternal Son, because He is of the eternal generation and equal with the Father as pertaining to His substance, His eternity, His love, His power, His grace, His goodness, and all of the attributes of deity, He is the channel through which God dispenses all His blessing.

If you could ask the deer that goes quietly down to the edge of the lake for a refreshing drink, "Have you received of the fullness of the lake?" the answer would be: "Yes and no. I am full from the lake but I have not received from the fullness of the lake. I did not drink the lake. I only drank what I could hold of the lake."

And so, of His fullness, out of the fullness of God, He has given us grace upon grace according to our need, and it is all through Jesus Christ, our Lord. When He speaks, when He provides, while He sustains, it is because it can be said that He upholds all things by the Word of His power and in Him all things consist. CES027-028

Jesus, thank You for giving me all that I need. I pray that today I would be receptive to Your grace and that it would impact my life for Your glory and the good of the world. Amen.

SEPTEMBER 11

A Selfish Lust: Man's Desire for First Place

And when the centurion . . . saw how he died, he said, "Surely this man was the Son of God!"

—MARK 15:39

When we come to Christ we enter a different world. The New Testament introduces us to a spiritual philosophy infinitely higher than and altogether contrary to that which motivates the world. According to the teaching of Christ, the poor in spirit are blessed; the meek inherit the earth; the first are last and the last first; the greatest man is the one that best serves others and the one who loses everything is the only one that will have everything at last. The successful man of the world will see his hoarded treasures swept away by the tempest of judgment; the righteous beggar goes to Abraham's bosom and the rich man burns in the fires of hell.

Our Lord died an apparent failure, discredited by the leaders of established religion, rejected by society, and forsaken by His friends. The man who ordered Him to the cross was the successful statesman whose hand the ambitious hack politician kissed. It took the resurrection to demonstrate how gloriously Christ had triumphed and how tragically the governor had failed. The resurrection and the judgment will demonstrate before all worlds who won and who lost. We can wait! EWT093

Lord, this world tries to teach me to be first, when You call me to be last. May I be a servant today like You and experience more of Your goodness. Amen.

SEPTEMBER 12

Preach a Whole Christ

God is faithful, who has called you into fellowship with his Son, Jesus Christ our Lord.
—1 CORINTHIANS 1:9

I reject the human insistence among us that Christ may sustain a divided relationship toward us in this life.

I am aware that this is now so commonly preached that to oppose it or object to it means that you are sticking your neck out and you had best be prepared for what comes.

But, I am forced to ask: How can we insist and teach that our Lord Jesus Christ can be our Savior without being our Lord?

How can so many continue to teach that we can be saved without any thought of obedience to our Sovereign Lord?

I am satisfied in my own heart that when a man or a woman believes on the Lord Jesus Christ, he or she must believe on the whole Lord Jesus Christ—not making any reservation! How can a teaching be justified when it encourages sinners to use Jesus as a Savior in their time of need, without owing Him obedience and allegiance?

I believe we need to return to preaching a whole Christ to our needy world! MWT078

Heavenly Father, I humbly acknowledge Your saving grace in my life, and it is an honor to obey and serve You. Amen.

SEPTEMBER 13

Revolve Around Christ

Since, then, you have been raised with Christ, set your hearts on things above, where Christ is, seated at the right hand of God.
—COLOSSIANS 3:1

This kind of an attachment to the person of Christ means that Christ is not just one of several interests. It means that He is the one exclusive attachment as the sun is the exclusive attachment of the earth. As the earth revolves around the sun, and the sun is its center and the core of its being, so Jesus Christ is the Son of righteousness, and to become a Christian by the grace of God means to come into His orbit and begin to revolve around Him exclusively.

In the sense of spiritual life and desire and devotion, it means to revolve around Him completely, exclusively—not partly around Him.

This does not mean that we do not have other relationships—we all do because we all live in a complex world. You give your heart to Jesus. He becomes the center of your transformed life. But you may be a man with a family. You are a citizen of the country. You have a job and an employer. In the very nature of things, you have other relationships. But by faith and through grace, you have now formed an exclusive relationship with your Savior, Jesus Christ. All of your other relationships are now conditioned and determined by your one relationship to Jesus Christ, the Lord. CES158-159

Lord Jesus, may You be the center of my life! May I remove anything in my life that would keep You from being my all in all. Amen.

SEPTEMBER 14

How Do We Know Him?

I know whom I have believed.
—2 TIMOTHY 1:12

I must ask this question in the context of today's modern Christianity: "Is it not true that for most of us who call ourselves Christians there is no real experience?"

We have substituted theological ideas for an arresting encounter; we are full of religious notions, but our great weakness is that for our hearts there is no one there!

Whatever else it embraces, true Christian experience must always include a genuine encounter with God. Without this, religion is but a shadow, a reflection of reality, a cheap copy of an original once enjoyed by someone else of whom we have heard.

It cannot but be a major tragedy in the life of any man or woman to live in a church from childhood to old age and know nothing more real than some synthetic god compounded of theology and logic, but having no eyes to see, no ears to hear—and no heart to love! MWT253

O Lord, I pray for the people in churches who may think they are Christians because they were raised in a religious environment. What a tragedy it would be if these men and women are not truly saved. Lord, I pray for each one, that they will receive Christ into their hearts. Amen.

SEPTEMBER 15

The Answer to Our Sin

If we confess our sins, he is faithful and just and will forgive us our sins and purify us from all unrighteousness.

—1 JOHN 1:9

There is no question about man's sin—therefore there is no question about his being lost. A man is lost if he is not converted—overwhelmed in the vast darkness of emptiness!

Man was created to know God but he chose the gutter. That is why he is like a bird shut away in a cage or like a fish taken from the water. That is the explanation of man's disgraceful acts—war and hate, murder and greed, brother against brother!

Is there still a good word for man in his lost condition? Is there an answer for man in whom there is that instinctive groping and craving for the lost image and the knowledge of the Eternal Being?

Yes, the positive answer is in the Word of God, teaching the sinner-man that it is still possible for him to know God. It all has to do with forgiveness and grace and regeneration and justification in Jesus Christ! EWT362

Lord Jesus, I praise and thank You for providing salvation! Grant that I would proclaim the news of Your work all my days, that others would be reconciled to the Father. Amen.

SEPTEMBER 16

The Unchanging One

And surely I am with you always, to the very end of the age.
—MATTHEW 28:20

He is the same today as before He went away. He's the same Jesus Christ the Lord. And if you turn to Him now, as Mary turned to Him, as the rich young ruler turned to Him, as Jairus and many others turned to Him, He will fill you. . . .

If you turn to Him for clearer light, you'll find He is the same Jesus as when He gave the blind their sight—the very same Jesus. He'll feed you as He fed the multitude, He'll calm you as He calmed the sea. He'll bless you as He blessed the children. He'll forgive you as He forgave the woman that fell at His feet in her shame. He'll give you eternal life as He gave eternal life to His people. He'll wash you as He washed their feet, back there. He's the same! The God we preach is the same God, unchanging and unchangeable, forever and ever.

I recommend to you Jesus Christ, the unchanging One. I recommend to you God's answer to your questions, God's solution to your problems, God's life for your dying soul, God's cleansing for your sin-cursed spirit, God's rest for your restless mind, and God's resurrection for your dying body. For your advocate above, I recommend Him to you. You will find Him to be all He ever was—the very same Jesus.
AOGII110-111

Lord Christ, You are the same person who walked this earth 2,000 years ago. I place my trust in You and confidently ask that You would move mightily in my life. Amen.

SEPTEMBER 17

God Will Not Play Along with Adam

In your relationships with one another, have the same mindset as Christ Jesus.

—PHILIPPIANS 2:5

There is great need for us to learn the truths of the sovereignty of God and the Lordship of Christ. God will not play along with Adam; Christ will not be "used" by any of Adam's selfish brood.

We had better learn these things fast if this generation of young Christians is to be spared the supreme tragedy of following a Christ who is merely a Christ of convenience and not the true Lord of glory at all!

I confess to a feeling of uneasiness about this when I observe the questionable things Christ is said to do for people these days. He is often recommended as a wonderfully obliging but not too discriminating Big Brother who delights to help us to accomplish our ends, and who further favors us by forbearing to ask any embarrassing questions about the moral and spiritual qualities of those ends.

In our eagerness to lead men to "accept" Christ we are often tempted to present for acceptance a Christ who is little more than a caricature of "that holy thing" which was conceived by the Holy Ghost, born of the virgin Mary, to be crucified and rise the third day to take His place on the right hand of the Majesty in the heavens.

The whole purpose of God in redemption is to make us holy and to restore us to the image of God! To accomplish this, He disengages us from earthly ambitions and draws us away from the cheap and unworthy prizes that worldly men set their hearts upon. EWT066

Lord, I repent of the ways in which I have made You a convenience rather than submitting to Your Lordship. May I recognize You more for who You truly are. Amen.

SEPTEMBER 18

Both Lord and Christ

God has made this Jesus . . . both Lord and Messiah.

—ACTS 2:36

No Christian believer should ever forget what the Bible says about the Person and the offices of the eternal Son, the Christ of God.

"God hath made the same Jesus, whom ye have crucified, both Lord and Christ" (Acts 2:36). Jesus means Savior; Lord means Sovereign; Christ means Anointed One.

The Apostle Peter did not proclaim Jesus only as Savior—he preached to them Jesus as Lord and Christ and Savior, never dividing His Person or His offices.

Remember, also, the declaration of Paul: "If thou shalt confess with thy mouth the Lord Jesus . . . thou shalt be saved" (Rom. 10:9).

Three times in the passage to the Roman Christians telling how to be saved, Paul calls Jesus "Lord." He says that faith in the Lord Jesus plus confession of that faith to the world brings salvation to us! MWT047

Sovereign Lord, You are the One I choose to serve. Help me to meditate on this truth as I journey through some mundane tasks today. Amen.

SEPTEMBER 19

Life's Greatest Honor

Therefore God exalted him to the highest place and gave him the name that is above every name.
—PHILIPPIANS 2:9

The humblest man who heeds the call to follow Christ has an honor far above that given to any king or potentate, for the nations of the earth can bestow only such honor as they possess, while the honor of Christ is supreme over all. God has given Him a name that is above every name!

This being true and being known to the heavenly intelligences, the methods we use to persuade men to follow Christ must seem to them extremely illogical if not downright wrong.

Evangelical Christians commonly offer Christ to mankind as a nostrum to cure their ills, a way out of their troubles, a quick and easy means to the achievement of their personal ends. The message is often so presented as to leave the hearer with the impression that he is being asked to give up much to gain more. And that is not good, however well intentioned it may be! . . .

Salvation comes not by "accepting the finished work" or "deciding for Christ." It comes by believing on the Lord Jesus Christ, the whole, living, victorious Lord who, as God and man, fought our fight and won it, accepted our debt as His own and paid it, took our sins and died under them, and rose again to set us free. This is the true Christ, and nothing less will do! EWT188

Lord, forgive me for the ways in which I have looked to You as simply a cure for my ills and troubles rather than following You wholeheartedly in reverence and obedience. Grant that I would live victoriously in You this day. Amen.

SEPTEMBER 20

Intimacies of the Trinity

Now this is eternal life: that they know you, the only true God, and Jesus Christ, whom you have sent.
—JOHN 17:3

That's the consummation. The infinite Godhead invites us into Himself to share in all the intimacies of the Trinity. And Christ is the way in.

The moon and earth turn in such a way that we only see one side of the moon and never see the other. The eternal God is so vast, so infinite, that I can't hope to know all about God and all there is about God. But God has a manward side, just as the moon has an earthward side. Just as the moon always keeps that smiling yellow face turned earthward, so God has a side He always keeps turned manward, and that side is Jesus Christ. Jesus Christ is God's manward face. Earth's Godward side, Jesus, is the way God sees us. He always looks down and sees us in Jesus Christ. Then we go back to the quotation from Lady Julian: "Where Jesus appeareth the blessed Trinity is understood." AOG015-016

Father, thank You for sending Your Son to save me and to bring me into fellowship with You and the Holy Spirit. Thank You for seeing me as one who is in Christ. May I be ever grateful. Amen.

SEPTEMBER 21

God's Express Image

The Son is the image of the invisible God.
—COLOSSIANS 1:15

I wish I could comprehend everything that the inspired Word is trying to reveal in the statement that Jesus, the eternal Son, is the "brightness of his glory, and the express image of his person" (Heb. 1:3). This much I do know and understand: Jesus Christ is Himself God. As a believer and a disciple, I rejoice that the risen, ascended Christ is now my High Priest and intercessor at the heavenly throne.

The writer to the Hebrews commands our attention with this descriptive, striking language:

> [God] hath in these last days spoken unto us by his Son . . . Who being the brightness of his glory, and the express image of his person, and upholding all things by the word of his power. (1:2–3)

Nothing anywhere in this vast, complex world is as beautiful and as compelling as the record of the Incarnation, the act by which God was made flesh to dwell among us in our own human history. This Jesus, the Christ of God, who made the universe and who sustains all things by his powerful word, was a tiny babe among us. He was comforted to sleep when He whimpered in His mother's arms. Great, indeed, is the mystery of godliness. JMI034-035

Son of God, thank You for becoming one of us to redeem us! I bask in the mystery of Your incarnation and worship You, holy God. Amen.

SEPTEMBER 22

The Godhead—Forever One

Father, into your hands I commit my spirit.

—LUKE 23:46

When Christ Jesus died on that unholy, fly-infested cross for mankind, He never divided the Godhead! We are assured from the earliest church fathers that the Father in heaven, His eternal Son, and the Holy Ghost are forever One—inseparable, indivisible—and can never be anything else.

Not all of Nero's swords could ever cut down through the substance of the Godhead to cut off the Father from the Son.

It was Mary's son who cried out, "Why hast Thou forsaken me?" It was the human body which God had given Him. It was the sacrifice that cried—the lamb about to die! The Son of Man knew himself forsaken. God dumped that vast, filthy, slimy mass of human sin on the soul of the Savior—and then backed away.

Believe it that the ancient and timeless Deity was never separated. He was still in the bosom of the Father when He cried, "Into thy hands I commend my spirit" (Luke 23:46).

Little wonder that we are amazed and marvel every day at the wonder of the ancient theology of the Christian Church! MWT076

Lord, sometimes You are a mystery to my limited thinking. But how grateful I am that You were willing to bear my sin—and that of the whole human race—on the cross of Calvary. Amen.

SEPTEMBER 23

We Are Convinced

In the beginning was the Word, and the Word was with God, and the Word was God.

—JOHN 1:1

We live in a society where we cannot always be sure that traditional definitions still hold. But I stand where I always have stood. And the genuine believer, no matter where he may be found in the world, humbly but surely is convinced about the person and position of Jesus Christ. Such a believer lives with calm and confident assurance that Jesus Christ is truly God and that He is everything the inspired writer said He is. He is "the brightness of his glory, and the express image of his person" (Heb. 1:3). This view of Christ in Hebrews harmonizes with and supports what Paul said of Jesus when he described Him as "the image of the invisible God, the firstborn of every creature" (Col. 1:15), in whom "dwelleth all the fulness of the Godhead bodily" (2:9).

Bible-believing Christians stand together on this. They may have differing opinions about the mode of baptism, church polity, or the return of the Lord. But they agree on the deity of the eternal Son. Jesus Christ is of one Substance with the Father—begotten, not created (Nicene Creed). In our defense of this truth we must be very careful and very bold—belligerent, if need be. JMI035-036

Lord Jesus, I stand firm today in the truth that You are fully God and fully man! May I never depart from this glorious truth. Amen.

SEPTEMBER 24

True Beauty

Let the king be enthralled by your beauty; honor him, for he is your lord.

—PSALM 45:11

When are we going to raise up a crop of preachers who will begin to preach the perfection of God and tell the people what they ought to hear—that Jesus Christ was born of the Virgin Mary and suffered under Pontius Pilate to die and rise again? He rose that He might save us from the everlasting monstrosities, the uglinesses that are far from God, that are not God. He will bring us to the beauty that is God. He came to call us away from all evil, away from the deformity and eternal ugliness that is hell, and toward holiness, perfection, and eternal beauty.

Jesus Christ is God come to us, for "God was in Christ, reconciling the world unto himself" (2 Cor. 5:19). Oh, how beautiful is the thought that God came to us in that lowly manger bed! How beautiful that He came to us and walked among us! He came with our shape and form, bearing on Himself our humanity, that He might cleanse, purify, purge, remake, and restore us, in order to take us back with Him again to that place that is the perfection of beauty. AOG192

Father, thank You for sending Your Son to live among us and die on our behalf. I pray that I and all Christians would embrace and proclaim the wonderful news that is His death and resurrection. Amen.

SEPTEMBER 25

Christianity Is What Christ Says It Is

Set your minds on things above, not on earthly things.
—COLOSSIANS 3:2

No one who knows what the New Testament is about will worry over the charge that Christianity is "otherworldly." Of course it is—and that is precisely where its power lies!

Christianity, which is faith in Christ, trust in His promises, and obedience to His commandments, rests down squarely upon the person of Christ.

What He is, what He did and what He is doing—these provide a full guarantee that the Christian's hopes are valid.

Christianity is what Christ says it is. His power becomes operative toward us as we accept His words as final and yield our souls to believe and obey.

Christ is not on trial; He needs no character witnesses to establish His trustworthiness!

He came as the Eternal God in time's low tabernacle. He stands before no human tribunal, but all men stand before Him now and shall stand for judgment at the last. . . . When Christ arose from death and ascended into heaven He established forever three important facts, namely, that this world has been condemned to ultimate dissolution, that the human spirit persists beyond the grave, and that there is indeed a world to come! EWT079

You determine what Christianity is and what my life should look like, O Lord. I submit myself to You today. Amen.

SEPTEMBER 26

Jesus Is What God Is Like

If you really know me, you will know my Father as well. From now on, you do know him and have seen him.

—JOHN 14:7

Some are still asking, "What is God like?" God Himself has given us a final, complete answer. Jesus said, "he that hath seen me hath seen the Father" (John 14:9).

For those of us who have put our faith in Jesus Christ, the quest of the ages is over. Jesus Christ, the eternal Son, came to dwell among us, being "the brightness of his glory, and the express image of his person" (Heb. 1:3). For us, I say, the quest is over because God has now revealed Himself to us. What Jesus is, the Father is. Whoever looks on the Lord Jesus Christ looks upon all of God. Jesus is God thinking God's thoughts. Jesus is God feeling the way God feels. Jesus is God now doing what God does.

In John's Gospel, we have the record of Jesus telling the people of His day that He could do nothing of Himself. He said, "The Son can do nothing of himself, but what he seeth the Father do: for what things soever he doeth, these also doeth the Son likewise" (John 5:19). It was on the strength of such testimony that the Jewish leaders wanted to stone Him for blasphemy.

How strange it is that some of the modern cults try to tell us that Jesus Christ never claimed to be God. Yet those who heard Him 2,000 years ago wanted to kill Him on the spot because He claimed to be one with the Father. JMI043-044

Lord Christ, how marvelous it is that when I see You I see the Father! Grant by Your Spirit that I would see You more clearly today and draw nearer to the Father. Amen.

SEPTEMBER 27

Truth Is a Person

Then you will know the truth, and the truth will set you free.
—JOHN 8:31–32

Let me say boldly that it is not the difficulty of discovering truth, but the unwillingness to obey it, that makes it so rare among men.

Our Lord said, "I am . . . the Truth" (John 14:6). And again He said, "The Son of man is come to seek and to save that which was lost" (Luke 19:10). Truth, therefore, is not hard to find for the very reason that it is seeking us!

So we learn that Truth is not a thing for which we must search, but a Person to whom we must hearken! In the New Testament, multitudes came to Jesus for physical help, but only rarely did one seek Him out to learn the Truth. The whole picture in the Gospels is one of a seeking Savior, not one of seeking men.

The Truth was hunting for those who would receive it, and relatively few did, for "many are called, but few are chosen" (Matt. 22:14). MWT048

Thank You for this truth, Lord, that You came "to seek and to save that which was lost." I don't want to keep this truth tucked in my back pocket. Give me an opportunity to share Your good news with someone today. Amen.

SEPTEMBER 28

Bridging the Gulf

All this is from God, who reconciled us to himself through Christ and gave us the ministry of reconciliation.
—2 CORINTHIANS 5:18

Paul encouraged the Athenians by reminding them that God was not far from any one of them, that it was He in whom they lived and moved and had their being. Yet men think of Him as farther away than the farthest star. The truth is that He is nearer to us than we are to ourselves!

But how can the conscious sinner bridge the mighty gulf that separates him from God in living experience? The answer is that he cannot, but the glory of the Christian message is that Christ did! Through the blood of His cross He made peace that He might reconcile all things unto Himself: "And you, that were sometime alienated and enemies in your mind by wicked works, yet now hath he reconciled In the body of his flesh through death, to present you holy and unblameable and unreproveable in his sight" (Col. 1:21–22).

The new birth makes us partakers of the divine nature. There the work of undoing the dissimilarity between us and God begins. From there it progresses by the sanctifying operation of the Holy Spirit till God is satisfied.

That is the theology of it, but even the regenerated soul may somctimes suffer from the feeling that God is far from him. Put away the evil from you, believe, and the sense of nearness will be restored. God was never away in the first place! EWT176

Thank You, Father, for bridging the gulf between me and You by the work of Your Son. May I grow in gratitude for what You have done and proclaim Your goodness to all I encounter. Amen.

SEPTEMBER 29

Lord of the Angels

So he became as much superior to the angels as the name he has inherited is superior to theirs.

—HEBREWS 1:4

The writer of the letter to the Hebrews gives his readers a vivid, vital portrait of Jesus, the eternal Son. He knows their familiarity, through the Old Testament, with the concept and ministry of angels. He trades on that knowledge to point out the overwhelming superiority of the victorious Jesus as He ministers in the heavenly world above:

> And again, when he bringeth in the firstbegotten into the world, he saith, And let all the angels of God worship him. And of the angels he saith, Who maketh his angels spirits, and his ministers a flame of fire. But unto the Son he saith, Thy throne, O God, is for ever and ever: a sceptre of righteousness is the sceptre of thy kingdom. (Heb. 1:6–8)

In this revealing comparison between angels and the Messiah-Savior, Jesus Christ, we need to bear in mind that the ministries of angels were very well known and highly respected among the Jews. It should be of great significance to us, then, that the writer would assure them that Jesus our Lord is infinitely above and superior to the brightest angels who inhabit the kingdom of God. Never has there been a created angelic being of whom it could be said, as it was said of Christ, He is "the brightness of his glory, and the express image of his person" (1:3). JMI048

Lord Christ, there is none beside You! You are great and greatly to be praised! Be glorified in my life, Lord of creation. Amen.

SEPTEMBER 30

Infinite Love Poured Out

Who have been chosen according to the foreknowledge of God the Father, through the sanctifying work of the Spirit, to be obedient to Jesus Christ and sprinkled with his blood.

—1 PETER 1:2

We are surely aware that as human beings we can never know all of the Godhead. If we were capable of knowing all of the Godhead perfectly, we would be equal to the Godhead.

The early fathers in the church, in illustrating the Trinity, pointed out that God the eternal Father is an infinite God, and that He is love. The very nature of love is to give itself, but the Father could not give His love fully to anyone not fully equal to Himself. Thus we have the revelation of the Son Who is equal to the Father and of the eternal Father pouring out His love into the Son, Who could contain it, because the Son is equal with the Father!

Further, those ancient wise men reasoned, if the Father were to pour out His love on the Son, a medium of communication equal both to the Father and to the Son would be required, and this was the Holy Ghost! So we have their concept of the Trinity—the ancient Father in the fullness of His love pouring Himself through the Holy Ghost, Who is in being equal to Him, into the Son Who is in being equal to the Spirit and to the Father!

Thus, all that man can know of God and His love in this life is revealed in Jesus Christ. EWT099

Lord Christ, I praise You for revealing to the world the love that exists eternally between You and the Father and the Spirit. May that love fill my heart this day. Amen.

OCTOBER

OCTOBER 1

Healing Silence

After leaving them, he went up on a mountainside to pray.
—MARK 6:46

Very few of us know the secret of bathing our souls in silence. It was a secret our Lord Jesus Christ knew very well. There were times when He had to send the multitudes away so He could retire alone into the silence of the mountainside. There He would turn the God-ward side of His soul toward heaven and for a long time expose Himself to the face of His Father in heaven. . . .

My eyes and ears and spirit are aware of the immaturities in the so-called evangelicalism of our time. The more noise we make, the more we advertise, the more bells we jingle, the happier we seem to be. All of the signs of immaturity are among us.

We are seeing a general abhorrence of being alone, of being silent before the Lord. We shrink from allowing our souls to be bathed in the healing silences. MMG103-104

Father, grant that we might not forsake the quest for solitude and silence until we have really mastered this discipline, no matter how busy our lives continue to be. Amen.

OCTOBER 2

Seek the Full Anointing

Your throne, O God, will last for ever and ever;
a scepter of justice will be the scepter of your kingdom.
You have loved righteousness and hated wickedness;
therefore God, your God, has set you above your companions
by anointing you with the oil of joy.
—HEBREWS 1:8–9

I am happy to tell everyone that the power of the Spirit is glad power! Our Savior, Jesus Christ, lived His beautiful, holy life on earth and did His healing, saving deeds of power in the strength of this oil of gladness.

We must admit that there was more of the holy oil of God on the head of Jesus than on your head or mine—or on the head of anyone else who has ever lived. That is not to say that God will withhold His best from anyone. But the Spirit of God can only anoint in proportion to the willingness He finds in our lives. In the case of Jesus, we are told that He had a special anointing because He loved righteousness and hated iniquity. That surely gives us the clue we need concerning the kind of persons we must be in order to receive the full anointing and blessing from Almighty God. JMI064

Lord God, I earnestly desire the full anointing of Your Spirit in my life, that I might be more like Christ. Empower me to love righteousness and hate iniquity. Amen.

OCTOBER 3

More Than Just the Bible

The Word became flesh and made his dwelling among us.
—JOHN 1:14

Christian believers make a great mistake when they refer only to the Bible as the Word of God.

True, the inspired Bible is the Word of God speaking to our hearts and to our souls. But in referring to the Word of God, we do not mean just the book—printed pages sewed together with nylon thread. Rather, we mean the eternal expression of the mind of God. We mean the world-filling breath of God!

God's Word and God's revelation are much more than just the Old and New Testament books. . . . God's Word is the revelation of divine truth that God Himself has given to us. It has come in the message and appeal of the sacred Scriptures. It comes in the conviction visited on us by the Holy Spirit. It comes in the person of Jesus Christ, God's Son, the living Word of God. JMI072-073

Heavenly Father, thank You for revealing Yourself in the Scriptures and ultimately in Your Son Jesus Christ. May I embrace Your Word—both written and living—and grow closer to You. Amen.

OCTOBER 4

Coming at Night

Now there was a Pharisee, a man named Nicodemus who was a member of the Jewish ruling council. He came to Jesus at night.
—JOHN 3:1–2

It is plain enough that Nicodemus came to Jesus by night—and that has resulted in a great deal of abuse being heaped on his memory throughout the centuries. But he came feeling his way. He came inquiring. He came asking questions. From our vantage point in time, we believe that he was spiritually sensitive and that he was seeking answers about the things of God which he himself did not know.

Let me tell you what his coming to Jesus suggests to me. It suggests that the soul of man is too nobly conceived and too highly born and too mighty and mysterious a universe in itself ever to be satisfied with anything less than Jesus the Christ, the eternal Son of God.

His coming to Jesus suggests that only Jesus Christ is enough; only in Jesus Christ are there adequate answers to the questions men have always asked about God and eternity, of life, forgiveness, and blessing.

I can stand and assure you without any embarrassment that no matter who you are, either now or later in your life or at death or in the world to come, you will find that only Jesus Christ is enough.
CES131-132

Dear Jesus, may I see that You are enough, that only in You are there adequate answers to all my questions. Give me strength to point others to You, that they may find the answers to all their questions. Amen.

OCTOBER 5

Christ Will Rule

May your whole spirit, soul and body be kept blameless at the coming of our Lord Jesus Christ.
—1 THESSALONIANS 5:23

I am not surprised that I still meet people who do not believe that Jesus Christ is going to return to earth. In fact, some of them, armed with their own Bibles and interpretations, are insistent on setting me "straight."

One gentleman has written saying that I have it all wrong, and that Paul did not mean what I had said he meant, as I applied Paul's statement to everyday life.

I took time to write a reply: "When it comes to saying what he meant, Paul's batting average has been pretty good up to now. So, I will string along with what Paul plainly, clearly said."

I did not figure I needed someone to straighten me out—particularly someone who had decided the Bible does not mean what it says.

No one is going to argue me out of my faith in what God has revealed and what God has said. As far as I am concerned, it is a fact that Jesus is coming again! The question I do raise is this: Are we prepared spiritually for His coming? Are we tolerating conditions in our midst that will cause us embarrassment when He does come? MWT038

Dear Lord, grant me courage to live today—indeed, every day of my life—as though You were coming back this afternoon. Amen.

OCTOBER 6

Beauty Centers Around Christ

One thing I ask from the LORD, this only do I seek: that I may dwell in the house of the LORD all the days of my life, to gaze on the beauty of the LORD and to seek him in his temple.

—PSALM 27:4

All beauty centers around Jesus Christ. That is why, apart from the commercialism, Christmas is such a beautiful thing. And that is why Easter is so beautiful. To me, Easter is more beautiful than Christmas because Easter celebrates a triumph, and Christmas celebrates the coming of Someone who hadn't yet fought. He had been born to fight, but He hadn't fought. But when Easter comes, we sing, "The three sad days are quickly sped; He rises glorious from the dead." And there's beauty there, though not the beauty of color, outline, or physical proportion. You can worship Him in a stable; you can worship Him in a coal mine; you can worship Him in a factory.

It's not the external beauty that is beautiful but the internal beauty. Heaven is beautiful because it is the expression of that which is the perfection of beauty. And while that is true of heaven, I must also say that hell is the place of unrelieved, monstrous ugliness, because there is no perfection; there is only monstrous moral deformity. There is nothing beautiful in hell. And in heaven, of course, there is supreme beauty.

Earth lies halfway between. Earth knows ugliness and beauty; it's halfway between heaven and hell. And the inhabitants of earth must decide whether they are to seek the beauty of heaven or the monstrous, unrelieved ugliness of hell. AOG190-191

Lord Jesus, You are the definition and picture of true beauty! May I stand in awe of Your majesty and make it known in my life today. Amen.

OCTOBER 7

His Cross Is My Cross

The student is not above the teacher, nor a servant above his master.
—MATTHEW 10:24

To take Jesus Christ into your life without reservation is to accept His friends as your friends and to know that His enemies will be your enemies! It means that we accept His rejection as our rejection. We knowingly accept His cross as our cross.

If you then find yourself in an area where Christ has no friends, you will be friendless—except for the one Friend who will stick closer than a brother. I made up my mind a long time ago. Those who declare themselves enemies of Jesus Christ must look upon me as their enemy, and I ask no quarter from them! And if they are friends of Christ, they are my friends—and I do not care what color they are or what denomination they belong to.

If the preachers would faithfully tell the people what it actually means to receive Christ and obey Him and live for Him, we would have fewer converts backsliding and foundering.

Preachers who are not faithful one day will stand before the judgment seat of Christ and answer to a faithful Savior why they betrayed His people in this way! MWT176

Lord, I pray that You will send encouragement to Your children today who live and/or serve in an area where Christ is not formally welcome. Amen.

OCTOBER 8

How to Be Christlike

But when he, the Spirit of truth, comes . . . He will glorify me because it is from me that he will receive what he will make known to you.

—JOHN 16:13–14

If we are going to reproduce Christ on earth and be Christ-like and show forth Christ, what is our greatest need? We must have the Spirit of Christ!

If we are going to be the children of God, we must have the Spirit of the Father to breathe in our hearts and breathe through us. That is why we must have the Spirit of God! That is why the church must have the Spirit of Christ!

The Christian church is called to live above her own ability. She is called to live on a plane so high that no human being can live like that of his own ability and power. The humblest Christian is called to live a miracle, a life that is a moral and spiritual life with such intensity and such purity that no human being can do it—only Jesus Christ can do it. He wants the Spirit of Christ to come to His people—an invasion from above affecting us mentally, morally, and spiritually!

The Holy Spirit brings the wonderful mystery that is God to us, and presents Him to the human spirit. The Spirit is our Teacher, and if He does not teach us, we never can know. He is our Illuminator, and if He does not turn on the light, we never can see. He is the Healer of our deaf ears, and if He does not touch our ears, we never can hear!

The Holy Ghost bestows upon us a beatitude beyond compare. He asks nothing except that we be willing to listen, willing to obey! EWT045

O Christ, fill me with Your Spirit this day, that I may be conformed to Your likeness and walk above my own ability. Amen.

OCTOBER 9

"Accepting Christ"

We also boast in God through our Lord Jesus Christ, through whom we have now received reconciliation.

—ROMANS 5:11

How can any man or woman, lost and undone, sinful and wretched, alienated from God, stand there and intimate that the death and resurrection of Jesus Christ and God's revealed plan of salvation do not take priority over some of life's other decisions?

Now, the particular attitude revealed here about "accepting Christ" is wrong because it makes Christ stand hat-in-hand, somewhere outside the door, waiting on our human judgment.

We know about His divine Person, we know that He is the Lamb of God who suffered and died in our place. We know all about His credentials. Yet we let Him stand outside on the steps like some poor timid fellow who is hoping he can find a job.

We look Him over, then read a few more devotional verses, and ask: "What do you think, Mabel? Do you think we ought to accept Him? I really wonder if we should accept Him."

And so, in this view, our poor Lord Christ stands hat-in-hand, shifting from one foot to another looking for a job, wondering whether He will be accepted.

Meanwhile, there sits the proud Adamic sinner, rotten as the devil and filled with all manner of spiritual leprosy and cancer. But he is hesitating; he is judging whether or not he will accept Christ. CES145-146

Lord Jesus, forgive me for the ways in which I have looked at You and debated whether I will fully accept You. Make me who You want me to be, so that You would accept me before Your Father in Heaven. Amen.

OCTOBER 10

Jesus Asks Us to Love the Unlovely

No one has ever seen God; but if we love one another, God lives in us and his love is made complete in us.

—1 JOHN 4:12

In his earthly ministry, our Lord Jesus loved babies, publicans, harlots, and sick people—and He loved them spontaneously and individually!

The person who claims to follow Christ cannot afford to do otherwise.

A peril always confronting the minister is that he may come unconsciously to love religious and philosophic ideas rather than saints and sinners. It is altogether possible to feel for the world of lost men the same kind of detached affection that the naturalist Fabre, say, felt for a hive of bees or a hill of black ants. They are something to study, to learn from, possibly even to help, but nothing to weep over or die for!

Where this attitude prevails it soon leads to a stilted and pedantic kind of preaching. The minister assumes that his hearers are as familiar with history, philosophy, and theology as he is, so he indulges in learned allusions, makes casual references to books and writers wholly unknown to the majority of people who listen to him, and mistakes the puzzled expression on the faces of his parishioners for admiration of his brilliance!

Why religious people continue to put up with this sort of thing, as well as to pay for it and support it, is beyond me. I can only add it to the long list of things I do not and probably never will understand. EWT374

Lord Jesus, help me today to love others as You have loved them, spontaneously and individually, that they would know Your goodness and You would be glorified. Amen.

OCTOBER 11

The Model Man

We are more than conquerors through him who loved us.
—ROMANS 8:37

Jesus is not said to be the victorious God—God is always victorious. How could the sovereign God be anything but victorious? Rather, we take our position with those earliest Christian believers who saw in Jesus a Man in the heavenlies. He is a victorious man, and if we are in Him, we too can be victorious.

Through the new birth, the miracle of regeneration, we have been brought by faith into the kingdom of God. As Christians we should recognize that our nature has been joined to God's nature in the mystery of the incarnation. Jesus has done everything He can to make His unbelieving people see that we have the same place in the heart of God that He Himself has. He does so not because we are worthy of it, but because He is worthy and He is the Head of the Church. He is the representative Man before God, representing us.

Jesus is the Model Man after which we are patterned in our Christian faith and fellowship. That is why He will not let us alone. He is determined that we will have eyes to see more than this world around us. He is determined that we will have eyes of faith to see God in the kingdom of heaven, and Himself—our Man in glory—seated there in victorious control! JMI080-081

Lord Christ, You are the victorious one! Grant that I would be conformed to Your image and walk in Your victory today. Amen.

OCTOBER 12

Question: How Much More Could I Have Done?

They all gave out of their wealth; but she, out of her poverty, put in everything—all she had to live on.

—MARK 12:44

While Christ was the perfect example of the healthy, normal man, He yet did not live a normal life. He sacrificed many pure enjoyments to give Himself to the holy work of moral rescue. His conduct was determined not by what was legitimate or innocent, but by our human need. He pleased not Himself but lived for the emergency; and as He was, so are we in this world!

It is in view of this that all our Christian service must be evaluated.

My old friend Tom Haire, the praying plumber, told me one day that he was going back home for a rest. "I am preached out," he said, "and I must wait on the Lord. There are some spiritual matters that I want to get straightened out. I want to appear before the judgment seat now while I can do something about it!" EWT061

Heavenly Father, grant by Your Spirit that I may follow the example of Christ, who came to serve and not to be served. Amen.

OCTOBER 13

Attachment to Christ

Therefore, if anyone is in Christ, the new creation has come:
The old has gone, the new is here!
—2 CORINTHIANS 5:17

I want to give you a definition for accepting Christ. To accept Christ in anything like a saving relation is to have an attachment to the person of Christ that is revolutionary, complete and exclusive.

What I am talking about is an attachment to the person of Christ, and that is so important. It is something more than getting in with a crowd that you like. . . . Accepting Jesus Christ is more than finding association with a group you like. It is not just going on a picnic or taking a hike. We have those activities in our church and I believe in them. But they are not the things that are as important as your acceptance of Jesus Christ. The answer you are seeking in Jesus Christ does not mean that you are just getting in with a religious group who may not be any better off than you are.

Accepting Jesus Christ, receiving Jesus Christ into your life means that you have made an attachment to the person of Christ that is revolutionary in that it reverses the life and transforms it completely.

It is an attachment to the person of Christ. It is complete in that it leaves no part of the life unaffected. It exempts no area of the life of the total man; his total being. CES157-158

Jesus, You are Lord of my life! Transform it completely to the glory of Your name. Amen.

OCTOBER 14

Bruised for Our Iniquities

He was pierced for our transgressions, he was crushed for our iniquities.

ISAIAH 53:5

The word *iniquity* is not a good word—and God knows how we hate it! But the consequences of iniquity cannot be escaped.

The prophet reminds us clearly that the Saviour was bruised for our iniquities.

We deny it, and say "No!" but the fingerprints of all mankind are plain evidence against us—the fingerprints of man found in every dark cellar and in every alley and in every dimly lighted evil place throughout the world. God knows man from man, and it is impossible to escape our guilt and place our moral responsibility upon someone else.

For our iniquities and our transgressions He was bruised and wounded—and Israel's great burden and amazing blunder was her judgment that this wounded one on the hillside beyond Jerusalem was being punished for His own sin!

The prophet foresaw this historic error in judgment, and he himself was a Jew, saying: "We thought He was smitten of God. We thought that God was punishing Him for His own iniquity for we did not know then that God was punishing Him for our transgressions and our iniquities."

For our sakes, He was profaned by ignorant and unworthy men!

EWT115

Lord Christ, I praise and thank You for suffering for my sake, for bearing my sins and iniquities. May I walk holy and upright today as one who has been forgiven and redeemed. Amen.

OCTOBER 15

God Cannot Love Sin

For you are not a God who is pleased with wickedness;
with you, evil people are not welcome.
—PSALM 5:4

The goodness of God means He cannot feel indifferent about anything. People are indifferent, but not God. God either loves with a boundless unremitting energy or He hates with consuming fire. It was said about the second person of the Trinity, "Thou hast loved righteousness, and hated iniquity; therefore God, even thy God, hath anointed thee with the oil of gladness above thy fellows" (Heb. 1:9). The same Lord Jesus that loved with boundless consuming love also hated with terrible consuming fire and will continue to do so while the ages roll. The goodness of God requires that God cannot love sin. . . .

Why would God the Eternal Son bleed for us? The answer is, out of His goodness and lovingkindness. "Therefore the children of men put their trust under the shadow of thy wings" (Ps. 36:7). Why would God forgive me when I've sinned and then forgive me again and again? Because God out of His goodness acts according to that goodness and does what His loving heart dictates that He do. AOG45

Holy Father, forgive me for the ways in which I have felt indifferent about sin. May I, like Your Son, love righteousness and hate iniquity, so that You would be glorified in my life. Amen.

OCTOBER 16

Words and Deeds

In my former book, Theophilus, I wrote about all that Jesus began to do and to teach until the day he was taken up to heaven, after giving instructions through the Holy Spirit to the apostles he had chosen.

—ACTS 1:1–2

Modern Christians are long on talk and short on conduct. We use the language of power but our deeds are the deeds of weakness.

Our Lord and His apostles were long on deeds. The gospels depict a Man walking in power, "who went about doing good, and healing all that were oppressed of the devil; for God was with him."

The moral relationship between words and deeds appears quite plainly in the life and teachings of Christ. . . .

Since in one of its aspects religion contemplates the invisible, it is easy to understand how it can be erroneously made to contemplate the unreal. The praying man talks of that which he does not see, and fallen human minds tend to assume that what cannot be seen is not of any great importance and probably not even real, if the truth were known.

So religion is disengaged from practical life and retired to the airy region of fancy where dwell the sweet insubstantial nothings which everyone knows do not exist but which they nevertheless lack the courage to repudiate publicly.

I could wish that this were true only of pagan religions; but candor dictates that I admit it to be true also of much that passes for evangelical Christianity. EWT291

Holy God, grant that I would embrace the teachings of Christ and excel in deeds more than in lofty speech. Amen.

OCTOBER 17

Decide for Themselves

Then Jesus said to his disciples, "Whoever wants to be my disciple must deny themselves and take up their cross and follow me."

—MATTHEW 16:24

There is a strange beauty in the ways of God with men. He sends salvation to the world in the person of a Man and sends that Man to walk the busy ways saying, "If any man will come after me." No drama, no fanfare, no tramp of marching feet or tumult of shouting. A kindly Stranger walks through the earth, and so quiet is His voice that it is sometimes lost in the hurly-burly; but it is the last voice of God, and until we become quiet to hear it we have no authentic message. He bears good tidings from afar but He compels no man to listen. "If any man will," He says, and passes on. Friendly, courteous, unobtrusive, He yet bears the signet of the King. His word is divine authority, His eyes a tribunal, His face a last judgment.

"If any man will come after me," He says, and some will rise and go after Him, but others give no heed to His voice. So the gulf opens between man and man, between those who will and those who will not. Silently, terribly the work goes on, as each one decides whether he will hear or ignore the voice of invitation. Unknown to the world, perhaps unknown even to the individual, the work of separation takes place. Each hearer of the Voice must decide for himself, and he must decide on the basis of the evidence the message affords. TRC153-154

Lord, thank You for Your simple, quiet invitation. It is the most important call in all the world. May I respond to it today with my whole being. Amen.

OCTOBER 18

Blessed Humility

Those who humble themselves will be exalted.
—LUKE 14:11

Watch out, Christian brothers and sisters, for the danger of arrogance, in assuming that you are somebody, indeed!

God will never let you high-hat somebody else if you are a Christian. He loves you far too much to let you get away with that.

You may ask: "What will the Lord do, then, if I get arrogant and presumptuous, full of pride over my victories and successes?"

Well, the Lord will remind you of His own example, and will rebuke and chasten you in His own way.

Our Lord Jesus Christ would not allow any success or temporary honor to lead Him astray.

The Lord had no servants. He bossed no one around. He was the Lord, but He never took the tyrannical attitude toward anyone.

I think it is very good spiritual advice that we should never tie ourselves up to public opinion and never consider any honors we may receive as being due us because of our superior gifts.

In that day of the triumphal entry into Jerusalem, the crowd acclaimed Him and cried, "Hosanna!" but on the very next Friday they joined in the shout, "Crucify him!" Humility is a blessed thing if you can find it. Early church fathers wrote that if a man feels that he is getting somewhere in the kingdom of God, that's pride—and until that dies, he is getting nowhere! EWT216

Heavenly Father, grant me strength and grace today to walk in the steps of Your Son, that I would be humble like Him. Amen.

OCTOBER 19

My Kingdom Go

Your kingdom come, your will be done, on earth as it is in heaven.
—MATTHEW 6:10

It may surprise you that Aldous Huxley, often a critic of orthodox and evangelical Christianity, has been quoted as saying: "My kingdom go is the necessary corollary to Thy kingdom come." . . .

Certainly His kingdom can never be realized in my life until my own selfish kingdom is deposed. It is when I resign, when I am no longer king of my domain that Jesus Christ will become king of my life.

Now, in confession, may I assure you that a Christian clergyman cannot follow any other route to spiritual victory and daily blessing than that which is prescribed so plainly in the Word of God. It is one thing for a minister to choose a powerful text, expound it, and preach from it—it is quite something else for the minister to honestly and genuinely live forth the meaning of the Word from day to day. A clergyman is a man—and often he has a proud little kingdom of his own, a kingdom of position and often of pride and sometimes with power. Clergymen must wrestle with the spiritual implications of the crucified life just like everyone else, and to be thoroughgoing men of God and spiritual examples to the flock of God, they must die daily to the allurements of their own little kingdoms of position and prestige.

WPJ173-174

Lord, I quit, I resign, I'm no longer "king of my domain." I die to "my own little kingdom of position and prestige." Christ, You are the true King. Reign in my life! Amen.

OCTOBER 20

Celebration of His Person

This is my body given for you; do this in remembrance of me.
—LUKE 22:19

Surely Jesus was identified with us. Everything He did was for us; He acted in our stead. He took our guilt. He gave us His righteousness. In all that Jesus did on earth, He acted for us because by His incarnation He identified Himself with the human race. In His death and resurrection He identified Himself with the redeemed human race.

As a blessed result, whatever He is we are. Where He is, potentially His people are. What He is, potentially His people are—only His deity excepted. . . .

Jesus Christ, our Lord, has acceptance at the throne of God. Although once "rejected by," He is now "accepted at"! The bitter rejection has turned into joyous acceptance. And the same is true for His people. Through Him we died. Identified with Him, we live. And in our identification with Him we are accepted at the right hand of God the Father.

The Lord's table, the Communion, is more than a picture on a wall, more than a set of beads reminding us of Jesus Christ and His death. It is a celebration of His person—a celebration in which we gladly join because we do remember Him. By it we testify to each other and to the world of Jesus' sacrificial, conquering death—until He comes! TRC075-076

Lord Jesus, how wonderful is the exchange You have set in place! You became one of us so that we might become like You. You took on our sin and gave us Your righteousness. All our poverty You took upon Yourself so that we might be made rich in You. And in Your death, we are made alive! I praise You, Lord! Amen.

OCTOBER 21

Our Anchor in the Storm

For who is God besides the LORD? And who is the Rock except our God?
—PSALM 18:31

We are in the midst of the storm of life. The believing saints of God are on board the ship. Someone looks to the horizon and warns, "We are directly in the path of the typhoon! We are as good as dead. We will surely be dashed to pieces on the rocks!"

But calmly someone else advises, "Look down, look down! We have an anchor!" We look, but the depth is too great. We cannot see the anchor. But the anchor is there. It grips the immovable rock and holds fast. Thus the ship outrides the storm.

The Holy Spirit has assured us that we have an Anchor, steadfast and sure, that keeps the soul. Jesus—Savior, Redeemer, and our great High Priest—is that Anchor. He is the One who has gone before us. He has already entered into the calm and quiet harbor, the inner sanctuary behind the curtain.

Where Jesus is now, there we will be—forever. The Spirit is saying to us, "Keep on believing. Pursue holiness. Show diligence and hold full assurance of faith to the very end. Follow those who through faith and patience inherit what has been promised. "He is faithful!"

JMI091-092

Lord Christ, You are my anchor in the storm of life. May I remain steadfast in my journey and faithfully serve You all my days. Amen.

OCTOBER 22

Christ's World of Nature

Then the devil left him, and angels came and attended him.
—MATTHEW 4:11

Jesus Christ came into our world in the fullness of time, and His own world, the world of nature, received Him, even though His own people received Him not!

It is my own feeling that when Jesus came, all of nature went out to greet Him. The star led the wise men from the East. The cattle in the stable stall in Bethlehem did not bother Him. His own things in created nature received Him.

Dr. G. Campbell Morgan believed that when Jesus went into the wilderness to be tempted of the devil, He was there with the wild beasts for forty days and nights. Dr. Morgan held that there had been a wrong conception, as if Jesus needed angelic protection from the animals.

Jesus was perfectly safe there. He was nature's Creator and Lord. Jesus was in total harmony with nature, and I am of the opinion that the deeper our Christian commitment becomes, the more likely we will find ourselves in tune and in harmony with the natural world around us! MWT398

Dear Lord, many people love nature, but they don't yet acknowledge the One who created it and sustains it. Lord, do something to impress upon those people that there had to be a Master Designer who set the physical world in motion. Amen.

OCTOBER 23

Take the Narrow Way

I say this because many deceivers, who do not acknowledge Jesus Christ as coming in the flesh, have gone out into the world.
—2 JOHN 1:7

Deception has always been an effective weapon and is deadliest when used in the field of religion.

Our Lord warned against this when He said, "Beware of false prophets, which come to you in sheep's clothing, but inwardly they are ravening wolves." These words have been turned into a proverb known around the world, and still we continue to be taken in by the wolves. There was a time, even in the twentieth century, when a Christian knew, or at least could know, where he stood. The words of Christ were taken seriously. A man either was or was not a believer in New Testament doctrine. Clear, sharp categories existed. Black stood in sharp contrast to white; light was separated from darkness; it was possible to distinguish right from wrong, truth from error, a true believer from an unbeliever. Christians knew that they must forsake the world, and there was for the most part remarkable agreement about what was meant by the world. It was that simple. The whole religious picture has changed. Without denying a single doctrine of the faith, multitudes of Christians have nevertheless forsaken the faith. Anyone who makes a claim to having "accepted Christ" is admitted at once into the goodly fellowship of the prophets and the glorious company of the apostles regardless of the worldliness of his life or the vagueness of his doctrinal beliefs. We can only insist that the way of the cross is still a narrow way! EWT152

Lord, I desire to travel the narrow way that leads to everlasting life. Grant that I would follow Christ and shun the world. Amen.

OCTOBER 24

Normal—or Nominal?

Where your treasure is, there your heart will be also.
—LUKE 12:34

Is the Lord Jesus Christ your most precious treasure in the whole world? If so, count yourself among "normal" Christians, rather than among "nominal" Christians!

My old dictionary gives this definition as the meaning of nominal:

> Existing in name only, not real or actual;
> hence so small, slight, as to be hardly
> worth the name.

With that as a definition, those who know they are Christians "in name only" should never make the pretense of being normal Christians. Thankfully those who are "normal" are constantly being drawn to praise and worship, charmed by the moral beauty which is found only in Jesus.

I cannot understand how anyone can profess to be a follower and a disciple of our Lord Jesus Christ and not be overwhelmed by His attributes. Those divine attributes faithfully attest that He is indeed Lord of all, completely worthy of our worship and praise! MWT084

Heavenly Father, You are the Creator of heaven and earth. You are holy and righteous in all Your ways. Your Son is my Treasure today and every day, and I follow Him. Amen.

OCTOBER 25

Prophet and Priest

Therefore, holy brothers and sisters, who share in the heavenly calling, fix your thoughts on Jesus, whom we acknowledge as our apostle and high priest.
—HEBREWS 3:1

Jesus was God's faithful witness. In effect He said: "I am a reporter. I have come down from heaven, and the things that I saw there I speak to you. I tell you the truth, but you will not receive it." He was the Prophet of all prophets, the summation of all of God's prophets.

But He was more. His ministry was that of the priest of God. He offered Himself. He was the only priest in all of history who could offer Himself as an offering and a sacrifice to God. The writer to the Hebrews says clearly that "Christ . . . through the eternal Spirit offered himself without spot to God" (9:14). Then God raised Him from the dead, and He is now our great High Priest at the right hand of God. JIV034

Holy Father, thank You for sending Your Son to reveal truth to humanity and serve as mediator between us and You. May I grow in my love for Your Son today. Amen.

OCTOBER 26

Christian Reproof

Brothers and sisters, if someone is caught in a sin, you who live by the Spirit should restore that person gently.

—GALATIANS 6:1

It is quite natural, and even spiritual, to feel sorrow and heaviness when we see the professed followers of Christ walking in the ways of the world. Our first impulse may be to go straight to them and upbraid them indignantly, but such methods are seldom successful. The heat in our spirit may not be from the Holy Spirit, and if it is not, then it can very well do more harm than good. . . .

We cannot fight sin with sin or draw men to God by frowning at them in fleshly anger, "for the wrath of man worketh not the righteousness of God."

Often acts done in a spirit of religious irritation have consequences far beyond anything we could have guessed. Moses allowed himself to become vexed with Israel and in a fit of pique smote the rock. With the same stroke he closed the land of promise against him for the rest of his life.

It is not an easy task to stand for God as we should in our generation and yet maintain a spirit of kindliness toward the very ones we are sent to reprove—but it is not impossible! In this as in everything else, Christ is our perfect example and He can do the impossible if we but yield and obey. He will surely show us how to oppose with kindness and reprove with charity, and the power of the Holy Spirit within will enable us to follow His blessed example! EWT367

Lord Christ, grant by Your Spirit that I would embody kindness and charity, as You have done, and so be a light in this dark world. Amen.

OCTOBER 27

People Apart

Do not conform to the pattern of this world, but be transformed by the renewing of your mind. Then you will be able to test and approve what God's will is—his good, pleasing and perfect will.
—ROMANS 12:2

We who call ourselves Christians are supposed to be a people apart. We claim to have repudiated the wisdom of this world and adopted the wisdom of the cross as the guide of our lives. We have thrown in our lot with that One who while He lived on earth was the most unadjusted of the sons of men. He would not be integrated into society. He stood above it and condemned it by withdrawing from it even while dying for it. Die for it He would, but surrender to it He would not.

The wisdom of the cross is repudiation of the world's "norm." Christ, not society, becomes the pattern of the Christian life. The believer seeks adjustment, not to the world, but to the will of God, and just to the degree that he is integrated into the heart of Christ is he out of adjustment with fallen human society. TRC147

Lord, consecrate me today, that I would be separated from the world and joined to You in holiness. Amen.

OCTOBER 28

Seek to Know Christ Better

Look to the Lord and his strength; seek his face always.
—PSALM 105:4

Are you aware that we have been snared in the coils of a modern spurious logic which insists that if we have found Christ we need no more seek Him?

This is set before us as the last word in orthodoxy, and it is taken for granted that no Bible-taught Christian ever believed otherwise. Thus the whole testimony of the worshiping, seeking, singing church on that subject is crisply set aside!

The experiential heart-theology of a grand army of fragrant saints is rejected in favor of a smug interpretation of Scripture which would certainly have sounded strange to an Augustine, a Rutherford, or a Brainerd.

In the midst of this great chill there are some, I rejoice to acknowledge, who will not be content with shallow logic. They will admit the force of the argument, and then turn away with tears to hunt some lonely place and pray, "O God, show me Thy glory!" They want to taste, to touch with their hearts, to see with their inner eyes the wonder that is God.

Complacency is a deadly foe of all spiritual growth. Acute desire must be present or there will be no manifestation of Christ to His people. He waits to be wanted!

Too bad that with many of us He waits so long, so very long, in vain! EWT303

Lord Christ, may I never be content with how much I currently know You. May Your Spirit give me the desire and ability to know and love You better. Amen.

OCTOBER 29

Ripped in Two

And when Jesus had cried out again in a loud voice, he gave up his spirit. At that moment the curtain of the temple was torn in two from top to bottom.

—MATTHEW 27:50–51

That ancient veil was not just a curtain. It was a special drape—a veil so thick and heavy that it took several men to pull it aside. As Jesus died, the finger of God rent that veil which had housed the earthly presence of the invisible God. Thus, God was indicating the beginning of a new covenant and a new relationship between mankind and Himself. He was demonstrating the passing of the old order and the transfer of authority, efficacy, and mediation to the new order.

The priesthood, the priests, the old covenants, the altars, the sacrifices—all that had been involved in the Old Testament system of law—was done away with. God had eliminated it as useless, powerless, without authority. In its place He instituted a new Sacrifice, the Lamb of God, the eternal Son, Jesus Christ. God instituted as well a new and efficacious altar, this one eternal in the heavens, where Jesus lives to intercede for God's believing children. JMI099-100

Lord Christ, thank You for removing all the barriers between me and the Father, that I would have direct access to Him. Amen.

OCTOBER 30

Be Like Jesus

Do not conform to the pattern of this world, but be transformed by the renewing of your mind. Then you will be able to test and approve what God's will is—his good, pleasing and perfect will.
—ROMANS 12:2

The Christian gospel is too often presented as a means toward happiness, to peace of mind or security. There are even those who use the Bible to "relax" them, as if it were a drug.

How far wrong all this is will be discovered easily by the simple act of reading the New Testament through once, with meditation. There the emphasis is not upon happiness but upon holiness. God is more concerned with the state of people's hearts than with the state of their feelings.

Undoubtedly, the will of God brings final happiness to those who obey, but the most important matter is not how happy we are but how holy!

The childish clamor after happiness can become a real snare. One may easily deceive himself by cultivating a religious joy without a correspondingly righteous life. For those who take this whole thing seriously I have a suggestion: Go to God and have an understanding. Tell Him that it is your desire to be holy at any cost and then ask Him never to give you more happiness than holiness! Be assured that in the end you will be as happy as you are holy; but for the time being let your whole ambition be to serve God and be Christlike! EWT136

Holy Father, grant by the power of Your Spirit that I would desire and pursue holiness more than happiness, that I would be conformed to the glorious image of Your Son. Amen.

OCTOBER 31

The Conditions of Peace

The jailer . . . rushed in and fell trembling before Paul and Silas . . . and asked, "Sirs, what must I do to be saved?"
—ACTS 16:29–30

In a world like ours, with conditions being what they are, what should a serious-minded man or woman do?

First, accept the truth concerning yourself. You do not go to a doctor to seek consolation, but to find out what is wrong and what to do about it.

Then seek the kingdom of God and His righteousness. Seek through Jesus Christ a right relationship to God and then insist upon maintaining a right relation to your fellow man.

Set about reverently and honestly to amend your doings. Magnify God, mortify the flesh, simplify your life. Take up your cross and learn of Jesus Christ, to die to this world that He may raise you up in due time.

If you will do these things in faith and love, you will know peace—the peace of God that passes all understanding.

You will know joy—the joy of resurrection. You will know too the comfort of the indwelling Spirit of God, for you have sought to do the will of God at any price! MWT193

Dear Lord, teach me and my family what it means to both live in this world and at the same time "die to this world" for the sake of Christ. Amen.

NOVEMBER

NOVEMBER 1

Once and for All

We have been made holy through the sacrifice of the body of Jesus Christ once for all.
—HEBREWS 10:10

The blood of Jesus Christ is of infinite value. The pouring out of blood indicates the termination of life. Because the blood of Jesus Christ, the eternal Son, the Lamb of God, was poured out, our acts of sin may be pardoned. . . .

In the Old Testament, the sacrifices and offerings and the poured-out blood of animals were efficacious in ceremonial symbolism. But the death of Jesus Christ was efficacious actually and eternally. (*Efficacious* is a word theologians like to use; it simply means that it works. It is effective. You can count on it.) When Jesus poured out His blood on Calvary, He guaranteed eternal redemption to all who would put their trust in Him. . . .

The atoning, vicarious death of Jesus Christ for sinful humanity is at the very foundation of the Christian faith. For those who think they can find a better way than God's way, it is not a popular teaching. But there is no other way. Jesus is the only way. JMI123-124

Lord, I praise You for Your all-sufficient sacrifice on the cross! How wonderful You are and how great is Your work of salvation. May I always be grateful for all that You have done. Amen.

NOVEMBER 2

Jesus Calls Us to His Rest

Be completely humble and gentle; be patient, bearing with one another in love.

—EPHESIANS 4:2

Jesus calls us to His rest, and meekness is His method! The meek man cares not at all who is greater than he, for he has long ago decided that the esteem of the world is not worth the effort. He develops toward himself a kindly sense of humor and learns to say, "Oh, so you have been overlooked? They placed someone else before you? They have whispered that you are pretty small stuff after all? And now you feel hurt because the world is saying about you the very things you have been saying about yourself? Only yesterday you were telling God that you were nothing, a mere worm of the dust. Where is your consistency? Come on, humble yourself, and cease to care what men may think!"

Rest is simply release from the heavy, crushing burden borne by mankind, and the word Jesus used for "burden" means a load carried or toil borne to the point of exhaustion. The "rest" is not something we do—it is what comes to us when we cease to do.

The meek man is not a human mouse afflicted with a sense of his own inferiority. Rather, he may be in his moral life as bold as a lion and as strong as Samson; but he has stopped being fooled about himself. He has accepted God's estimate of his own life. He knows he is as weak and helpless as God has declared him to be, but paradoxically, he knows at the same time that he is in the sight of God of more importance than angels. In himself nothing; in God, everything. He rests perfectly content to allow God to place His own values! EWT288

Lord Jesus, thank You for the rest You offer me. May I enter into it more fully today and know You more. Amen.

NOVEMBER 3

The Art of True Worship

Then I heard every creature in heaven and on earth and under the earth and on the sea, and all that is in them, saying: "To him who sits on the throne and to the Lamb be praise and honor and glory and power, for ever and ever!"
—REVELATION 5:13

It remains only to be said that worship as we have described it here is almost (though, thank God, not quite) a forgotten art in our day. For whatever we can say of modern Bible-believing Christians, it can hardly be denied that we are not remarkable for our spirit of worship. The gospel as preached by good men in our times may save souls, but it does not create worshipers. . . .

How few, how pitifully few are the enraptured souls who languish for love of Christ. . . .

If Bible Christianity is to survive the present world upheaval, we shall need to recapture the spirit of worship. We shall need to have a fresh revelation of the greatness of God and the beauty of Jesus. We shall need to put away our phobias and our prejudices against the deeper life and seek again to be filled with the Holy Spirit. He alone can raise our cold hearts to rapture and restore again the art of true worship. TIC130-131

Lord, help us to "raise our cold hearts to rapture and restore again the art of true worship." May it no longer be said that true worship is "a forgotten art." Amen.

NOVEMBER 4

The Adequacy of Christ

For the foolishness of God is wiser than human wisdom, and the weakness of God is stronger than human strength.
—1 CORINTHIANS 1:25

Science and philosophy are more arrogant and bigoted than religion could ever possibly be, and still they try to brand evangelical Christians as bigots.

But I have never taken my Bible and gone into the laboratory and tried to tell the scientist how to conduct his experiments, and I would thank him if he didn't bring his test tube into the holy place and tell me how to conduct mine! The scientist has nothing he can tell me about Jesus Christ, our Lord. There is nothing he can add, and I do not need to appeal to him.

Studying the philosophers may clarify my thinking and may help me broaden my outlook, but it is not necessary to my salvation. I have studied Plato and the rest of them from the time I was knee-high to a rubber worker in Akron, Ohio. But I have never found that Plato added anything, finally, to what Jesus Christ has said.

You know what Jesus said: "I am the Light that lighteth every man. I am the Bread that feedeth every man. I am the One who came from the heart of the Father, and I am the Eternal Word which was in the beginning with God, and which was and is God, and that's who I am."

So, we are assured in the Word that it is Jesus only and He is enough! It is not Jesus plus a lot of other religions. It is not Jesus plus a lot of other philosophies. He is the Eternal Word, and so we must listen to Him! EWT044

Christ, I praise You for being sufficient! May I rest in the knowledge that You are all I need. Amen.

NOVEMBER 5

Delight Within the Trinity

Father, I want those you have given me to be with me where I am, and to see my glory, the glory you have given me because you loved me before the creation of the world.

—JOHN 17:24

God is boundlessly enthusiastic. I'm glad somebody is, because I don't find very many Christians who are. If they are, they're not enthusiastic about the things that matter. If they're going to a movie, they can get all steamed up about that. If they're going on a moonlight cruise, they get all worked up over that. But if you just say, "Look, look, behold God, behold God!" you can't get much enthusiasm.

God is enthusiastic. He's enthusiastic for Himself in the Persons in the Godhead. The Persons of the Godhead are infinitely delighted with each other. The Father is infinitely delighted with the Son, and the Son is infinitely delighted with the other two Persons of the Godhead. He is delighted with His whole creation, and especially with men made in His image. Unbelief comes and throws a cloud over us and shuts out the light of God, and we don't believe that God is delighted, infinitely delighted with us. AOG031-032

Triune God, You are full of delight, and I want to experience that same delight. Jesus, thank You for making a way back to the Father, that I may experience the wonderful love and joy He has together with You and the Spirit. Amen.

NOVEMBER 6

Christ's Words Are for the Children of God

I have hidden your word in my heart that I might not sin against you.
—PSALM 119:11

The gracious words of Christ are for the sons and daughters of grace, not for the Gentile nations whose chosen symbols are the lion, the eagle, the dragon, and the bear!

So, the notion that the Bible is addressed to everybody has wrought confusion within and without the church. The effort to apply the teaching of the Sermon on the Mount to the unregenerate nations of the world is one example of this. Courts of law and the military powers of the earth are urged to follow the teachings of Christ, an obviously impossible thing for them to do. To quote the words of Christ as guides for policemen, judges, and generals is to misunderstand those words completely and to reveal a total lack of understanding of the purposes of divine revelation.

Not only does God address His words of truth to those who are able to receive them, He actually conceals their meaning from those who are not. The parables of Christ were the exact opposite of the modern "illustration" which is meant to give light: the parables were "dark sayings" and Christ asserted He sometimes used them so that His disciples could understand and His enemies could not.

The natural man must know in order to believe; the spiritual man must believe in order to know! EWT237

Holy Spirit, illuminate the eyes of my heart so that I would understand the words of Christ, and give me the ability to obey them to the glory of the Father. Amen.

NOVEMBER 7

Administrator of a New Will

For this reason Christ is the mediator of a new covenant, that those who are called may receive the promised eternal inheritance—now that he has died as a ransom to set them free from the sins committed under the first covenant.
—HEBREWS 9:15

What no mortal has done, Jesus Christ, the eternal Son of God, has achieved. He has accomplished this kind of enduring administration and divine beneficence. Jesus died to activate the terms of the will to all its beneficiaries; Jesus rose in victory from the grave to administer the will.

Is that not beautiful? Jesus did not turn God's will over to someone else to administer. He Himself became the Administrator. Many times He declared, "I will be back. I will rise again on the third day!" He came back from the dead. He rose on the third day. He lives to carry out for His people all the terms of His will.

We must continue to trust this Living One who is now our great High Priest in the heavens. There is not a single argument in liberal theology strong enough to pry us from our faith. We have a living hope in this world, and that living hope is equally valid for the world to come. JMI126

Lord Jesus, Administrator of God's will, I praise You for Your accomplished work and the hope You offer me today. Grant by Your Spirit that I would live in hope and faithfulness until I receive the inheritance You have secured for me. Amen.

NOVEMBER 8

Our Hiding Place

Kiss his son, or he will be angry and your way will lead to your destruction, for his wrath can flare up in a moment. Blessed are all who take refuge in him.

—PSALM 2:12

We are accepted by [God] because of Christ Jesus. But we also have the right to hide in God and be safe. That too is our privilege because Jesus, our great High Priest, perfectly represents us at God's right hand. When we are united to Christ, no one can take this right and privilege away from us. We are safe! We are safe!

Someone was quoted as saying, "I do not want to hide from life. I want to face up to life every day." Knowing the nature of humankind, I would call such talk bold and brave. . . .

What we are hiding from is not life. We are hiding from a sinful world, from a sinister devil, from vicious temptation. We are hiding in the only place there is to hide—in God. It is our right and our privilege to know the perfect safety He has promised.

The trusting child of God is safe in Jesus Christ. When the lambs are safe in the fold, the wolf can growl and snarl outside, but he cannot get into the fold. When the child of God enters the Father's house, the enemy of his or her soul can roar and threaten, but he cannot enter. Such a shelter is our high privilege! JMI137-138

Heavenly Father, thank You that I can hide safely in Your Son from the dangers of this world. Grant that I would always flee to Him, my only place of security. Amen.

NOVEMBER 9

We Are Amazed

For I am the least of the apostles. . . . But by the grace of God I am what I am.

1 CORINTHIANS 15:9–10

Every humble and devoted believer in Jesus Christ must have his own periods of wonder and amazement at this mystery of godliness—the willingness of the Son of Man to take our place in judgment so that the people of God could be a cleansed and spiritual people!

If the amazement has all gone out of it, something is wrong, and you need to have the stony ground broken up again!

The Apostle Paul, one of the holiest men who ever lived, was not ashamed of his times of remembrance and wonder over the grace and kindness of God. He knew that God did not hold his old sins against him forever!

Knowing the old account was all settled, Paul's happy heart assured him again and again that all was well.

He could only shake his head in amazement and confess: "I am unworthy to be called, but by His grace, I am a new creation in Jesus Christ!"

I make this point about the faith and assurance and rejoicing of Paul in order to say that if that humble sense of perpetual penance ever leaves our justified being, we are on the way to backsliding! EWT116

I am amazed at what You have done for me, Lord Christ! Thank You for the grace You have given to me. May I honor and love You more today. Amen.

NOVEMBER 10

Don't Turn Back

No one who puts a hand to the plow and looks back is fit for service in the kingdom of God.

—LUKE 9:62

God has given every one of us the power to make our own choices. I am not saying that we are forced to bow our necks to this yoke and we do not have to apply it to ourselves. It is true that if we do not like it, we can turn our backs on it.

The record in the New Testament is plain on this point—many people followed Jesus for a while and then walked away from Him. Once Jesus said to His disciples: "Except ye eat my body, my flesh, and drink my blood, there is no life in you." Many looked at one another and then walked away from Him. Jesus turned to those remaining and said, "Will you also go away?" Peter gave the answer which is still my answer today: "Lord, if we wanted to go away, where would we go? Thou alone hast the words of eternal life."

Those were wise words, indeed, words born of love and devotion.

So, we are not forced to obey in the Christian life, but we are forced to make a choice at many points in our spiritual maturity.

We have that power within us to reject God's instructions—but where else shall we go? TSII059

Lord Christ, I know that You alone have the words of eternal life. Grant by Your Spirit that I would remain in You always and persevere through life's trials. Amen.

NOVEMBER 11

Discerning Our Cross

Whoever wants to be my disciple must deny themselves and take up their cross daily and follow me.
—LUKE 9:23

I must point out here the fallacy of thinking that in following Jesus we can easily go up on the hillside and die—just like that! I admit that when Jesus was here on earth, the easiest and cheapest way to get off was to follow Jesus physically. Anyone could get out of work and say goodbye with the explanation, "I am going to follow Jesus." Multitudes did this. They followed Him physically, but they had no understanding of Him spiritually. Therefore, in that day the cheapest, easiest way to dispose of the cross was to carry it physically.

But brethren, taking our cross is not going to mean the physical act of following Jesus along a dusty pathway. We are not going to climb the hill where there are already two crosses in place and be nailed up between them.

Our cross will be determined by whatever pain and suffering and trouble which will yet come to us because of our obedience to the will of God. The true saints of God have always borne witness that wholehearted obedience brings the cross into the light quicker than anything else. ITB102

Lord, I acknowledge that following You is no easy task. Yet I also know that You give me grace and strength to do so, to carry my own cross. Help me to see my cross clearly and to carry it in joyful obedience. Amen.

Christ Does in Us What We Cannot Do

When Christ, who is your life, appears, then you also will appear with him in glory.

—COLOSSIANS 3:4

Writing to the Corinthian believers, Paul promised full spiritual deliverance and stability in the knowledge that Jesus Christ "is made unto us wisdom, righteousness, sanctification and redemption." He also assured the Colossian believers: "You are complete in Him!"

Our great need, then, is simply Jesus Christ. He is what we need. He has what we need. He knows what we need to know. He has the ability to do in us what we cannot do—working in us that which is well-pleasing in God's sight.

But no matter who we are, we must acknowledge that it is a gracious plan and provision for men and women in the kindness and wisdom of God. Brothers and sisters, we get Christ and glory and fruitfulness, a future and the world to come and the spirits of just men made perfect; we get Jesus, mediator of a new covenant, and the blood of the everlasting covenant; an innumerable company of angels and the church of the firstborn and the New Jerusalem, the city of the living God!

And before we get all that, we have the privilege and the prospect of loving and joyful service for Christ and for mankind on this earth!

EWT143

Christ my Lord, I knowledge that You have all that I need and that I am complete in You. Keep me from relying on my own efforts rather than trusting in Your work alone. Amen.

NOVEMBER 13

Getting God in Focus

But Stephen, full of the Holy Spirit, looked up to heaven and saw the glory of God.
—ACTS 7:55

While many are busy trying to set forth satisfactory definitions of the word faith, we do well to simply consider that believing is directing the heart's attention to Jesus!

It is lifting the mind to "behold the Lamb of God," and never ceasing that beholding for the rest of our lives. At first this may be difficult, but it becomes easier as we look steadily at His wondrous Person, quietly and without strain.

Distractions may hinder, but once the heart is committed to Him, the attention will return again and rest upon Him like a wandering bird coming back to its window.

I would emphasize this one great volitional act which establishes the heart intention to gaze forever upon Jesus. God takes this intention for our choice and makes what allowances He must for the thousand distractions which beset us in this evil world. So, faith is a redirecting of our sight, getting God in our focus, and when we lift our inward eyes upon God, we are sure to meet friendly eyes gazing back at us! MWT362

Lord Jesus, I pray that the inward eyes of my soul will put You in clear focus throughout this day. Amen.

NOVEMBER 14

Innocent and Honest

Let the little children come to me.

—MARK 10:14

I believe that our attitudes must be a great grief to God Himself, as He tries to move us to praise and delight and devotion.

I surely believe that it is the nature of God to delight in enthusiasm and I do not refer to the extreme aspects of fanaticism.

I refer back to the record concerning the warmth and brightness and enjoyment of our Lord when He walked with us on this earth. I read and study and am assured that the Lord Jesus Christ had a special fondness for the babies and the small children and I think I know why.

These little ones are always vigorous and buoyant and unsophisticated and fresh. Their reactions are unmediated, candid, and truthful. They do just what they do out of simplicity showing the immediate response of their young hearts.

Jesus called the children and laid His hands upon them and blessed them, and then taught that "for of such is the kingdom of God" (Mark 10:14).

As a result, the theologians have been tossing that statement around ever since wanting to know what it all means!

The simple-hearted people knew that Jesus just loved the babies because they were innocent and honest and unspoiled. They responded to Him and to His love without stopping to consider and measure all of the consequences. CES097-098

Lord Jesus, You love simplicity and honesty and integrity of heart. May I have the faith of a child! Amen.

NOVEMBER 15

A Beautiful Reality

These have come so that the proven genuineness of your faith . . . may result in praise, glory and honor when Jesus Christ is revealed. Though you have not seen him, you love him.

—1 PETER 1:7–8

The Apostle Peter, who had seen Jesus Christ in the flesh with his own eyes, passed along to every believing Christian the assurance that it is possible for us to love the Savior and to live a life that will glorify Him even though we have not yet seen Him!

It is as though Peter is urging: "Love Him and work for Him and live for Him. I give you my testimony that it will be worth it all when you look upon His face—for I have seen Him with my own eyes, and I know!"

In his epistle, Peter, who had known Jesus in the flesh, was moved to write to the strangers scattered abroad—the Christians of the dispersion—to remind them that they should love Jesus Christ even though they had not seen Him in the flesh.

The Lord Jesus Himself had set His own stamp of approval and blessing upon all Christians who would believe, never having seen Him in the time of His own flesh. He told Thomas after the resurrection, "Because thou hast seen me, thou hast believed: blessed are they that have not seen, and yet have believed."

God has seen fit to give us wonderful and mysterious faculties, and I truly believe that God has ordained that we may actually know Jesus now, and love Him better never having seen Him, than Peter did when he saw Him! EWT118

Sweet Savior and Redeemer, I love You even though I have not seen You. Grant that my faith in You would increase this day. Amen.

NOVEMBER 16

Genuine Christianity

I want to know Christ—yes, to know the power of his resurrection and participation in his sufferings, becoming like him in his death, and so, somehow, attaining to the resurrection from the dead.
—PHILIPPIANS 3:10–11

As believers, we are supposed to have died with Jesus Christ our Lord. When we were joined to Him in the new birth, we were joined to His death. When we were joined to His rising again, it should have been plain to us that sin is now a moral incongruity in the life of a Christian.

The sinner sins because he is out there in the world—and he has never died. He is waiting to die and he will die once and later he will die the second death.

But a Christian dies with Christ and dies in Christ and dies along with Christ, so that when he lays his body down at last the Bible says he will not see death. . . .

I believe the gospel of Jesus Christ saved me completely—therefore He asks me for total commitment. He expects me to be a disciple totally dedicated.

Joined to Jesus Christ, how can we be other than what He is? What He does, we do. Where He leads, we go. This is genuine Christianity! EFE044

Lord Jesus, I want to give You all that I am and be totally committed to You. Grant me the ability to identify with You fully that I may experience the fullness of Your resurrection life. Amen.

NOVEMBER 17

Jesus Lives Eternally

Therefore he is able to save completely those who come to God through him, because he always lives to intercede for them.
—HEBREWS 7:25

All that I have been saying may seem complex and involved. This much we must understand: Jesus our Lord, God's Christ and our Savior, lives forevermore! As God is timeless and ageless, so also is Jesus Christ. And Jesus lives to intercede for us! His eternal interest is to be our surety. We sing of it with faith and joy: "Before the throne my Surety stands; My name is written in His hands." And then we continue with the rest of those stirring words from the vision and heart of Charles Wesley:

The Father hears Him pray,
His dear anointed One;
He cannot turn away
The presence of His Son.
His Spirit answers to the blood
And tells me I am born of God.

How different is our vision of Jesus Christ from that of the ones who put Him to death, saying, "That is the end of him!" Our vision is of a risen, victorious, all-powerful, and all-wise High Priest. Quietly, triumphantly, He pleads the worth and value of His own life and blood for the preservation and victory of God's believing children.
JMI101-102

Lord Jesus, I praise You for Your power, victory, compassion, and love. Thank You for interceding for me. I ask today that You would pray that I would be preserved and be victorious. Amen.

NOVEMBER 18

Break with This World

"Come out from them and be separate, says the Lord."
—2 CORINTHIANS 6:17

I dare to say that Christians who have genuinely come to love and trust Jesus Christ have also renounced this world and have chosen a new model after which to pattern their lives.

Further, we should say that this is the aspect of the Christian life that most people do not like. They want comfort. They want blessing. They want peace. But they recoil from this radical, revolutionary break with the world.

To follow Christ in this rough and thoroughgoing way is too much for them!

Actually, the true Christian dissents from the world because he knows that it cannot make good on its promises. As Christ's believing disciple, he is not left without a "norm" to which he seeks to be adjusted. The Lord Jesus Christ is Himself the norm, the ideally perfect model, and the worshiping soul yearns to be like Him. Indeed, the whole drive behind the Christian life is the longing to be conformed to the image of Christ! MWT100

Dear Lord, it is difficult to be a future citizen of heaven yet live and function in this present world. Help me live each day in a manner worthy of Jesus Christ (see Phil. 1:27). Amen.

NOVEMBER 19

Kneel at Jesus' Feet

My brothers and sisters, believers in our glorious Lord Jesus Christ must not show favoritism.

—JAMES 2:1

A system of literature has grown up around the notion that Christianity may be proven by the fact that "great men" believe in Christ!

A magazine article carries the caption that "Senator So-and-So Believes in Christ." The implication is that if the senator believes in Christ, then Christ must be all right.

When did Jesus Christ have to ride in on the coattail of a senator, or a governor, or some other well-known man?

No, no, my brother! Jesus Christ stands alone, unique and supreme, self-validating, and the Holy Ghost declares Him to be God's eternal Son. Let all the presidents and all the kings and queens, the senators, and the lords and ladies of the world, along with the great athletes and great actors—let them kneel at His feet and cry, "Holy, holy, holy is the Lord God Almighty!"

Only the Holy Ghost can do this, my brethren. . . . If Christ is to be the Christ of God rather than the Christ of intellect, then we must enter in beyond the veil, until the illumination of the Holy Spirit fills our hearts and we are learning at the feet of Jesus—not at the feet of men! EWT142

Lord Christ, You stand alone above all others! I kneel at Your feet today and ask that You would empower me to share the gospel with those who have not bowed to You. Amen.

NOVEMBER 20

Christ Is the Pattern

And we all, who with unveiled faces contemplate the Lord's glory, are being transformed into his image with ever-increasing glory, which comes from the Lord, who is the Spirit.
—2 CORINTHIANS 3:18

The gospel not only furnishes transforming power to remold the human heart; it provides also a model after which the new life is to be fashioned, and that model is Christ Himself. Christ is God acting like God in the lowly raiments of human flesh. Yet He is also man; so He becomes the perfect model after which redeemed human nature is to be fashioned.

The beginnings of that transformation, which is to change the believing man's nature from the image of sin to the image of God, are found in conversion when the man is made a partaker of the divine nature. By regeneration and sanctification, by faith and prayer, by suffering and discipline, by the Word and the Spirit, the work goes on till the dream of God has been realized in the Christian heart. Everything that God does in His ransomed children has as its long-range purpose the final restoration of the divine image in human nature. Everything looks forward to the consummation.

In the meantime the Christian himself can work along with God in bringing about the great change. Paul tells us how: "But we all, with open face beholding as in a glass the glory of the Lord, are changed into the same image from glory to glory, even as by the Spirit of the Lord" (2 Cor. 3:18). ROR072

Heavenly Father, thank You for revealing what it means to be truly human. Grant by Your Spirit that I would be conformed to the image of Christ and become who You intend me to be. Amen.

NOVEMBER 21

Who Will Come to Jesus?

Let the one who wishes take the free gift of the water of life.
—REVELATION 22:17

God's invitation to men is broad but not unqualified. The words "whosoever will may come" throw the door open, indeed, but the church is carrying the gospel invitation far beyond its proper bounds, turning it into something more human and less divine than that found in the sacred Scriptures.

What we tend to overlook is that the word "whosoever" never stands by itself. Always its meaning is modified by the word "believe" or "will" or "come."

According to the teachings of Christ no one will or can come and believe unless there has been done within him a prevenient work of God enabling him to do so.

In the sixth chapter of John, Jesus teaches us that no one can come of himself; he must first be drawn by the Father. "It is the spirit that quickeneth; the flesh profiteth nothing," Jesus said (6:63).

Before any man or woman can be saved, he or she must feel a consuming spiritual hunger. Where a hungry heart is found, we may be sure that God was there first—"Ye have not chosen me, but I have chosen you" (John 15:16). MWT051

Heavenly Father, I pray today for evangelists and missionaries around the world who are representing You in teeming cities and remote areas. Through them, I ask that You will draw many people to Yourself who have never heard the gospel message. Amen.

NOVEMBER 22

Manifestation of the Trinity

Father, the hour has come. Glorify your Son, that your Son may glorify you.

—JOHN 17:1

We must get into our heads and hearts that Jesus Christ is the full, complete manifestation of the Trinity: "He that hath seen me hath seen the Father" (John 14:9). He set forth the glory of the Triune God, all the God there is! Where Jesus appears, God is. And where Jesus is glorified, God is.

I wouldn't quote anybody unless there were Scripture to confirm it, and Scripture does indeed confirm that the Trinity will fill our hearts. "No man hath seen God at any time. If we love one another, God dwelleth in us, and his love is perfected in us. Hereby know we that we dwell in him, and he in us, because he hath given us of his Spirit" (1 John 4:12–13). There you have the Father and the Spirit. "And we have seen and do testify that the Father sent the Son to be the Saviour of the world. Whosoever shall confess that Jesus is the Son of God, God dwelleth in him, and he in God" (4:14–15). There you have the Father and the Son, or the Trinity. AOG002-003

Son of God, Jesus Christ, You are the perfect image of the Father, and You indwell me by Your Spirit. May I stand continually in awe of who You are and the revelation You give. Amen.

NOVEMBER 23

Christ's Call

Then Peter spoke up, "We have left everything to follow you!"
MARK 10:28

Jesus Christ is a Man come to save men. In Him the divine nature is married to our human nature, and wherever human nature exists there is the raw material out of which He makes followers and saints!

Our Lord recognizes no classes, high or low, rich or poor, old or young, man or woman: all are human and all are alike to Him. His invitation is to all mankind.

In New Testament times, persons from many and varied social levels heard His call and responded: Peter the fisherman; Levi the publican; Luke the physician; Paul the scholar; Mary the demon possessed; Lydia the businesswoman; Paulus the statesman. A few great and many common persons came. They all came and our Lord received them all in the same way and on the same terms.

In those early Galilean days, Christ's followers heard His call, forsook the old life, attached themselves to Him, began to obey His teachings, and joined themselves to His band of disciples. This total commitment was their confirmation of faith. Nothing less would do!

And it is not different today. From any and every profession or occupation men and women may come to Him if they will. He calls us to leave the old life and to begin the new. There must never be any vacuum, never any place of neutrality where the world cannot identify us as truly belonging to Him! ETW121

Lord, I recognize Your call to follow after You. Grant by Your Spirit that I would not look back and that I would invite others to walk in Your steps. Amen.

NOVEMBER 24

Where God Releases Grace

For if the many died by the trespass of the one man, how much more did God's grace and the gift that came by the grace of the one man, Jesus Christ, overflow to the many!

—ROMANS 5:15

If I want to know this immeasurable grace, this overwhelming, astounding kindness of God, I have to step under the shadow of the cross. I must come where God releases grace. I must either look forward to it or I must look back at it. I must look one way or the other to that cross where Jesus died. Grace flowed out of His wounded side. The grace that flowed there saved Abel—and that same grace saves you. "No man cometh unto the Father, but by me," said our Lord Jesus Christ (John 14:6). And Peter said, "There is none other name under heaven given among men, whereby we must be saved," except the name of Jesus Christ (Acts 4:12).

The reason for that is, of course, that Jesus Christ is God. Law could come by Moses and only law could come by Moses.

But grace came by Jesus Christ. And it came from the beginning. It could come only by Jesus Christ because there was no one else who was God who could die. No one else could take on Him flesh and still be the infinite God. And when Jesus walked around on earth and patted the heads of babies, forgave harlots, and blessed mankind, He was simply God acting like God in a given situation. In everything that God does, He acts like Himself. TRC174-175

Lord Jesus, I praise You for the grace You have poured out on me! Outside You there is no salvation, for You are the only source of life and grace. May I point others to You today. Amen.

NOVEMBER 25

Salvation's Price

Without faith it is impossible to please God.
—HEBREWS 11:6

Too many Christian leaders, acting like enthusiastic promoters, are teaching that the essence of faith is this: "Come to Jesus—it will cost you nothing!"

The price has all been paid—"it will cost you nothing!"

Brethren, that is a dangerous half-truth. There is always a price connected with salvation and with discipleship.

God's grace is free, no doubt about that. No one in the wide world can make any human payment toward the plan of salvation or the forgiveness of sins.

I take issue on Bible grounds with the statement that "everyone in the world has faith—all you have to do is turn your faith loose."

That is truly a misconception of what the Bible teaches about men and God and faith. Actually, faith is a rare and wonderful plant that lives and grows only in the penitent soul.

The teaching that everyone has faith is simply a form of humanism in the guise of Christianity. I warn you that any faith that belongs to everybody is not the faith that saves. It is not that faith which is a gift of God to the broken and contrite heart! MWT027

Lord Jesus, I praise You for extending Your grace so freely to me. I repent of any sins I have committed, both knowingly and unknowingly. Help my faith in You to grow today. Amen.

NOVEMBER 26

Confused About Worship

For we are the temple of the living God.
—2 CORINTHIANS 6:16

To really know Jesus Christ as Savior and Lord is to love and worship Him!

As God's people, we are so often confused that we could be known as God's poor, stumbling, bumbling people, for we are most prone to think of worship as something we do when we go to church on Sunday!

We call it God's house. We have dedicated it to Him. So, we continue with the confused idea that it must be the only place where we can worship Him.

We come to the Lord's house made of brick and stone and wood. We are used to hearing the call to worship: "The Lord is in His holy temple—let us kneel before Him!" This is on Sunday and in church—very nice!

But on Monday, as we go about our different duties, are we aware of the continuing Presence of God? The Lord desires still to be in His holy temple, wherever we are; for each of us is a temple in whom dwells the Holy Spirit of God! MWT376

Lord Christ, I want all the rooms in my temple to be clean, not only for Your abiding presence but also to be a shining testimony to those I encounter during the week. Amen.

NOVEMBER 27

Bringing Us to Glory

In bringing many sons and daughters to glory, it was fitting that God . . . should make the pioneer of their salvation perfect through what he suffered.

—HEBREWS 2:10

As Christian believers (I am assuming you are a believer), you and I know how we have been changed and regenerated and assured of eternal life by faith in Jesus Christ and His atoning death. On the other hand, where this good news of salvation by faith is not known, religion becomes an actual bondage. If Christianity is known only as a religious institution, it may well become merely a legalistic system of religion, and the hope of eternal life becomes a delusion.

I have said this much about reality and assurance to counter the shock you may feel when I add that God wants to fully prepare you in your daily Christian life so that you will be ready indeed for heaven! Many of us have been in God's household for a long time. Remember that God has been trying to do something special within our beings day after day, year after year.

Why? Because His purpose is to bring many sons—and daughters too—unto glory! MWT032

Dear Jesus, thank You for Your faithfulness in my life—even when I ignore You. Today I want to be especially attuned to Your holy presence in each of my activities. Amen.

NOVEMBER 28

Our Remedy

Who gave himself for our sins to rescue us from the present evil age, according to the will of our God and Father.

—GALATIANS 1:4

Our Lord did not come into the world 2,000 years ago to launch Christianity as a new religion or a new system. He came into this world with eternal purpose. He came as the center of all things. Actually, He came to be our religion, if you wish to put it that way.

He came in person, in the flesh, to be God's salvation to the very ends of the earth. He did not come just to delegate power to others to heal or cure or bless. He came to *be* the blessing, for all the blessings and the full glory of God are to be found in His person. Because Jesus Christ is the center of all things, He offers deliverance for the human soul and mind by His direct, personal, and intimate touch. This is not my one-man interpretation. It is the basic teaching of salvation through the Messiah-Savior, Jesus Christ. It is a teaching that runs throughout the Bible! . . .

Into the midst of all this came the Light that was able to light every man that was to come into the world. He could say and teach, "I am the light of the world," because He shone so brightly, dispelling the darkness.

Jesus Christ came in the fullness of time to be God's salvation. He was to be God's cure for all that was wrong with the human race.

TSII386-387

Lord Jesus, may I always turn only to You for all my needs. You are my remedy, my life, my salvation. Amen.

NOVEMBER 29

The Great Physician

When Jesus saw him . . . he asked him, "Do you want to get well?"
—JOHN 5:6

If you are a discouraged and defeated Christian believer, you may have accepted the rationalization that your condition is "normal for all Christians."

You may now be content with the position that the progressive, victorious Christian life may be suitable for a few Christians—but not for you! You have been to Bible conferences; you have been to the altar—but the blessings are for someone else.

Now, that attitude on the part of Christian believers is neither modesty nor meekness. It is a chronic discouragement resulting from unbelief. It is rather like those who have been sick for so long that they no longer believe they can get well.

Jesus is still saying, as He said to the man lying by the gate at the Jerusalem pool, "Do you want to be made whole?" (see John 5:6). Jesus made him whole—because of his desire! His need was great, but he had never lapsed into that state of chronic discouragement. MWT085

Thank You, Lord Christ, that a victorious Christian life can be the norm—even in the midst of this chaotic, malevolent world. Fill me anew with Your Spirit, and shine through me today. Amen.

NOVEMBER 30

Listen to God

When Jesus spoke again to the people, he said, "I am the light of the world. Whoever follows me will never walk in darkness, but will have the light of life."

—JOHN 8:12

If while hearing a sermon we can fix on but one real jewel of truth, we may consider ourselves well rewarded for the time we have spent.

One such gem was uncovered during a sermon which I heard some time ago. From the sermon I got one worthy sentence and no more, but it was so good that I regret that I cannot remember who the preacher was, that I might give him credit. Here is what he said, "Listen to no man who fails to listen to God." . . .

No man has any right to offer advice who has not first heard God speak. No man has any right to counsel others who is not ready to hear and follow the counsel of the Lord. True moral wisdom must always be an echo of God's voice. The only safe light for our path is the light which is reflected from Christ, the Light of the World. . . .

God has His chosen men still, and they are without exception good listeners. They can hear when the Lord speaks. We may safely listen to such men. But to no others. ROR017-019

Don't ever let me speak empty, worthless words, Lord. I pray that whenever I open my mouth, I would speak truth that accords with the revelation You have given in Jesus Christ. Amen.

DECEMBER

DECEMBER 1

God's Sovereign Plan

Then the end will come, when he hands over the kingdom to God . . . For he must reign.
—1 CORINTHIANS 15:24–25

Many people continue to live in daily fear that the world "is coming to an end."

Only in the Scriptures do we have the description and prediction of the age-ending heavenly and earthly events when our Lord and Savior will be universally acknowledged as King of kings and Lord of lords.

God's revelation makes it plain that in "that day" all will acclaim Him "victor"!

Human society, generally, refuses to recognize God's sovereignty or His plan for His redeemed people. But no human being or world government will have any control in that fiery day of judgment yet to come.

John's vision of things to come tells us clearly and openly that at the appropriate time this world will be taken away from men and placed in the hands of the only Man who has the wisdom and authority to rightly govern.

That Man is the eternal Son of God, the worthy Lamb, our Lord Jesus Christ! MWT402

Dear Lord, I pray today for the remaining people groups in the world who have not yet heard the gospel message. Without knowing You, Father, many will be lost eternally when the end of the world comes. Lord, raise up specific individuals to take Your Word to those remaining peoples. Amen.

DECEMBER 2

The Worth of a Soul

Or what can anyone give in exchange for their soul?
—MATTHEW 16:26

We may learn how dear and precious we are to Christ by what He was willing to give for us!

Many Christians are tempted to downgrade themselves too much. I am not arguing against true humility and my word to you is this: Think as little of yourself as you want to, but always remember that our Lord Jesus Christ thought very highly of you—enough to give Himself for you in death and sacrifice!

If the devil comes to you and whispers that you are no good, don't argue with him. In fact, you may as well admit it, but then remind the devil: "Regardless of what you say about me, I must tell you how the Lord feels about me. He tells me that I am so valuable to Him that He gave Himself for me on the cross!"

So the value is set by the price paid—and in our case, the price paid was our Lord Himself, and the end that the Savior had in view was that He might redeem us from all iniquity, that is, from the power and consequences of iniquity.

One of Wesley's hymns speaks of "the double cure" for sin. The wrath of God against sin and the power of sin in the human life—both of these were dealt with when Christ gave Himself for us. He redeemed us with a double cure! EWT112

Lord Christ, thank You for coming to earth and saving me! The price You paid was great, and I give my life to You anew today. Amen.

DECEMBER 3

It Was a Joy

For the joy set before him he endured the cross, scorning its shame, and sat down at the right hand of the throne of God.
HEBREWS 12:2

There was no moral necessity upon God to redeem mankind. He didn't have to send His Son Jesus Christ to die for mankind. He sent Him, but at the same time Jesus did it voluntarily. If God was willing, it was the happy willingness of God.

A mother doesn't have to get up and feed her baby at two in the morning. There's no law compelling her to do it. The law probably would compel her to take some care of the little tyke, but she doesn't have to give him that loving care that she does. She wants to do it. I used to do it for our little fellows, and I enjoyed doing it. A mother and a father do what they do because they love to do it. . . .

The incarnation, too, was not something that Jesus Christ did gritting His teeth and saying, "I hate this thing—I wish I could get out of it." One of the dear old hymn writers said, "He abhorred not the virgin's womb." The writer thought about this and said, "Wait a minute here. The womb of the creature? How could the everlasting, eternal, infinite God, whom space cannot contain, confine Himself inside one of His creatures? Wouldn't it be a humiliation?" Then he smiled and said, "No, He abhorred not the virgin's womb," and he wrote it and we've been singing it for centuries. The incarnation of Jesus Christ's immortal flesh was not a heavy thing. The second person of the Trinity, the everlasting Son, the eternal Word made Himself flesh—joyously! When the angels sang about the incarnation, they sang joyously about it. AOG008-010

Lord, thank You for coming to earth to save me. You are a selfless, loving God. May my life be pleasing to You. Amen.

DECEMBER 4

Display of Eternal Glory

The Word became flesh and made his dwelling among us.
We have seen his glory, the glory of the one and only Son,
who came from the Father, full of grace and truth.
—JOHN 1:14

The Apostle John speaks for all of us also when he writes of the eternal Son and reminds us that *we beheld his glory.*

It is right that we should inquire, "What was this glory? Was it the glory of His works?"

Jesus was not only a worker—He was a wonder worker!

Every part of nature had to yield to Him and His authority.

He turned the water into wine and many people miss the point of His power and authority and argue about the difference between grape juice and wine. It mattered little—He turned water into wine. It was a miracle.

When our Lord came to the sick, He healed them. When He came to the devil-possessed, He commanded the devils to go out. When our Lord stood on the rocking deck of a tiny boat tossed by fierce winds and giant waves, He spoke to the water and rebuked the wind and there came a great calm.

Everything our Lord did was meaningful in the display of His eternal glory. CES023-024

O Lord, may I behold Your glory today! Fill me with Your Spirit and open the eyes of my heart, that I might know You perfectly. Amen.

DECEMBER 5

Arguing about Christ's Return

For the Lord himself will come down from heaven, with a loud command, with the voice of the archangel and with the trumpet call of God, and the dead in Christ will rise first.
—1 THESSALONIANS 4:16

The believing Christian should be living in joyful anticipation of the return of Jesus Christ, and that is such an important segment of truth that the devil has always been geared up to fight it and ridicule it. In fact, one of his big successes is being able to get people to argue and get mad about the details of the Second Coming—rather than looking and waiting for it.

Suppose a man has been overseas two or three years, away from his family. Suddenly, a cable arrives for the family with the message: "My work completed here; I will be home today."

After some hours he arrives at the front door with his bags. But in the house the family members are in turmoil. There has been a great argument as to whether he would arrive in the afternoon or evening and what transportation he would be using. So, no one is actually watching for his arrival.

You may say, "That is only an illustration."

But what is the situation in the various segments of the Christian community?

They are fighting with one another and glaring at each other. They are debating whether He is coming and how He is coming. That is the work of the devil—to make Christian people argue about the details of His coming so they forget the most important thing! EWT304

Lord, forgive Your church for arguing needlessly over details of Your return. May we in unity look forward to that glorious day and encourage one another in good deeds until then. Amen.

DECEMBER 6

What We Shall Be

For those God foreknew he also predestined to be conformed to the image of his Son.
ROMANS 8:29

We must take a high view of what God has done for us in consummating the plan of salvation for a lost race!

The supreme work of Christ in redemption is not just to save us from hell, but to restore us to Godlikeness again. Paul has confirmed this in Romans 8:29, "Whom he did foreknow, he also did predestinate to be conformed to the image of his Son."

While perfect restoration to the divine image awaits the day of Christ's appearing, the work of restoration is going on now. There is a slow but steady transmutation of the base metal of human nature into the gold of Godlikeness effected by the faith-filled gaze of the soul at the glory of God—the face of Jesus Christ!

We have already moved from what we were to what we are, and we are now moving toward what we shall be. To become like God is and must be the supreme goal of all moral creatures! MWT303

Lord, there are days when I feel I am losing ground in my spiritual growth. Help me today to move closer to the image of God's Son. Amen.

DECEMBER 7

The Hope We Have

We have this hope as an anchor for the soul, firm and secure.
It enters the inner sanctuary behind the curtain.
HEBREWS 6:19

Hope is the music, the drift and direction of the whole Bible. It sets the heartbeat and atmosphere of the Bible, meaning as it does desirable expectation and pleasurable anticipation!

Human hopes will fail and throw us down. But the Christian's hope is alive. The old English word "lively" meant what the word "living" means now; the word coming from God Himself for it is the strongest word in the Bible for life. It is the word used of God Himself when it says He is the Living God. So it is that God takes a Christian's hope and touches it with Himself and imparts His own "livingness" to the hope of the believer. The true Christian hope is a valid hope! We have been born of God. There has been a new creation. No emptiness there, no vanity, no dreams that can't come true. We have no great place of beauty in this world—Taj Mahal, Buckingham Palace, or the White House—that can compare with the glory that belongs to the true child of God who has known the major miracle, who has been changed by an inward operation of supernatural grace unto an inheritance, a living hope!

Your expectation should rise and you should challenge God, and begin to dream high dreams of faith and spiritual anticipation. Remember, you cannot out-hope the living God! EWT379

Heavenly Father, thank You for the hope You have given me in Christ! I praise You that with His coming, I may be confident of the good work You are doing in this world and that You will complete it someday. Amen.

DECEMBER 8

Take the Right Stance

For the Lord himself will come down from heaven, with a loud command, with the voice of the archangel and with the trumpet call of God.

—1 THESSALONIANS 4:16

We may take one of only two stances in regard to this prophetic "unveiling"—this portraying of the future return of Jesus Christ to this earth, to this world that once rejected Him as Messiah and crucified Him at Calvary. We may ignore it, in effect despising it and jeering at the prospect of a future divine intervention affecting the entire world. Or we may embrace it, cheering for the promised victory of a righteous Ruler, the coming King of kings.

Those who ignore Revelation take their place with the many who believe a humanistic view of life is sufficient: that men and women are responsible captains of their own souls. They take their place with the defiant multitude who shout the age-old refrain: "We will not have this Man to rule over us!"

Those who take Revelation seriously are convinced of an actual heavenly realm as real as the world we now inhabit. They are persuaded that the day of consummation nears when "the kingdoms of the world" become "the kingdoms of our Lord, and of his Christ," who "shall reign for ever and ever" (Rev. 11:15). JIV002

King Jesus, grant that I would take seriously Your second coming and look forward to it with eager anticipation. Amen.

DECEMBER 9

True Man

This is how you can recognize the Spirit of God: Every spirit that acknowledges that Jesus Christ has come in the flesh is from God.
—1 JOHN 4:2

Certain religious teachers in apostolic times refused to believe that Jesus was actually God come in the flesh. They were willing to exhaust the language of unctuous flattery to describe His glorious manhood, but they would have none of His deity. Their basic philosophy forbade them to believe that there could ever be a union of God and human flesh. Matter, they said, is essentially evil. God, who is impeccably holy, could never allow Himself contact with evil. Human flesh is matter; therefore, God is not come in the flesh.

Certainly it would not be difficult to refute this negative teaching. One would only need to demonstrate the error of the major premise, the essential sinfulness of matter, and the whole thing would collapse. But that would be to match reason against reason and take the mystery of godliness out of the realm of faith and make of it merely another religious philosophy. Then we would have rationalism with a thin Christian veneer. How long before the veneer wore off and we had only rationalism?

There is nothing unreasonable about the Christian message, but its appeal is not primarily to reason. At a specific time in a certain place God became flesh, but the transcendence of Christ over the human conscience is not historic; it is intimate, direct, and personal. WOS098

Father God, thank You for sending Your Son to become human, so that I might be saved. I pray today that I would be full of faith, trusting Your Word rather than my own logic, and thus grow closer to Your Son. Amen.

DECEMBER 10

Lukewarm About Christ's Return

Therefore keep watch, because you do not know the day or the hour.

—MATTHEW 25:13

The longing to see Christ that burned in the breasts of those first Christians seems to have burned itself out. All we have left are the ashes. It is precisely the "yearning" and the "fainting" for the return of Christ that has distinguished the personal hope from the theological one. Mere acquaintance with correct doctrine is a poor substitute for Christ, and familiarity with New Testament eschatology will never take the place of a love-inflamed desire to look on His face. . . .

In these times religion has become jolly good fun right here in this present world, and what's the hurry about heaven anyway? Christianity, contrary to what some had thought, is another and higher form of entertainment. Christ has done all the suffering. He has shed all the tears and carried all the crosses; we have but to enjoy the benefits of His heartbreak in the form of religious pleasures modeled after the world but carried on in the name of Jesus. So say the same people who claim to believe in Christ's second coming. . . .

Our present preoccupation with this world may be a warning of bitter days to come. God will wean us from the earth some way—the easy way if possible, the hard way if necessary. It is up to us. BAM158-160

Lord Christ, create within me a burning desire for Your return to earth, and grant that I would live faithfully until You do. Amen.

DECEMBER 11

Know the Lord as Perfectly as Possible

The throne of God and of the Lamb will be in the city, and his servants will serve him. They will see his face.

—REVELATION 22:3–4

When the work of Christ has been completed in His people, however, it will be possible, even natural, for redeemed men to behold their Redeemer. This is stated plainly by the Apostle John: "But we know that, when he shall appear, we shall be like him: for we shall see him as he is" (1 John 3:2).

This rapturous experience has been called the Beatific Vision and will be the culmination of all possible human blessedness. It will bring the glorified saint into a state of perpetual bliss which to taste for even one moment will banish forever from his mind every memory of grief or suffering here below.

I suppose the vast majority of us must wait for the great day of the Lord's coming to realize the full wonder of the vision of God Most High. In the meantime, we are, I believe, missing a great measure of radiant glory that is ours by blood-covenant and available to us in this present world if we would but believe it and press on in the way of holiness. EWT401

I eagerly await Your return, King Jesus, the day when I will see and know You more clearly! Until then, grant that I would seek to know You as fully as possible. Amen.

DECEMBER 12

Worshipers from Rebels

Not only is this so, but we also boast in God through our Lord Jesus Christ, through whom we have now received reconciliation.
—ROMANS 5:11

Sometimes evangelical Christians seem to be fuzzy and uncertain about the nature of God and His purposes in creation and redemption. In such instances, the preachers often are to blame. There are still preachers and teachers who say that Christ died so we would not drink and not smoke and not go to the theater.

No wonder people are confused! No wonder they fall into the habit of backsliding when such things are held up as the reason for salvation.

Jesus was born of a virgin, suffered under Pontius Pilate, died on the cross, and rose from the grave to make worshipers out of rebels! WHT011

Lord, keep the cross in the forefront of our evangelistic preaching, and fill us with Your longing for sinners to become worshipers. Amen.

DECEMBER 13

Longing to See Jesus

I am coming soon. Hold on to what you have, so that no one will take your crown.
—REVELATION 3:11

There is no doubt in my mind that millions of Christians in our day yearn within themselves to be ready to see the Lord Jesus when He appears. These are the saints of God who have a real understanding that what our Lord Jesus Christ is to us in our personal lives, moment by moment, is more important than merely dwelling on "what He did for us"!

I say this because a great segment of Christian theology emphasizes the "utility" of the cross on which Jesus died, rather than the Person who died on that cross for our sins.

Because of that view, many really have no emotional yearning for the return of Jesus. The best hope they know is a kind of intellectual, theological hope. But an intellectual knowledge of what the New Testament teaches about the return of Christ is surely a poor substitute for a love-inflamed desire to look on His face!

While we await Him, our Lord expects us to love one another, to worship Him together, and to send this gracious gospel to the ends of the earth. MWT288

Lord Jesus, what You did on the cross for us is mind-staggering, but to know that the "story" doesn't end there is cause for great exulting! I know that You are risen, because You live in me today! Amen.

DECEMBER 14

Savior and Judge

This will take place on the day when God judges people's secrets through Jesus Christ, as my gospel declares.
—ROMANS 2:16

What is your concept of Jesus Christ as Saviour and Judge? If the "ten-cent-store Jesus" that is being preached by a lot of men, the plastic, painted Christ who has no spine and no justice and is pictured as a soft and pliable friend to everybody—if He is the only Christ there is, then we might as well close our books and bar our doors, and make a bakery or garage out of the church!

But that Christ that is being preached and pictured is not the Christ of God, nor the Christ of the Bible, nor the Christ we must deal with.

The Christ we must deal with will be the judge of mankind—and this is one of the neglected Bible doctrines in our day!

The Father judges no man. When the Lord, the Son of Man, shall come in the clouds of glory, then shall be gathered unto Him the nations, and He shall separate them.

God has given Him judgment, authority to judge mankind, so that He is both the Judge and Savior of men.

That makes me both love Him and fear Him! I love Him because He is my Savior and I fear Him because He is my Judge. EWT309

Holy Lord, I acknowledge that You are both Savior and Judge! One day, You will return to judge the nations and all will stand before You. May I serve You with my whole heart until then. Amen.

DECEMBER 15

The Rightful Owner Will Take Over

Then Jesus came to them and said, "All authority in heaven and on earth has been given to me."
—MATTHEW 28:18

The crux of the whole matter is this: our wonderful, created world will be restored to its rightful Owner. I for one look forward to that day. I want to live here when Jesus Christ owns and rules the world. Until that hour, there will be conflict, distress and war among the nations. We will hear of suffering and terror and fear and failure. But the God who has promised a better world is the God who cannot lie. He will shake loose Satan's hold on this world and its society and systems.

Our heavenly Father will put this world into the hands that were once nailed to a cross for our race of proud and alienated sinners.

It is a fact. Jesus Christ is returning to earth. The Revelation teaches it. Daniel teaches it. Isaiah teaches it. Jeremiah teaches it. Go to the Gospels written by Matthew, Mark, Luke, and John. They teach it. Read the promises in the Acts. Read them in Romans and the rest of Paul's epistles. Find the same message in Peter's important two letters to the churches. Jesus Christ is returning to earth! JIV023-024

Lord Christ, You have authority over all things! You are just and good, and I long for the day when You will return to earth to make all things new and right. Amen.

DECEMBER 16

Giving Christ His Place

Every tongue [will] acknowledge that Jesus Christ is Lord,
to the glory of God the Father.
—PHILIPPIANS 2:11

Christianity at large and the Church, generally speaking, are afflicted with a dread, lingering illness that shows itself daily in the apathy and spiritual paralysis of its members.

How can it be otherwise when twentieth-century Christians refuse to acknowledge the sharp moral antithesis that God Himself has set between the Church, as the Body of Christ, and this present world with its own human systems?

The differences between the churchly world and the followers of the Lamb are so basic that they can never be reconciled or negotiated. God has never promised His believing people that they would become a popular majority in this earthly scene.

I wonder how many believers would join me in a clear-cut manifesto to our times? I want it to be a declaration of our intentions to restore Christ to the place that is rightfully His in our personal lives, in our family situations, and in the fellowship of the churches that bear His name.

Are we willing to demonstrate the standards of godliness and biblical holiness as a rebuke to this wicked and perverse generation? MWT245

Lord, though the Church and the world often collide, I pray that each member of the Body of Christ will be so full of integrity that many unsaved people in the world will be pointed to Jesus Christ. Amen.

DECEMBER 17

Servants of Truth

So it is with everyone born of the Spirit.
—JOHN 3:8

Only the servants of truth can ever know truth. You can fill your head full of knowledge but the day that you decide that you are going to obey God, it will get down into your heart. You shall know!

I once read a book about the inner life of a man who was a sharp intellectual. By his own admission, he stood outside and examined spiritual people from the outside but nothing ever reached him. And that's possible!

You cannot argue around this. Read your Bible—any version you want—and if you are honest you will admit that it is either obedience or inward blindness. You can repeat the book of Romans word for word and still be blind inwardly. You can know the doctrine of justification by faith and take your stand with Luther and the Reformation and still be blind inwardly.

For it is not the body of truth that enlightens: it is by the Spirit of truth. If you are willing to obey the Lord Jesus, He will illuminate your spirit, inwardly enlighten you; and the truth you have known will then be known spiritually, and power will begin to flow up and out and you will find yourself changed—marvelously changed.

It is rewarding to believe in a Christianity that really changes men and women. In that great day of Christ's coming, all that will matter is whether we have been inwardly illuminated, inwardly regenerated, inwardly purified! The question is: do we really know Jesus in this way? EWT064

Lord Christ, grant that I would be illumined by Your Spirit and serve the Truth, and so be ready for Your glorious return. Amen.

DECEMBER 18

Why He Came

For God did not send his Son into the world to condemn the world, but to save the world through him.

—JOHN 3:17

Why would the Son of God come to our race? Our own hearts—sin and darkness and deception and moral disease—tell us what His mission should be. The sin we cannot deny tells us that He might have come to judge the world! . . .

Men and women are condemned in their own hearts because they know that if the Righteous One is coming, then we ought to be sentenced.

But God had a greater and far more gracious purpose—He came that sinful men might be saved. The loving mission of our Lord Jesus Christ was not to condemn but to forgive and reclaim. . . .

Thus, I believe it was a morally logical decision, that when Jesus Christ became incarnate it was in the flesh and body of a man because God had made man in His image.

I believe that although man was fallen and lost and on his way to hell, he still had a capacity and potential that made the Incarnation possible, so that God Almighty could pull up the blankets of human flesh around His ears and become a Man to walk among men.

There was nothing of like kind among angels and fallen creatures—so He came not to condemn but to reclaim and to restore and to regenerate. CES104-105

Jesus, thank You for coming to our lost race, for stooping so low to save us. I pray that I would always reach out to those who have not accepted You so that they may know the joy of Your salvation. Amen.

DECEMBER 19

Heir to All Creation

God . . . has spoken to us by his Son, whom he appointed heir of all things.

—HEBREWS 1:1–2

In this life, we are experiencing only unfinished segments of God's great eternal plan. Certainly we are not able to comprehend fully the glory that will be ours in that future day when, leaning on the arm of our heavenly Bridegroom, we are led into the presence of the Father in heaven with exceeding joy!

The writer to the Hebrews has tried to help us in the proper exercise of our faith, with the amazing statement that our Lord Jesus Christ is the heir of all things in God's far-flung creation.

All things created have been ordered and laid out so they become the garment of deity and the universal living expression of Himself to this world!

What does "heir of all things" really mean? It includes angels, seraphim, cherubim, ransomed men and women of all ages, matter, mind, law, spirit, value, meaning. It includes life and events on varied levels of being—and God's great interest embraces them all!

Surely God has left nothing to chance in His creative scheme—whether it be the tiniest blade of grass or the mightiest galaxy in the distant heavens above! MWT264

Lord of the Harvest, there are still people in this world who have never heard the name of Jesus. Nor, therefore, have they heard that He will be the rightful "heir of all things." I pray that Your Spirit will hasten the sending of the gospel to the remaining unreached peoples of the world. Amen.

DECEMBER 20

Do We Really Long for Our Lord to Come?

For the Son of Man is going to come in his Father's glory with his angels.
—MATTHEW 16:27

The joyful and personal element in what we call the "blessed hope," the return of Christ to earth, seems to be altogether missing in our day.

If the tender yearning is gone from the advent hope, there must be reasons for it, and I think I know what they are.

One is simply that popular fundamentalist theology has emphasized the utility of the cross rather than the beauty of the One who died on it. The saved man's relation to Christ has been made contractual instead of personal. The "work" of Christ has been stressed until it has eclipsed the person of Christ, and what He did for me seems to be more important than what He is to me! Redemption is seen as an across-the-counter transaction which we "accept," and the whole thing lacks emotional content. We must love someone very much to stay awake and long for his coming, and that may explain the absence of power in the advent hope even among those who still believe in it.

History reveals that times of suffering for the Church have also been times of looking upward. Tribulation has always sobered God's people and encouraged them to look for and yearn after the return of their Lord. God will wean us from the earth some way—the easy way if possible, the hard way if necessary! EWT204

Lord, grant me a greater expectation for Your return and that I may live diligently until then or until I die. Amen.

DECEMBER 21

Christ Came for All

For God did not send his Son into the world to condemn the world, but to save the world through him.
—JOHN 3:17

Brethren, let us treasure this: God sent His Son to the people. He is the people's Savior. Jesus Christ came to give life and hope to people like your family and like mine.

The Savior of the world knows the true value and worth of every living soul. He pays no attention to status or human honor or class. Our Lord knows nothing about this status business that everyone talks about.

When Jesus came to this world, He never asked anyone, "What is your IQ?" He never asked people whether or not they were well traveled. Let us thank God that He sent Him—and that He came! Both of those things are true. They are not contradictory. God sent Him as Savior! Christ, the Son, came to seek and to save! He came because He was sent and He came because His great heart urged Him and compelled Him to come. CES103

Lord, thank You for coming for all of us! You show no partiality and have redeemed us all by Your undeserved grace. Grant that I would love all people indiscriminately and so honor You. Amen.

DECEMBER 22

Lord of Righteousness

It is because of him that you are in Christ Jesus, who has become for us wisdom from God—that is, our righteousness, holiness and redemption.
—1 CORINTHIANS 1:30

In the midst of all the confusions of our day, it is important that we find out that Jesus Christ is the Lord of all righteousness and the Lord of all wisdom.

Righteousness is not a word easily acceptable to lost men and women in a lost world. Outside of the Word of God, there is no book or treatise that can give us a satisfying answer about righteousness, because the only One who is Lord of all righteousness is our Lord Jesus Christ, Himself. A scepter of righteousness is the scepter of His kingdom. He is the only One in all the universe who perfectly loved righteousness and hated iniquity.

Our great High Priest and Mediator is the righteous and Holy One—Jesus Christ, our risen Lord. He is not only righteous, He is the Lord of all righteousness!

Then, there is His wisdom. The sum total of the deep and eternal wisdom of the ages lies in Jesus Christ as a treasure hidden away. All the deep purposes of God reside in Him because His perfect wisdom enables Him to plan far ahead! Thus history itself becomes the slow development of His purposes. MWT079

Lord, I admit that my mind at times has difficulty wrapping around the concept of Your depth of wisdom and knowledge. I am humbled that You think of me, care for me, and love me. Amen.

DECEMBER 23

God's Best Gift

He sacrificed for their sins once for all when he offered himself.
—HEBREWS 7:27

God's gifts are many; His best gift is one. It is the gift of Himself. Above all gifts, God desires most to give Himself to His people. Our nature being what it is, we are the best fitted of all creatures to know and enjoy God. "For Thou madest us for Thyself, and our heart is restless, until it repose in Thee" (from The Confessions of St. Augustine). . . .

To know God, this is eternal life; this is the purpose for which we are and were created. The destruction of our God-awareness was the master blow struck by Satan in the dark day of our transgression.

To give God back to us was the chief work of Christ in redemption. To impart Himself to us in personal experience is the first purpose of God in salvation. To bring acute God-awareness is the best help the Spirit brings in sanctification. All other steps in grace lead up to this.

Were we allowed but one request, we might gain at a stroke all things else by praying one all-embracing prayer: Thyself, Lord! Give me Thyself and I can want no more. WTA071-072

Holy Father, I thank You for giving me Yourself in the person of Your Son. May I embrace Him, the best gift of all, with my whole being. Amen.

DECEMBER 24

Christmas Is Real

The mystery from which true godliness springs is great:
He appeared in the flesh.
—1 TIMOTHY 3:16

The birth of Christ was a divine declaration, an eternal statement to a race of fallen men and women.

The advent of Christ clearly established:

First, that God is real. The heavens were opened, and another world than this came into view.

Second, that human life is essentially spiritual. With the emergence into human flesh of the Eternal Word of the Father, the fact of man's divine origin is confirmed.

Third, that God indeed had spoken by the prophets. The coming of the Messiah Savior into the world confirmed the veracity of the Old Testament Scripture.

Fourth, that man is lost but not abandoned. Had men not been lost, no Savior would have been required. Had they been abandoned, no Savior would have come.

Finally, that this world is not the end. We are made for two worlds and as surely as we now inhabit the one, we shall also inhabit the other! MWT395

Heavenly Father, the historical fact of Your divine visitation gives the world reason for hope and joy. I pray that the significance of Your birth will impact the lives of many people who are searching for the meaning of life. Amen.

DECEMBER 25

The Happy Morn

Today in the town of David a Savior has been born to you; he is the Messiah, the Lord.

—LUKE 2:11

When we sing, "The Light of the world is Jesus," there should be a glow on our faces that would make the world believe indeed that we really mean it!

The Incarnation meant something vast and beautiful for John Milton—and he celebrated the coming of Jesus into the world with one of the most beautiful and moving expressions ever written by a man:

This is the month, and this the happy morn,
Wherein the Son of Heaven's eternal King,
Of wedded maid, and Virgin mother born,
Our great redemption from above did bring.

That glorious form, that Light insufferable,
And that far beaming blaze of majesty,
He laid aside, and here with us to be,
Forsook the courts of everlasting Day,
And chose with us a darksome house of mortal clay.

Oh! run; present them with thy humble ode,
And lay it lowly at His blessed feet,
Have thou the honor first thy Lord to greet
And join thy voices with the Angel quire,
From out His secret altar touched with hallowed fire! MWT397

Lord Jesus, I worship You today for choosing to put on mortal flesh for the sole purpose of redeeming mankind. I praise You for Your single-minded dedication to that most difficult task. Amen.

DECEMBER 26

He Came!

He was in the world, and though the world was made through him, the world did not recognize him. He came to that which was his own, but his own did not receive him.

—JOHN 1:10–11

In earlier verses in John's Gospel record, we have read in remarkably brief and simple words of the eternal past and of the eternal Son. We are told that from the beginning He was God; that He made all things, and that in Him was Light and that in Him was life.

Surely, these powerfully simple words and phrases are at the root of all theology. They are at the root of all truth.

How thrilling it is for us, then, to receive in these two words, *He came,* the confirmation of the Incarnation, God come in the flesh!

I confess that I am struck with the wonder and the significance of the limitless meaning of these two words, *He came.* Within them the whole scope of divine mercy and redeeming love is outlined.

All of the mercy God is capable of showing, all of the redeeming grace that He could pour from His heart, all of the love and pity that God is capable of feeling—all of these are at least suggested here in the message that *He came!*

Beyond that, all of the hopes and longings and aspirations, all of the dreams of immortality that lie in the human breast, all had their fulfillment in the coming to earth of Jesus, the Christ and Redeemer.

CES058-059

I am filled with gratitude, O Son of God, that You came to us to save us! You are our hope! Amen.

DECEMBER 27

United with Deity

For Christ's love compels us, because we are convinced that one died for all, and therefore all died. And he died for all, that those who live should no longer live for themselves but for him who died for them and was raised again.

—2 CORINTHIANS 5:14–15

When Christ became humanity, He made it possible for us to get up into deity—not to become deity but to be united with deity.

God counts Christ's death to be my death and He counts the sacrifice Christ laid down to be mine. . . .

When will we realize and confess that every sin is now a moral incongruity? As believers, we are supposed to have died with Jesus Christ our Lord. When we were joined to Him in the new birth, we were joined to His death. When we were joined to His rising again, it should have been plain to us that sin is now a moral incongruity in the life of a Christian.

The sinner sins because he is out there in the world—and he has never died. He is waiting to die and he will die once and later he will die the second death.

But a Christian dies with Christ and dies in Christ and dies along with Christ, so that when he lays his body down at last the Bible says he will not see death. TRC117-118

Glorious Son of God, how marvelous that You would become human so that we might be joined to God. May the union we share with You today be strengthened and confirmed. Amen.

DECEMBER 28

Very God of Very God

The Son is the image of the invisible God, the firstborn over all creation.
—COLOSSIANS 1:15

Now, the Bible has a great deal to say about the manner in which sinful man may come into the fellowship and the presence of God, and it all has to do with forgiveness and grace and regeneration and justification in Jesus Christ! It all boils down to the teaching that Jesus Christ is everything that the Godhead is! The image of the invisible God, the brightness of His glory, the express image of His person—all of these we find in and through Jesus Christ!

We believe with rejoicing that Jesus Christ was the begotten of the Father, before all ages, that He is God of God, Light of light, very God of very God, begotten and not made, of one substance with the Father, and it is by Him that all things were made! . . .

He was and is and can never cease to be God, and when we find Him and know Him, we are back at the ancient fount again! Christ is all that the Godhead is! ITB021

How amazing is Your plan of redemption, Lord, that through finding Christ we find You. Let me know Him more, that I may enter into fellowship with You. Amen

DECEMBER 29

Faith and Holiness

We know that when Christ appears, we shall be like him, for we shall see him as he is.

1 JOHN 3:2

The Bible does not approve of modern curiosity that plays with the Scriptures and which seeks only to impress credulous and gullible audiences!

I cannot think of even one lonely passage in the New Testament which speaks of Christ's revelation, manifestation, appearing, or coming that is not directly linked with moral conduct, faith, and spiritual holiness.

The appearing of the Lord Jesus on this earth once more is not an event upon which we may curiously speculate—and when we do only that we sin! The prophetic teacher who engages in speculation to excite the curiosity of his hearers without providing them with a moral application is sinning even as he speaks.

There have been enough foolish formulas advanced about the return of Christ by those who were simply curious to cause many believers to give the matter no further thought or concern. But Peter said to expect "the appearing of Jesus Christ."

Paul said there is a crown of righteousness laid up in glory for all those who love His appearing. John spoke of his hope of seeing Jesus and bluntly wrote: "Every man that hath this hope in him purifieth himself, even as he is pure."

Are you ready for the appearing of Jesus Christ? Or are you among those who are merely curious about His coming? EWT234

Heavenly Father, grant that I would be ready for the return of Jesus by living by faith and in holiness. Amen.

DECEMBER 30

Jesus Will Come

And he swore by him who lives for ever and ever . . . and said, "There will be no more delay!"
—REVELATION 10:6

We are living in a period when God waits in grace and mercy. In His faithfulness, God is calling out a people for His name—those who will in faith cast their lot with Jesus Christ! Then, at a time known only to God, the end of this age will come, and Jesus Christ will return to earth for His own believing people—His church.

The event is certain—the timing is uncertain. When the mighty angel of Revelation shouts his signal and raises his hand heavenward, it will be eternally too late for unrepentant sinners.

When the time comes in heaven for that announcement, three worlds will hear it. Heaven will hear it, with full agreement that the time of judgment has indeed come. The underworld of hell will hear the shout, and there will be fright. And on earth, the saints, the believing Body of Christ, will hear it and be glad! Meanwhile, the church is not simply a religious institution. It is an assembly of redeemed sinners, men and women called and commissioned to spread Christ's gospel to the ends of the earth. MWT237

Lord, while I look forward to Your return to restore justice and order to this fallen world, my heart is burdened for my friends and loved ones who haven't accepted You yet. Lord, I pray that each one will yield to Your Spirit. Amen.

DECEMBER 31

Come, Lord Jesus

He who testifies to these things says, "Yes, I am coming soon." Amen. Come, Lord Jesus.
REVELATION 22:20

The people of God ought to be the happiest people in all the wide world!

Fellow Christian, consider the source of our joy and delight: redeemed by the blood of the Lamb, our yesterdays behind us, our sin under the blood forever and a day, to be remembered against us no more forever! God is our Father, Christ is our Brother, the Holy Ghost our Advocate and Comforter!

Our Brother has gone to the Father's house to prepare a place for us, leaving with us the promise that He will come again!

Don't send Moses, Lord, don't send Moses! He broke the tablets of stone.

Don't send Elijah for me, Lord! I am afraid of Elijah—he called down fire from heaven.

Don't send Paul, Lord! He is so learned that I feel like a little child when I read his epistles.

O Lord Jesus, come Yourself! I am not afraid of Thee. You took the little children as lambs to Your fold. You forgave the woman taken in adultery. You healed the timid woman who reached out in the crowd to touch You. We are not afraid of You! EWT403

Amen! Come, Lord Jesus!

Reference Codes For Books and Booklets by A. W. Tozer

AOG	*The Attributes of God*
BAM	*Born after Midnight*
CES	*Christ the Eternal Son*
COU	*The Counselor*
EFE	*Echoes from Eden*
FBR	*Faith Beyond Reason*
EWT	*Evenings with Tozer*
GTM	*God Tells the Man Who Cares*
HTB	*How to Be Filled with the Holy Spirit*
ICH	*I Call It Heresy*
ITB	*I Talk Back to the Devil*
JAF	*Jesus, Author of Our Faith*
JIV	*Jesus Is Victor*
JMI	*Jesus, Our Man in Glory*
KDL	*Keys to the Deeper Life*
MDP	*Man: The Dwelling Place of God*
MMG	*Men Who Met God*
MWT	*Mornings with Tozer*
NCA	*The Next Chapter after the Last*
OCN	*The Old Cross and the New*
OGM	*Of God and Men*
POG	*The Pursuit of God*
POM	*God's Pursuit of Man*
PON	*The Price of Neglect*
PTP	*Paths to Power*
QTB	*The Quotable Tozer, Volume 2*
RDA	*Renewed Day by Day, Volume 1*
RDB	*Renewed Day by Day, Volume 2*

ROR	*The Root of the Righteous*
RRR	*Rut, Rot or Revival*
SAT	*Success and the Christian*
SIZ	*The Size of the Soul*
SOS	*The Set of the Sail*
TAM	*Those Amazing Methodists*
TCC	*Total Commitment to Christ*
TET	*The Early Tozer: A Word in Season*
TIC	*That Incredible Christian*
TTPI	*The Tozer Pulpit, Volume 1*
TTPII	*The Tozer Pulpit, Volume 2*
TRA	*Tragedy in the Church*
TRC	*The Radical Cross*
TSII	*Tozer Speaks, Volume 2*
TSS	*Tozer Speaks to Students*
TWE	*Tozer on Worship and Entertainment*
TWP	*This World: Playground or Battleground?*
WHT	*Whatever Happened to Worship?*
WMJ	*Worship: the Missing Jewel*
WOS	*The Warfare of the Spirit*
WPJ	*Who Put Jesus on the Cross?*
WTA	*We Travel an Appointed Way*

CONTINUE WORSHIPING ALONGSIDE TOZER WITH THE REST OF HIS TRINITARIAN DEVOTIONS

Spend a year dwelling on the awesomeness of God with A. W. Tozer. He will expand your faith in a God so great that words fall short to describe Him. He will nourish you with truth. Encounter Tozer's heart and wisdom like never before in this newly revised edition.

978-0-8024-1968-2

Spend a year encountering the Son of God alongside A. W. Tozer. In this 365-day devotional, you can intentionally pursue Christ daily. Encounter the character of Christ, His work on the cross, and His limitless love for you. With each page, may your heart be filled and your worship increased.

978-0-8024-1970-5

Spend a year unearthing the wonder of the Holy Spirit alongside A. W. Tozer. This devotional explores many of the defining characteristics of the Holy Spirit. Each day seeks to stoke the believer's internal desire to hunger and thirst after the Spirit of God.

978-0-8024-1969-9

MOODY Publishers®

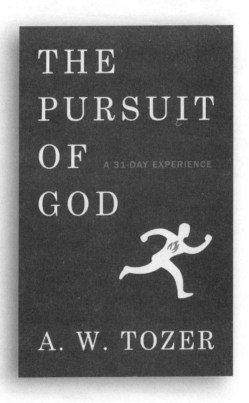

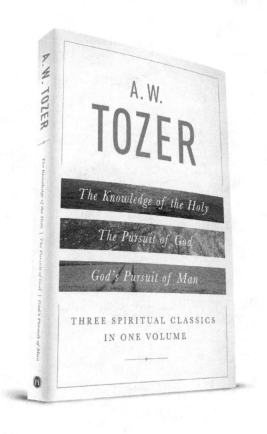